Common Sense Faith

Common Sense Faith

Patrick J. Brennan

ORBIS BOOKS

Maryknoll, New York 10545

Founded in 1970, Orbis Books endeavors to publish works that enlighten the mind, nourish the spirit, and challenge the conscience. The publishing arm of the Maryknoll Fathers and Brothers, Orbis seeks to explore the global dimensions of the Christian faith and mission, to invite dialogue with diverse cultures and religious traditions, and to serve the cause of reconciliation and peace. The books published reflect the views of their authors and do not represent the official position of the Maryknoll Society. To learn more about Maryknoll and Orbis Books, please visit our website at www.maryknollsociety.org.

Library of Congress Cataloging-in-Publication Data

Brennan, Patrick J.
    Common sense faith / Patrick J. Brennan.
        p. cm.
    ISBN 978-1-57075-977-2 (pbk.)
    1. Catholic Church—Doctrines.   2. Christian life—Catholic authors.   I. Title.
    BX1754.B725 2013
    230—dc23
                                                            2012036314

CONTENTS

PREFACE

PART 1
Jesus
He Saw It Coming   1
Who Is Your Sovereign?   4
Paralysis   7
Why My Funeral Will Rock   10
He Is! And He Is Here! Hooray!   13
Remembering Paddy O'Cinnamon   17
The Kingdom . . . Is Like . . .   21
Radical Faith in a Surprising God   24
"The Kingdom of God Will Be Taken away from You"   27
Veneration of the Cross   30
New Life . . . Eternal Life   34
The Cleansing of the Temple   38
Jerusalem, Our Destiny   42

PART 2
Conversion
Hate . . . Really?   47
Temptation and Potential   51
Lost and Found   54
Decisions, Decisions   58
Dirt . . . or Down to Earth   62
This Too Shall Pass   66

Help! 68

Changed Minds, Changed Hearts, Changed Behavior 72

Spiritual Intelligence 75

The Power of Surrender 78

The End 81

Repentance 86

Prodigal Son, Compassionate Father, Resentful Brother 90

John 3:16 96

Women and Salvation 99

Look in the Mirror 102

Job Moments 104

The Dangers of Religion 106

Do Not Be Afraid 110

Discipleship Should Cost 113

Searchin' 117

Paying Attention 120

Moral Courage 123

Turning 127

Never Forget 131

New Beginnings 135

Burdens and Kate Smith 139

Part 3

Church

Roots or Up in the Air? 143

Happiness and Hell 146

A Deserted Place 150

Good Shepherding 154

Part 4

Sacraments and Prayer

All Saints Day 159

All Souls 161

Learning from Two Blind Men 163

Supply Concerns   166

My Body and Blood: Do This in Remembrance of Me   169

Ash Wednesday   173

Hungers and Thirsts   176

The Bath of Rebirth   179

Motivation   183

A Creed   186

Delusion versus Mutuality   188

Corpus Christi   192

Part 5

Relationships

Forgiveness and Doubt   197

Mindfulness   201

Think It Out   204

All You Need Is Love   207

Knowing   210

Part 6

Mercy and Justice

Truth and Consequences   215

A Spirituality of Cultural Resistance   218

Bigger Barns   222

Socialist?   226

Heaven—Now and Later   231

Lepers   235

PREFACE

I have always valued communication: writing, public speaking, preaching, acting, and using radio, television, and the Internet. I have written a number of books on community, spirituality, counseling, and church that I hope readers have found helpful. This is my latest contribution.

I put a lot of effort into preaching, and over the years I have placed my homilies in the parish bulletin. In 2009 I left Holy Family Parish in Inverness, Illinois, after serving for seventeen years, fourteen as pastor. I began ministering at the Clare, a continuing care retirement community in downtown Chicago, and also at St. Thomas the Apostle in Naperville, Illinois. Before I left Holy Family, a friend and former director of operations at the parish, Rita Tresnowski, planted the seed that I should continue sharing my homiletic reflections using the Internet to create a kind of virtual community. She helped me begin the *National Center for Evangelization Newsletter*, in which I have shared reflections for the past three years. This book is a compilation of reflections from the those years, as well as others from my years at Holy Family. I am very grateful to Rita for her help in editing this book. I would like to dedicate this book to her and her family, as well as to the residents of the Clare and the people of St. Thomas, all of whom have been my faith home for the past three years. I also include in the dedication Dawn Mayer, colleague and friend for over thirty-five years, who helped with the text—and also Annaliese, her beautiful daughter and my godchild.

In my many years of working in evangelization, I have found that what people are most hungry and thirsty for in terms of faith and spirituality are preaching that offers people livable spirituality, communities that are welcoming, ministries that address real-life needs, and worship that offers people genuine religious experience. I have always tried to shape my writing and my preaching around these hungers and thirsts. At times people have been kind enough to tell me that when they hear me speak or read my writings it is almost as if I am in their home, discovering/knowing what they are experiencing. Of course I am not, but I have always felt that it is important to approach God, faith, and spirituality from the vantage point of human experience. I write and speak from human experience, including my own. At times this approach has not pleased religious authorities.

I did my master's degree and doctorate at the Adler School of Professional Psychology. While I am an eclectic in teaching psychology and doing psychotherapy, using the best from many different schools of psychology, I am, at root, an Adlerian. Alfred Adler and his followers distinguished between common sense and private logic. Common sense, for Adlerians, is a kind of shared wisdom that leads to mental health. Private logic often is filled with mistaken notions about life and relationships that keep people from discovering the love and happiness that they desire. Common sense, shared wisdom is something that I have pursued most of my adult life. I have tried to be discerning regarding private logic and mistaken notions in myself, and in people I have tried to help. I hope that you find in this book some common sense faith that helps you on your journey. The reflections are divided into six thematic sections: Jesus, Conversion, the Church, Prayer and Sacraments, Relationships, and Mercy and Justice.

My thanks to Michael Leach, editor at large of Orbis Books, who has supported me and published my books for many years. I am grateful to him for suggesting that I attempt a book more about spirituality and less about parish pragmatics, which I have written about for so long. Thanks to Mike also for his patience in waiting for the manuscript to be completed. May God bless all of you with common sense faith.

In Jesus,

Pat Brennan

Part 1

JESUS

HE SAW IT COMING

He saw it coming. Jesus knew that his preaching and teaching about the reign of God, and his attention-getting miracles, were disturbing the scribes and the Pharisees. They were envious of the attention he was getting. He was threatening the status quo of their collaborative relationship with the Roman government. Jesus knew that the vision and way of life that he named the "reign of God" was a more meaningful approach to life than 613 laws that the Pharisees espoused. He knew he was rocking the foundation of their control and manipulation of the poor Jewish people. Jesus, nonetheless, continued his mission and ministry, knowing that it was going to lead to a confrontation that would result in his death.

The Gospel of Luke adds psychological detail that suggests that Jesus almost forced the confrontation. Why? Why did he so passionately move toward Jerusalem and his final confrontation with his enemies? I think he knew that it was the final and full revelation of the nature of the reign of God. It was the final piece of his mission. He had to reveal not only all the other truths he had revealed in his preaching, teaching, and miracles; he had to reveal that the mystery of the cross, which is present in each person's life, always leads to new life here on earth, and eternal life on the other side of the experience of death.

Structurally, the eighth chapter of Mark is the turning point of that

Gospel. Up until this point, we have experienced many teachings and miracles from Jesus, but now he asks the twelve apostles, "Who do you say I am?" Peter speaks what has been evolving and developing in the apostles' consciousness, "You are the Christ." Jesus goes on to teach them what being the Christ will involve: he will suffer and die, but he will rise from the dead on the third day. Peter disagrees with Jesus, saying that a messiah should never have to suffer and die.

In turn, Jesus challenges Peter, saying that he is a devil. He calls him Satan, who judges by human standards rather than by God's. Jesus refers to himself as the "Son of Man." We hear of this title also in the book of Daniel. It is an enigmatic, apocalyptic image referring to someone through whom the reign of God is going to be fully revealed and given to the human family. We see employed in this Markan passage another literary device that Mark uses several times. It is called the "Messianic secret." Not wanting his role as Messiah to be confused, Jesus tells the apostles not to tell anyone about him. The Messianic secret is clarified in the crucifixion scene when the pagan Roman soldier looks at the dead Jesus and says, "Truly this was the Son of God."

The cross is the central symbol of Christianity. In teaching about his cross, Jesus is also trying to teach us about our own. Through the prophet Isaiah we hear of the kind of faith that Jesus had. In the book of Isaiah, there are four songs known as the servant songs or the suffering servant songs. Though the identity of the servant is unclear, the servant is someone who has great suffering enter his life, yet he remains convinced and convicted that God is with him—that God will vindicate him and lead him to new life.

Twice the servant says in Isaiah 50, "The Lord is my help." He goes on to say, "God is near; I will not be disgraced." The other servant songs can be found in Isaiah chapters 42, 49, and 52–53. Jesus could face the greatest of sufferings because he believed in the power of God with him, working all things for his benefit.

We are called to the same kind of faith. Not only are we called to the same kind of faith, we are called in Mark 8 to invest in the gospel, to live our lives for the gospel, to invest in getting the message to other people of the paschal nature of life, that all of life is about life, death, and resurrection.

I frequently say that the cross enters our life in different ways. Some crosses happen to us. In the mystery of things, suffering that we have not chosen and perhaps would never choose enters the story of our lives. In these situations, however long or short the experience might be, we are called to the faith of Jesus; we are called to the faith of the suffering servant of Isaiah.

Sometimes we *chose* crosses as Jesus chose the cross of confronting the religious leaders to fulfill his mission in revealing the resurrection. Sometimes in choosing a cross, perhaps ours is not as large scale and heroic as Jesus's choice was. Sometimes the crosses that we choose are some sort of therapeutic, disciplinelike crosses that hopefully lead to growth, conversion, and new life.

Finally, there is the cross of physical death. None of us are mature or fully developed until we have confronted the truth of our own mortality and the mortality of the people whom we love. In the face of the mystery of the cross of death, again we are called to the faith of Jesus and the faith of the suffering servant in Isaiah.

Peter and the other apostles certainly have their expectations changed about the nature of Jesus being the Christ and the nature of what it means to be Messiah. They also have their expectations changed as to what it means to be a disciple. To be a disciple of Jesus is to embrace this mystery, in faith, as he did, trusting in the paschal process.

The cross, however and whenever it appears in our lives, always leads to new life. The ultimate cross of physical death promises us eternal life.

In the letter from James 2 we receive a different perspective on the cross. If we say that we have faith, that must always manifest itself in acts of love, mercy, and justice toward our fellow person. Faith manifests itself in works. Since the time of the Reformation, a needless dichotomy arose between some Protestant groups emphasizing the importance of faith alone and accusing Catholics of being too preoccupied with works in an attempt to earn our own salvation. This

James passage keeps this theological question in healthy balance. True faith embraces the self-sacrificing love of the cross in making ourselves uncomfortable so that we might be of service toward other people, especially those in need.

Let us be conscious of the cross as it comes to us in many different ways, and let us try to practice the faith of Jesus and the suffering servant in embracing the cross. I told someone recently that this experience of transition that I have been in has made me feel at times like a Hurricane Katrina victim. So many pieces of my life have been washed away or are in storage. My identity has changed and my roles in life have changed. But the anxiety and depression are beginning to wane, somewhat, as I grow in faith that this cross that has happened to me is leading me to new life, resurrection.

WHO IS YOUR SOVEREIGN?

I still chuckle at the *Honeymooners* episodes that are consistently rerun on TV. I enjoy watching those classic Jackie Gleason, Art Carney, Audrey Meadows, and Joyce Randolph episodes. If you are old enough, you probably remember Ralph Kramden, the Gleason character, as being the preeminent sexist. At times, he would go into a rage with Alice, his wife, about how their dingy apartment was "his castle." He was the "king of the castle" and she was a "mere servant." Alice, the Audrey Meadows character, usually deflated the balloon of his hot air with a terse word or two. I think the show still intrigues me, because Ralph and Alice always have reminded me so much of my parents and their relationship: loving, but at times volatile.

Kings . . . As people who have grown up in a democratic republic, the language of monarchies does not do much for us. Many people were intrigued by the life and death of Princess Diana some years ago, as well as the marriage of William and Kate, but royalty in the strict sense of that term is something we are not accustomed to. Perhaps, then, it might take us a while to get a feel for the importance of the Feast of Christ the King. A king, in nations that still have such rulers, is someone who claims to be the sovereign authority in people's lives. He—or in the case of a queen, she—is normative. Lives are to be lived relative to the king's leadership. The Feast of Christ the King reminds us that Jesus seeks to be the sovereign authority in our lives. He describes his kingdom in the Gospel of John as "a kingdom of truth." As disciples of Jesus Christ, with Christ as our king, with Christ as our sovereign authority, we are people who in the ideal order are always seeking the truth of Jesus Christ as the foundational direction for our lives.

Daniel is apocalyptic literature. "Apocalyptic" refers to revelations—prophetic revelations. Daniel speaks in highly symbolic language of the coming of a new kind of kingdom. In Daniel's apocalyptic vision, four beasts appear from the netherworld. These four beasts represent four prevailing pagan empires of the world at the time of Daniel's writing: the Babylonians, the Medes, the Persians, and the Greeks. None of these peoples or countries was tied to the God of the Old Testament Jews, Yahweh.

In this vision, the ancient one, representing God or Yahweh, takes his seat in the heavenly court, and there emerges in the heavenly court "one like a Son of Man" coming on the clouds of heaven, in contrast to the beasts who come from the underworld or from that area named as evil. The Son of Man imagery, referring to Christ, speaks of Jesus as being both divine and in the form of a human. This Son of Man, which later became a regular title for the Christ, "received dominion, glory, and kingship; all peoples, nations, and languages serve him. His dominion is an everlasting dominion that shall not be taken away; his kingship shall not be destroyed." Christians have taken this passage, which seems to refer to the coming Messiah, and interpreted it as pointing to Christ. Christ is the Son of Man who is being anointed king. The Son of Man image also stands for the kingdom to which he is going to give birth.

The author of Revelation says that Jesus Christ, the firstborn of the dead and ruler of the kings of the earth, "has made *us* into a kingdom, priests for his God and Father." This is a further clarification of that Son of Man imagery that indeed we now are a part of the kingdom that Jesus Christ has revealed.

A fact in the Gospels is that Jesus is not usually pointing to his own kingship, though he and Pilate discuss it. Jesus is always pointing to that countercultural vision of life and way of life that he called the "reign of God." If Jesus Christ is king, as king he is pointing always to another large reality: God's reign. He calls us to help with the emergence of God's reign in the world. He calls us to be members of that kingdom of truth that he refers to in the Gospel of John.

The Feast of Christ the King was instituted on December 11, 1925, by Pope Pius XI with his encyclical *Quas Primas*. Many Christian churches besides the Roman Catholic Church observe this feast. Since 1969 the Feast of Christ the King has been celebrated on the last Sunday of the liturgical year. The discipline of having this feast on the last Sunday of the liturgical year began during the pontificate of Pope Paul VI.

Going back to *Quas Primas* by Pope Pius XI, the pontiff quoted St. Cyril of Alexandria stating that Jesus's kingship "has dominion over all creatures, a dominion not seized by violence nor usurped, but his by essence and by nature." Pius XI was trying to remind Christians, in starting this feast, that their allegiance was to their spiritual ruler, Jesus, as opposed to the earthly supremacy being claimed by Benito Mussolini and later Hitler. The feast was also instituted as a response to World War I, calling the world to the peace that Jesus embodies. Today is a good opportunity for us to recommit ourselves to Jesus Christ as norm and sovereign of our lives, as Lord and Redeemer, as our King who points to a great reality, the reign of God.

In the Gospel of John, Jesus says that his kingdom is not of this world; his kingdom is not here. Already we have spoken about how Jesus describes his kingdom as a kingdom of truth. If we join Johannine theology to the theology of Matthew's Gospel, we find ourselves in a tension or a dialectic regarding the world. The essence of the reign of God is concerned with values and behaviors that are countercultural to many of the mores and customs of the dominant culture; because of this we can say that the reign of God is not in the world. But in Matthew 28, the Great Commissioning, Jesus says to apostles, disciples, and all of us, "Go into the world, make disciples, and teach them everything I taught you." As people who are the reign of God, as the book of Revelation tells us, "We are His kingdom"; we definitely are sent into the world around us to facilitate and help with the emergence of God's reign.

Recently at the Clare, along with the Eucharist, we celebrated the Sacrament of the Anointing of the Sick. Our tradition teaches us that in this sacrament, God's healing power, as mediated through a caring community, is extended to those of us who are in our senior years, and who may be suffering chronic or acute health problems; but this sacrament also functions in a parallel way to the Sacrament of Reconciliation. God's forgiveness of sin is extended to those who are anointed. One understanding of the Sacrament of the Anointing of the Sick that we do not hear too often is that the sacrament asks those who are receiving the anointing to place themselves in the posture of making a recommitment to God, to Jesus, to the reign of God. To those who share in the anointing, the person who receives the sacrament is saying, "I am recommitted to the reign of God despite the pain, the weakness, and the challenge that the senior years or illness may have brought my way." The Anointing of the Sick, at least in part, is an altar call, calling the anointed to recommitment or to be born again in Jesus Christ, our King.

PARALYSIS

Part of my childhood took place before the polio vaccine was created and made available. Children in the early to mid-1950s (and in previous years) were afflicted with polio in large numbers. I remember being in a restaurant that had an apartment above it. Someone said that a child upstairs had recently contracted polio. I remember my mother whisking my brother and me out of the restaurant quickly. I grew up with a phobia—the fear of being paralyzed, the fear of not being able to freely move parts of my body.

One of my classmates in grade school, a girl by the name of Kathy, was paralyzed from the waist down with polio. Her two legs were in braces, which she had to adjust to sit down for class. She walked with the aid of two steel crutches that came up to her elbows. Kathy was a very positive, bright girl, and she always exhibited an accepting attitude toward her affliction. But she must have suffered greatly, physically and emotionally, because of her paralysis. Though I liked Kathy I was uncomfortable being in her presence, because I feared her paralysis.

Many of us remember the accident that Christopher Reeve had some years ago that rendered him a quadriplegic. Cardinal Francis George was afflicted with polio as a child and still suffers with some symptoms. Franklin Roosevelt was paralyzed with polio from the waist down at the time he was president, but the media kept this a secret from the public. Many people did not realize Roosevelt's condition until after he died. Someone just told me a story of a young man who was recently paralyzed from the shoulders down in a recent accident.

Not being able to move—what a terrible loss! In some cases of polio, the paralysis impeded people's breathing, and they had to be placed in an iron lung. Perhaps many of us take for granted the gifts of movement and breathing. To be deprived of them must be truly awful, though people like Roosevelt and Reeve inspired many others with their courage in the face of paralysis.

In the Gospel of Mark we read the story of a paralytic man. Four men were carrying him on a mat. They were committed to bringing the man to Jesus; they seemed convinced that Jesus could do some kind of healing miracle for him. They were unable to get through the front door of the home to Jesus, because of the crowd. Many houses at this time had stairs that went to the roof of the house. The men took the paralytic up the stairs to the roof. The roofs of Palestinian homes at this time were customarily made of wooden beams, with thatching and mud. The four men opened up the roof and lowered the man down within reach of Jesus.

We are told that Jesus was struck by the faith of the paralytic man and the four men assisting him. He called the paralytic "child," a term of affection. The first thing that Jesus said to the paralytic was, "Your sins are forgiven." It seems that Jesus was trying to address a deeper form of paralysis than just physical paralysis. Jesus knew that we can be paralyzed *within*. We can experience a lack of movement within us. We can be paralyzed by patterns of sin and feelings that our sin is unforgivable. We can be paralyzed with an unwillingness to forgive others who have hurt us. We can be paralyzed with resentment or excessive anger. We can be paralyzed with the inability or unwillingness to express sorrow when we have hurt others. We can be paralyzed by broken relationships in need of healing and reconciliation. We can be paralyzed by fear, stress, and depression. We can be paralyzed by addictions, obsessions, and compulsions. We can be paralyzed in relationships by unresolved conflict. Jesus understood and understands that there are patterns of interior paralysis that are as real and painful as physical paralysis. Jesus used this encounter to address both physical and interior paralysis.

Jesus went on to heal the man's physical paralysis. He said: "Rise, pick up your mat, and go home!" We are told that the man rose and picked up his mat at once and went away. It seems that Jesus used the healing of physical paralysis to point to a deeper level of paralysis, the paralysis within that many of us experience.

The paradox of the story and its meaning is that many of us who fear or are uncomfortable with physical paralysis can be or have been paralyzed within, and we do not know it or have not known it. I know that such is the case with me: I have struggled with interior paralysis in many different ways. This gospel reminds us that Jesus can heal us of the paralysis that lies within us, at times not noticed or seen by us. Paradoxically, the scribes who took exception to Jesus saying that he can forgive sin, suffered from interior paralysis: they were stuck in their legalisms, and their concept of a remote and punishing God.

The gospel teaches us to make deliberate attempts to "get to Jesus," as the paralytic and the four men did in opening up the roof. We are called to develop the same kind of faith they had. Some things we cannot do ourselves; rather we need the healing power of God, as it comes through Jesus. We need to be persistent in seeking the healing touch of Jesus. Jesus can heal us and free us from our paralysis and stagnation. As Paul said in the second letter to the Corinthians: Jesus is always a yes for us when it comes to healing and helping us. We need not ever carry a burden alone.

A passage from Isaiah 43 is a mirror reflection of some of the themes that we find in the gospel. This passage is from Deutero-Isaiah, the second book of Isaiah, known as the book of Consolation. These chapters are addressed to the Jewish people in exile in Babylon. God says through the prophet that the exodus from Babylon will be greater than the exodus from Egypt. Therefore the people are to "Remember not the events of the past, the things of long ago. . . . See I am doing something new. . . . You burdened me with your sins. . . . It is I, I who wipe out . . . your offenses; your sins I will remember no more." God is ready and willing to always forgive the interior paralysis of sin, liberate us, and give us new interior freedom.

If you are feeling interior paralysis in any way, imagine yourself being lowered down on a mat by people who love you, into the presence of the healing Jesus. Hear Jesus say to you: "Your sins are forgiven. . . . Rise; pick up your mat, and walk." If we know of others who are suffering interior paralysis, let us imaginatively and prayerfully place those people in the presence of Jesus, so that he may heal them also.

Why My Funeral Will Rock

Joel Stein wrote an interesting article in the January 16, 2012, issue of *Time* magazine. It was titled "Over My Dead Body: Why My Funeral Will Rock." Stein reflected on the death of his grandmother, Mama Ann, a woman who was ninety years old. She died the same week as Kim Jong-il, of North Korea. Stein said only four people attended Mama Ann's funeral. She had been a wonderful woman who had a self-sacrificing love for the people in her life. Because of her age, not many people still knew her and related to her. On the other hand, Kim Jong-il, who had been a merciless tyrant, had a huge state funeral, with orchestrated, effusive mourning over him.

Stein's article is tongue-in-cheek, humorous; but he raises a sober issue. He does not want to have a funeral like his grandmother's. He wants his funeral to be a true celebration of his life.

In the article, Stein talks about consulting with Lisa Takuechi Cullen, the author of *Remember Me: A Lively Tour of the New American Way of Death*. She encouraged him to hire, ahead of time, professional mourners; she promised this would heighten the emotions at his funeral. She also recommended that he move to New Orleans where they have jazz funerals with marching brass bands, parades, and dancing mourners twirling parasols. Stein's wife said no to such a move. He said that he may plan to have gift bags handed out to mourners at his funeral. He concluded that while he did not want to die uncelebrated and unmourned, maybe it was nobler to die the way Mama Ann did.

Stein's article is obviously facetious, but it contains enough truth to get one wondering. It is written about the same theme that Paul wrote about in 1 Corinthians and many of his letters: the inevitability of death and how we should be preparing for that transition. Paul and many early Christians believed that the end of time was near. Some of them eventually changed their minds about this, but nonetheless, eschatology has remained an important part of Christian spirituality and theology. I believe that talk about "the end," in our tradition, refers to several things: the end of time, in the sense of the end of the world; the fall of Jerusalem, which Jesus predicted; the second coming of Jesus; and the end of our own personal time—our personal deaths. In Christian eschatology we look at the end without fear, but rather with hope, trust, and faith.

In 1 Corinthians, Paul encouraged his readers, and now he encourages us, to prioritize in our lives, based on our knowledge of our coming deaths. Realizing that each of us will face death, what really matters in life? What should we be attending to? What should we be invested in?

There is an urgency in Paul's writing. He warned us that time is running out; therefore we should be living in terms of that last transition. We should be striving to live an "eternal life lifestyle," so that this eternal life lifestyle may continue on the other side of death.

I frequently quote Steven Covey's *The 7 Habits of Highly Effective People.* One of the seven habits is to live with the end in mind. Covey encourages people to live with a sense of mission and purpose. What are we trying to accomplish in life? We should always keep this before us: we should live with the end in mind. In our tradition, while each of us can have many different ends or purposes throughout our lifetimes, one end or purpose—the end purpose—is to live the reign of God here on earth and continue that lifestyle in eternity.

Let Stein's article and Paul's wisdom challenge us to face the mystery of death soberly and responsibly. Death is a mystery that always throws us back to the question of how we are living now, in the present. Death is a horizon that calls us to repentance and conversion now.

As we do that reflection on the present moment of our lives, let two other notions from Scripture speak to us. First, in the Gospel of Mark, Jesus performed an exorcism in the synagogue in Capernaum. We are told that a man in the synagogue was possessed by an unclean spirit. When the man addressed Jesus he asked, "What have you to do with *us*? . . . Have you come to destroy *us*?" I find it interesting in this passage that the possessed man uses the plural: *us*, rather than *me*. The word "diabolical" speaks to me of that which divides or scatters us; evil separates us, disconnects us. The possessed man was more than one; he had become many, divided, torn apart because of the presence of evil in his life. Jesus commanded the unclean spirit to come out of the man. We are told that the unclean spirit came out of him. Jesus made the man whole, one again—with himself, with his fellow person, and with God.

What is the diabolical in each of our lives? What divides us, what keeps us from personal integrity? What keeps us from unity and communion with others and with God? As we reflect on the mystery of death that focuses us on the present, where might we need Jesus's exorcizing power?

Second, prophecy is spoken of in the book of Deuteronomy. Moses is presented as the first in a line of prophets to come. All the prophets lead up to the ultimate prophet, Jesus. Sometimes we confuse prophecy with the ability to foretell the future. The fact is that prophecy is very much about the present. A prophet is a person who has a developed sense of connection and communication with God. In addition, a prophet is very aware of situations, needs, and crises in the world. A prophet connects God's word and will with people and events in the present moment. This does not mean that prophecy has nothing to do with the future. The present is always prologue to the future. But an underappreciated understanding of prophecy is that of highly developing spiritual sensitivity. Prophets use this spiritual sensitivity to get in touch with God's word and will, and speak God's word and will to other people in the world.

When we were baptized, we were anointed to become priests, prophets, and kings. I translate that as we were anointed to become people of holiness, people of prophetic truth, and people who will lead in church and society. Ronald Heifetz and Marty Linsky say, in *Leadership on the Line*, that leadership is an innate ability in all of us waiting to be developed. So also is prophecy an innate ability in all of us waiting to be developed. Prophecy is spiritual sensitivity, intuition, proclamation, and behavior—a way of life.

May we all have funerals that rock, because we lived lives that rocked—spiritually and prophetically.

HE IS! AND HE IS HERE! HOORAY!

I think I was twelve—Christmas 1959. I was standing on the threshold of adolescence. Elvis and rock and roll were the new culture. Two of my aunts, Moll and Margaret, gave me the best, coolest Christmas gift ever: an Emerson transistor radio. Transistor radios actually were invented in the late 1940s, but they did not become popular until the price of them went down through mass production in the late 1950s, and then the 1960s and '70s. I walked through the house most of Christmas Day listening to my new transistor radio. I had a bookshelf in the headboard of my bed; I planned to put my new transistor radio on that bookshelf and listen to the radio even at night. Thank God for Moll and Margaret.

Moll and Margaret were my mother's sisters. Later Christmas Day, my uncle, the Chicago fireman John Brennan, came over for dinner. He was sitting at the kitchen table before dinner began, and of course I was eager to show him my new transistor radio. I handed it to him, and as he reached for it he dropped it on the linoleum floor. I looked down and saw that one of the corners of my beautiful, violet-colored Emerson radio had broken in the fall. It still played, but on Christmas day, the day I received it, it was broken. I was angry at John Brennan, and I felt like crying. But twelve-year-old Irish boys on the south side of the city did not do such things in public. John Brennan said to my mother, "Hey, Helen, do you have any Scotch tape around here?" She answered yes, got it, and gave it to him. He put tape on one side of the broken corner, and put tape on the other side of the broken corner. He smoothed out the tape, turned on the radio, and gave it back to me, saying, "There—good as new!" But it was not as good as new. I went to my bedroom, very sad that the coolest gift ever was broken. I put it on the bookshelf in the headboard of my bed.

I learned some things about Christmas gifts that Christmas. I learned that we exchange gifts at Christmas time to say to each other, " I love you." But I also learned that Christmas gifts do not last. They break; we outgrow them; we lose them; they become outdated—like transistor radios did in the 1970s. What is most important is that the love in our relationships that prompts gift giving does not break, that we do not outgrow or lose that love, that love does not become outdated.

It is Christmas 2011, and we continue to give gifts that say, "I love you." Remember that our gifts of love are a reflection of the gift of love given to us by God in the mystery of the Incarnation, the birth of Jesus, God entering our world and taking on the identity of being one of us, a person. We are reminded of God's great love for us in gifting us with Jesus in the words of Jesus in John 3:16, "God so loved the world that he gave his only son; so that everyone who believes in him might not perish but might have eternal life."

How is Jesus a gift to us? He is *The Way*: he reveals how we should be, how we should live, ideally what our world should look like. He assures us of the deep-down *meaning* in all of life, in all human experiences, in our joys, sorrows, sicknesses, and even our deaths. He has revealed to us the hope and the promise of *eternal life*. Life's most threatening and fear-producing events can be transformed by faith in Jesus and his promise of resurrection. Jesus is the revelation of that new vision and way of life that he called the *reign of God*. Jesus is the first Christmas gift that can never be broken, and who is everlasting.

Keep in mind that the mystery of the Incarnation is not just a historical event that we remember and celebrate. Christmas is not just a birthday. It is a celebration of a present reality: Jesus Christ is mysteriously always being born again. This is the mystery of the Incarnation.

Jesus is born again through the work and ministry of the Church. He is born again when we proclaim his truth through evangelization and catechesis. He is born again when we gather together for worship and the sacramental life. He is born again when we care for each other in need through acts of pastoral care. He is born again when we minister to our adolescents and young adults. He is born again when we engage in activities of mercy and justice. He is born again in the responsible administration of our faith communities. He is born again when we gather to share faith and prayer in Small Christian Communities. Jesus is born again when we, his Church, work to transform our world into God's reign.

Jesus is born again when we try to live God-centered lives. He is born again when we live lives of faith and hope. He is born again when we extend love and mercy to one another. He is born again when we extend charity to those in need. Jesus is born again when we strive to live vigilant and discerning lives. He is born again when we live lives of contrition, forgiveness, and reconciliation. He is born again when we are convinced of the truth of the paschal mystery—that life is about living, dying, and rising over and over again, to new life here on earth, and eternal life on the other side of death. He is born again when we discover him in new ways at every stage of human development.

Jesus is born again when we are born again and again and again. . . .

"The people who walked in darkness have seen a great light; upon those who dwelt in the land of gloom a light has shown. You have brought them abundant joy and great rejoicing. . . . For the yoke that burdened them, the pole on their shoulder, and the rod of their taskmaster you have smashed. . . . For a child is born to us, a son is given us; upon his shoulder dominion rests. They name him Wonder-Counselor, God-Hero, Father-Forever, Prince of Peace." These famous words from Isaiah 9 probably referred to the coming birth of King Hezekiah, whom Isaiah hoped would be a noble king for the people, leading them to new God-centeredness. The early Christians interpreted this passage as referring to Jesus. In a sense Isaiah himself did not completely understand the profound nature of his prophecy. In chapter 11, Isaiah speaks of a coming king who seems to be in the more remote future.

Luke's mentioning that the child Jesus was wrapped in swaddling clothes is a reflection of Wisdom 7:4–6, where Solomon is described as having been wrapped in swaddling clothes at his birth. Swaddling clothes were the garments that were put on ordinary babies at their birth (an emphasis on the humanity of Jesus), but the connection with Solomon is obviously an attempt to connect Jesus with David, Solomon's father. Jesus being placed in a manger, a food trough, is a strong statement that in many ways Jesus is food and nourishment for a hungry world.

So, Jesus can be born again in many different ways. He is born again every time we intentionally decide for him and invite him into our lives and hearts. I recall a Christmas card that I sent out many years ago that said very simply, "*He Is! And He Is Here! Hooray!*" Some of my friends thought that the card was a little goofy. For me, it simply says it all about the mystery of the Incarnation.

If you feel so moved, I invite you to join me in inviting Christ into our lives this Christmas. Pray with me:

Jesus, I am an imperfect, sinful person. I know that you are God's gift to us. You are Lord and Savior. I invite you into my heart, my mind, my spirit, and my way of life. Please be born again in me; and help me to be born again in you.

Remembering Paddy O'Cinnamon

This week I watched a show on WTTW, a public broadcasting channel, on the history of the Chicago Loop. The show put me in a nostalgic mood. I began to have memories of my childhood at Christmastime. I spontaneously remembered a radio show that became a television show: *The Cinnamon Bear*. My brother and I watched it with great devotion. It was the story of a bear, Paddy O'Cinnamon, who with two children, Judy and Jimmy, went on a search for the star for the children's Christmas tree, a star that had been taken by another, less than pleasant character. Paddy O'Cinnamon sang a song: "I'm the Cinnamon Bear with the shoe button eyes." It was a pretty song. He spoke and sang with a brogue, and everything turned out all right in the end; the star was retrieved.

I remembered also a TV show and a popular symbol at Christmastime titled Uncle Mistletoe. In 1946 Marshall Field's created Uncle Mistletoe to compete with Montgomery Ward's Rudolph the Red-Nosed Reindeer. The triweekly television program *The Adventures of Uncle Mistletoe* lasted for four seasons around Christmastime. I know now that both the Cinnamon Bear and Uncle Mistletoe were early devices of commercialization and marketing to get people into stores to shop. Indeed, the marketing went toward the kids, who in turn would influence adults.

My memories of the Cinnamon Bear and Uncle Mistletoe seem warmer and less harsh than the imagery and language we use around Christmastime now. We talk about Black Friday, now beginning on Thanksgiving night, in which people will stampede each other to get to deals at stores, to push businesses out of the red and into the black. Now we also have Small Business Saturday, the Saturday after Thanksgiving, in which we are encouraged to go and spend money in smaller stores. And of course there is the ever-popular and growing Cyber Monday, through which people spend a lot of money shopping via the Internet. Yes, the Cinnamon Bear and Uncle Mistletoe were cousins to Black Friday, Small Business Saturday, and Cyber Monday, but the season of Advent invites us to enter into realities that are more important and profound than selling and buying stuff.

For a number of years, the Office for Chicago Catholic Evangelization, which I codirected with Dawn Mayer, offered a day on evangelization in the African American Catholic community. We called it "Comfort My People Day," a day that offered the spiritual comfort which comes from a relationship with Jesus Christ for people dealing with the unique socioeconomic challenges of the African American community. The day was based on this passage from Isaiah 40: "Comfort, give comfort to my people, says your God. Speak tenderly to Jerusalem." This passage is taken from the second book of Isaiah, known as Deutero-Isaiah and as the book of Consolation. Written by an author other than the original Isaiah, the book is for Jewish exiles in Babylon, offering them encouragement and hope that someday their exile would end and they would be allowed to return home.

Whenever I read something from the book of Consolation (Isaiah 40–55), I am reminded of how much comfort and consolation faith brings into my life. I have struggled and still do struggle with my own painful emotions. Over the years, God's unconditional love for me and for all people has brought great healing and hope into my life. Sensing that I am not alone, that God's Spirit is always with me—with us—gives me strength and courage for life. When I am conscious of my sinfulness, God's word and the Sacrament of Reconciliation mediate to me God's mercy and forgiveness. Jesus's revelation of the mystery of life, death, and resurrection has convinced me of the meaning and purpose of life. This process of life, death, and resurrection is going on in each of our lives over and over again. We are constantly invited to new life here on earth and to eternal life when our physical lives come to an end.

One of the realities that faith in God/Abba, Jesus, and the Spirit brings into our lives is comfort. As Isaiah 40 promises, God is still bringing comfort to his people. How does God bring comfort and consolation to you? Sometimes the comfort of God comes to us through the presence, kindness, and words of other people. Let us be grateful for God's comforting ways, for God's patience with us as is talked about in 2 Peter.

But being a disciple of Jesus Christ is not just about being on the receiving end of God's comfort and consolation. Jesus and his teaching about the reign of God are also sources of great challenge. Many of us develop mistaken notions about life that are critiqued and challenged by the person and message of Jesus. As we seek during Advent to "prepare the way of the Lord," spoken of by Isaiah and John the Baptist, we are called to simultaneously wait for a new coming of Jesus into our lives and to facilitate that coming by repentance. Second Peter calls us to both wait and repent, and John the Baptist calls us to repentance in the Gospel of Mark. The call to ongoing repentance is one of the challenges of Christian discipleship.

Repentance presumes the reality of sin. Perhaps in the busyness of our lives we become unconscious of the reality of sin, or we become desensitized to sin. One of the things that the Scriptures teach us is that part of human nature is to engage in sin. There are sins that we commit; there also are sins of omission, in which we neglect to do the right, good, holy, just thing.

A word that helps me understand sin is "alienation." To be alienated is to be separated, estranged from everyone, someone, or something. We can be alienated from the best self that God is calling us to become. We can become alienated from other people. Similarly we can become distant or alienated from God.

One of the first steps in the process of repentance is to do what Mark says the people did in response to John's preaching: "They acknowledged their sins." To repent we need to do inventory as to how, where, and why we are alienated. We need to acknowledge our sins—for ourselves and to ourselves, to God, and when appropriate, to other people. This first step of acknowledging sin is a very important part of the process of repentance.

After acknowledging our sins, admitting and confessing them, we need to seek out God's forgiveness. We need also to do real-life, existential contrition and forgiveness work in our own relationships.

A very important part of the repentance process involves changing our minds and our hearts. Usually unconscious thinking patterns and assumptions lead us to justify sinful ways. True metanoia involves a process of changing patterns of thinking and feeling that lead to sinful alienation. Perhaps the most challenging part of repentance is changing behavior patterns that lead to or are involved in sin. Often we cannot accomplish this holistic conversion or repentance through our own power. Rather we need to turn to the Holy Spirit for the grace and strength to change.

In his book *Good to Great*, Jim Collins wrote that the biggest obstacle to organizations becoming great is complacency. Many organizations get comfortable with being "good enough." What is true of organizations and companies can be true of us also as disciples. We can become complacent. We can think, feel, and act as if we are good enough, not fulfilling the spiritual potential to which Jesus calls us. Jim Collins has a new book out titled *Great by Choice*, in which he speaks of the importance of decision making in moving in a direction of growth and transformation. Jesus in his reign of God preaching and teaching is constantly calling us to new decisions that lead us to follow him more intentionally in a life of discipleship. Jesus is certainly comfort, but he also is great challenge.

In chapter 9 of his book *Jesus: A New Vision*, Marcus Borg writes of Jesus as challenge. He says that Jesus's ministry and teaching challenged the conventional wisdom and dominant consciousness of his day. The alternative consciousness of Jesus (his call to the reign of God) collided with the dominant consciousness of his culture, wherein religion, politics, and militarism mutually supported each other in creating systems that dominated average and poor people. Borg feels that Jesus was executed by domination systems because of the challenge he brought to those systems. He needed to be out of the way. Similarly, we can get Jesus out of the way by our complacency, by our failure to attend to his challenge. If we are to truly prepare a way for the Lord to be reborn in us during Advent and Christmas, then we must not just embrace the comfort of Jesus but also his challenge, his call to holistic repentance.

When we allow Jesus to be both comfort and challenge in our lives, we are moving toward what Peter calls "new heavens and a new earth."

THE KINGDOM . . . IS LIKE . . .

Jesus knew Pharisaical law; he probably studied and learned it as a child, adolescent, and young man. But some scholars believe that Jesus and his cousin John became involved in a monastic group in their young adulthood, perhaps the Essenes. Spending time with these desert monks changed the faith and vision of these two cousins. John became an ascetical, prophetic preacher calling people to repentance. Jesus continued some of John's approach, calling people to repentance. Jesus, however, stepped beyond John—so much so that John sent representatives to Jesus—Luke 7; Matthew 11—asking his cousin if he, Jesus, is the one, or should people be looking for another? The ministry of Jesus became critical of the organized religion of his time. The ministry of Jesus became focused on a reality that he called the "kingdom of God" or the "reign of God."

In teaching about the reign of God, Jesus used a device called a parable. The word "parable" comes from the Greek, *parabole*, which refers to placing things side by side for comparison. A parable is a developed simile; a simile compares one thing to another of a different kind. The similarity is expressed by *like* or *as*. Often Jesus said, "The kingdom of God or the reign of God is like . . ." In Matthew's Gospel, Jesus speaks of the kingdom of heaven. The Gospel of Matthew was intended for a Jewish audience, converting to Christianity. Jewish people at the time were uncomfortable using the name of God with frequency. Out of respect for the name of God, the author of Matthew replaced "God" with "heaven."

The parables of Jesus fall into three categories. Some are advent parables. The reference to advent has nothing to do with the liturgical season of Advent. Rather, "advent" refers to the Latin infinitive *advenire*, which means "to come." Advent parables try to describe how God comes into and acts in our lives. Another classification of parables is parables of reversal. In these parables, our expectations of how God is and how life is are challenged and reversed. Action parables are parables that call us to do something, once we have discovered the mystery of the reign of God. Many of the parables are hybrids, combining the three different dynamics of the parables.

In the parable from Matthew 13, Jesus tells us that the kingdom of heaven is like a man who sowed good wheat seed in his field. Secretly his enemy sowed weeds throughout the wheat. His servants wanted to remove the weeds, but the householder told them that the weeds and the wheat were to grow together. At harvest time they would be separated: with the weeds thrown into a fire to be burned, and the wheat gathered into the barn. Jesus seems to be saying that the reign of God is the experience of good and evil, saints and sinners being allowed to coexist during our days on earth. However, there will be a harvest: the end of time, the final judgment. At this time God will allow people to experience the fulfillment of the lifestyles that they chose on earth. Some people will go on after death to eternal life, and some to eternal unhappiness.

In this first parable, we seem to have a definite hybrid. We are given hints of how God is with us in the world (advent parable). In addition, our expectations about God and the reign of God are reversed (parable of reversal). We are also called to act and live in expectation of the final harvest, the last judgment (action parable).

In telling parables, Jesus used imagery that people knew. In listening to the second parable, people would have been familiar with the small mustard seed. The people also knew that a small mustard seed grew to be a quite sizable bush. So it is with life in the reign of God. The reign of God can be a very small part of our lives. But if we give that mustard seed time and nurture, the reign of God can become a very significant part of our lives. As the growing bush becomes home to the birds of the sky, so also the reign of God becomes a place of comfort and hospitality to many people. All are welcome. Clearly, this is an advent parable, teaching us about the quiet, subtle ways God and the reign of God emerge in our lives.

In the final parable, we seem to be dealing with another advent parable: how God comes into and acts in our lives. Jesus tells us that the kingdom of heaven is like yeast that a woman took and mixed with three measures of wheat flour until the whole batch was leavened. A commentary I read regarding this passage said that yeast and three measures of wheat flour would have produced a substantial loaf of bread. Jesus is again teaching us that the reign of God is a reality that can grow and expand in our lives. Think about a loaf of bread: when we see a loaf of bread, we cannot see the yeast, but the yeast makes the whole loaf rise. God is like that. Sometimes God's presence is very hard to discern. Nonetheless, God's presence and activity in our lives are very real and tremendously influential in who we are and how we live.

The book of Wisdom reminds us that God teaches God's people, giving us hope, calling us to repentance. Paul reminds us in Romans 8 that the Spirit of God helps us in our weakness. These themes and many others are presented in the advent, reversal, and action parables of Jesus.

From my study, I believe that Jesus would not explain his parables. When I see or hear Jesus explaining the parables in the Gospels, I believe that those explanations are later additions, made by others in a later editing and development of the Scriptures. When Jesus told parables, I think he engaged people, got them caught up in the story, and allowed the meaning of the parable to gradually emerge in the mind of the listener.

Many of us were disturbed about the story of Caylee Anthony, the little two-year-old girl who was murdered and placed in a swamp. Her mother, Casey, was accused of the crime, but a jury acquitted her and she was released from prison. Many people are upset with both the verdict and Casey's liberation. Perhaps Jesus's parables, especially the one about the weeds and the wheat growing together, speak to us about this situation. As we witness this horrible story of a crime and injustice being done to a child, Jesus reminds us that the nature of life is that weeds and wheat often coexist in this life. But we all are moving toward a harvest of justice, in which God will do to the weeds what ought to be done. In the face of such apparent injustice on earth, let us trust in the weeds and wheat, mustard seed, yeast, God.

RADICAL FAITH IN A SURPRISING GOD

Have you ever had an apparent failure turn into a success or a blessing? That has happened to me a number of times. Significant losses, apparent failures, and struggles have become growth, transformation, conversion, and wisdom. There is a book titled *Adapt: Why Success Always Starts with Failure*, by Tim Harford, about how success flows from failure, often multiple failures. The author writes: "It seems to be the hardest thing in the world to admit that we've made a mistake and try to put it right. . . . Yet admitting our mistakes holds the key to solving the planet's most intractable problems." He says that success emerges from trial and error. Every wrong attempt discarded is one more step forward. Failure is necessary, useful, and must be tolerated. Evolution is a process driven by the failure of the less fit. This paradoxical thinking, that good and growth can emerge from that which is perceived to be negative, is a theme in Isaiah 45.

To review, remember that Isaiah is broken up into three separate parts. Chapters 1–39 were written by the original Isaiah. Chapters 40–55 are known as Deutero-Isaiah, or Second Isaiah. These chapters were written by another prophetic figure, addressed to the Jewish people in exile in Babylon. These chapters are also known as the book of Consolation, since they seek to offer hope and comfort to the exiled Jews, promising them a return to their homeland. Chapters 56–66, Trito-Isaiah, were written by another prophetic figure, addressing the Jews after they have returned to Jerusalem. Isaiah 45 offers this new-life-from-struggle paradox. The Babylonians had taken the Jews into exile for fifty years. But Cyrus, the king of Persia, defeated the Babylonians. Cyrus, in turn, would release God's people from exile, and allow them to go home to rebuild their lives. In the eyes of the

Jews, Cyrus was a pagan. He did not share in the faith of the Jewish people. Nonetheless, Isaiah speaks of him as an instrument of God. Speaking through Isaiah, God refers to Cyrus as "his anointed." God says that for the sake of Israel he has called Cyrus, though Cyrus does not know God. God, speaking through Isaiah, says, "There is no God besides me. . . . I am the LORD, there is no other."

This passage from Isaiah teaches us that God can work through any circumstance, in and through any and all people. God can choose unlikely people, like a pagan king, to effect new life and salvation for people. Our God is a surprising God, who works in surprising ways. God is a mystery to us, but God is present to and within us, ordering all circumstances to our growth and benefit. I am sure that the Jewish people were baffled and confused that Cyrus became the source of their liberation. The story of the Jewish people is about people of faith encountering this mysterious God over and over again and coming to hope and believe in and trust this benevolent God. Whether it was the exodus event, the giving of the commandments and the covenant, the rise of the monarchy, the teaching of the prophets, or this liberation from exile—experience and intuition taught the Jewish people to trust in God. This God was and is surprising; God's ways are not our ways.

Sometimes I have resisted, and do resist, the unfolding circumstances and events of life. I am particularly uncomfortable with change and transition. I favor continuity, stability, and the familiar. But I have discovered that sometimes it is in discomfort, in uninvited circumstances and events, with people whom I have not chosen to be with, that I have experienced great growth, learning, and spiritual transformation. As William Bridges has taught and written, it is often in the neutral zone, after a painful ending and before a new beginning, that a new beginning has actually already started.

With the people who first heard Isaiah 45 and its call to trust in the surprising God, we also are called to conviction and trust in the God of mystery and paradox. There are Cyrus-like people in our lives right now through whom God is working, leading us to new life. In the mystery of things we also are Cyrus figures for others. God is working through us, helping people, whom perhaps we are not aware of, to move to new life and new places.

Barbara Okun and Joseph Nowinski write beautifully about the paradox of new life coming from struggle in their book *Saying Goodbye: How Family Can Find Renewal Through Loss*. They say that with the advances in medicine, the seriously ill and dying are staying with us longer than such people did in the past. Much of our grief is now anticipatory grief; we grieve for a long time before someone leaves us in death. Okun and Nowinski state that the new grief process involves five stages:

1. The crisis of receiving the news of serious illness and impending death.
2. A new unity that emerges among loved ones concerning the sick person.
3. Upheaval, in which the new unity is lost and loved ones experience chaos and alienation.
4. Resolution, in which family members and friends have the opportunity to resolve long-standing issues, heal wounds, and redefine relationships.
5. Renewal, a time of renewed relationship with the one who has died and those loved ones still remaining here on earth.

We can use different words to describe the process, but what we are talking about here is the paschal mystery, the paschal process of life, death, new life, eternal life.

The call to radical, monotheistic faith is echoed in the gospel from Matthew. After having been challenged by Jesus's series of parables, Pharisees and Herodians sought to trap Jesus in his speech, to get him in trouble with the Romans and the Jewish leaders. They asked Jesus whether Jewish people should have to pay tax to the Roman government. The Pharisees were against such taxes; the Herodians, in collusion with Rome, supported the tax. Jesus, intuiting their deviousness, asks for a coin. In asking for a coin, Jesus was revealing how some of them already had given their allegiance to Caesar and Rome. As Jesus often masterfully did, he sidestepped their question and made a statement: "Repay to Caesar what belongs to Caesar and to God what belongs to God." Jesus is being practical: there is a certain government in charge at the time that can legitimately ask for taxes. But no government or political leader can serve as the foundation of our lives. We can build our lives on God alone. We hear that call again to radical, monotheistic faith. We are to purge from our lives all false gods, all false security, all examples of contemporary idolatry.

I have been leading a discussion on Rushworth Kidder's book *Moral Courage* at the Clare, where I direct pastoral care. Kidder says in his book that moral courage is made up of three realities: principles that we adhere to, dangers involved in living the principles, endurance through the painful results of living those principles and being moral. Jesus, in all his encounters with those who wanted to destroy him, always exhibited moral courage. He derived moral courage from his radical faith in the God of paradoxes and surprises. Let us allow that same God, in whom we have radical conviction and trust, to transform us into people of moral courage.

"The Kingdom of God Will Be Taken away from You"

Presidential elections have become a little like Christmas. We start on them earlier and earlier each time they come around. Nevertheless, presidential elections and elections in general are exciting times. They are an opportunity for people in a democratic republic like ours to look at the state of our nation, the fruitfulness of those in office, and to make decisions whether we support the status quo of what is going in our country. If we think that such fruitfulness is not there, we can choose to give the roles and responsibilities of leadership to others.

One thing that was obvious with the 2012 election was how concerned people were with the economy and jobs in our country. I gave a talk recently for a group of pastoral care workers on "Baby Boomers Becoming Senior Citizens." I mentioned that some of the research I came across said that aging baby boomers have two significant concerns at this time in their growth: whether their memories will become impaired with dementia and whether they will have enough financial resources to get through until the end of their lives—whether they will outlive their financial resources. Many are saying that a significant number of baby boomers probably will not be able to retire, or retire when they want to, because of our poor economy. I was in a meeting recently in which a man actually broke into tears over his financial situation. He is not a high-living, high-rolling man. He is a simple, holy man who is wondering if he is going to be able to support himself. In our socioeconomic/political situation, some in political office always run the risk of losing elections.

I thought of the elections as I studied today's readings from Isaiah and the Gospel of Matthew. The central image in both passages is God's vineyard standing perhaps for what Jesus meant by God's reign. Certainly in Isaiah and in the Gospel, the Jewish people of God are the focus, as those who have been blessed with the vineyard, with God's reign. In Isaiah and in the Gospel, there is a focus on how those who have been given the reign of God have not been good stewards of the gift that has been given them. In the Isaiah passage, there is a violent warning. God says he will destroy the vineyard or at least those who have had stewardship over it and transform it into something else. Those who are not fruitful in the vineyard will have the vineyard taken from them, as political office can be taken from some people today.

Similar imagery appears in the Gospel. Jesus seems to be saying to the religious people of his day—the chief priests and the elders—that the vineyard has been given to them historically, but the vineyard owner, God, sent servants to the tenants of the vineyard to teach them how to produce fruit in the vineyard. These servants seem to represent the prophets, and we are told that the tenants of the vineyard killed the servants, the prophets. The vineyard owner, God, decided to send his son to the vineyard, hoping that the son would have greater influence on the tenants than the servants did. But in mistaken, ignorant rage, the tenants killed the son of the vineyard owner in the hope of taking control of the vineyard themselves. They forgot about the reality of stewardship, that they have been given the vineyard for a while, to take care of it and to produce fruit. The Gospel passage closes with the chief priests, the temporary tenants of the vineyard, mindlessly indicting themselves as "wretched" and recommending that the vineyard be given to other tenants who will produce fruit. Jesus closes the Gospel by saying, "The kingdom of God will be taken away from you and given to a people who will produce its fruit."

So, while some politicians can lose their vineyard in election season, Jesus is warning so-called religious people that the vineyard can be taken from them also and given to people who produce greater fruit. I was reading an article recently by a bishop on the importance of returning to evangelization in the Catholic Church to help people hear and live the good news. The bishop lamented many contemporary issues that the Church has to deal with in doing the work of evangelization: consumerism, materialism, individualism, relativism. Religious leaders speak frequently of these isms as forces that contribute to the weakening of people's faith. The bishop went on in the article to say that the role of bishops in the Church is providing *authentication* to the message of the gospel. He talked of the importance of the teaching office of the Church, that Christ's message has been handed down, preserving its integrity and its vitality through the Church, beginning with the apostles and carried in each age by their successors, the bishops.

While I have great respect for the bishop who wrote that article, he seems to overemphasize the importance of the bishops' role in doing the work of evangelization. I believe that some of the missteps of bishops in recent years have resulted in counterevangelization—people not experiencing Jesus alive and active in our Church. Some of these people have chosen other faith expressions besides the Catholic Church in their search for Jesus. Some people have abandoned organized religions altogether and are doing reign-of-God work in other ways.

I read recently that Jesus preached the gospel by healing people. I think that many people are doing reign-of-God work outside of organized religion, outside of the institutional Roman Catholic Church.

This reign-of-God work is being done by doctors and nurses, counselors, psychotherapists, psychologists, spiritual directors, teachers, coaches, parents, spouses, families, and many other people who are involved in healing the brokenness of others, and helping others discover the meaning of life.

Bishops and other leaders in organized religion need to be warned by the gospel today. The vineyard can be—and in some ways is—being taken from them, and "given to a people that will produce its fruit."

I always find courage when I read the passage today from Philippians 4. Paul tells the Philippians and us, "Have no anxiety. . . . By prayer and petition with thanksgiving, make your requests known to God. Then the peace of God . . . will guard your hearts and minds in Christ Jesus." Paul goes on to teach us that we are to focus on what is true, honorable, just, pure, lovely, gracious, and excellent. We are to think about these things, and we are to keep on *doing* what we have learned and received. "Then the God of peace will be with you." We are reminded again by Paul that changing our minds—changing our hearts—through prayer and the imagery of our faith tradition, and changing our behavior to conform with the ideals of the reign of God can ultimately bring us inner peace in an age of anxiety and depression. This is the message that contemporary people are hungry and thirsty for, and they are often not hearing it in the preaching and liturgical celebration of a Church that, at times, is failing to produce fruit for the reign of God.

VENERATION OF THE CROSS

When I became the pastor of Holy Family Parish in Inverness, Illinois, in 1995, I inherited a huge fundraising and building campaign that my predecessor began. I spent many winter nights that first year going to people's homes, asking them to donate funds for the construction of the Bernardin Center for Spirituality and Ministry, as well as to acquire religious art for the worship space. The church did not have a crucifix or Stations of the Cross. Negotiations had already begun with an artist in California for the cross. It was a unique design. It was to be made of acrylic, which really resembles crystal, and it was to depict Jesus rising from the cross, extending his hand toward the congregation, seemingly inviting the community into the mystery of life, death, and resurrection. In other words, instead of separating out those three elements—life, death, and resurrection—the cross portrayed them as part of one mystery, the paschal or passage mystery.

The emergence of this new cross took me to the West Coast to meet the artist and see a mold that he was using to design the cross. Unfinished, the cross was baked in an instrument used to produce fighter jets. It then was sent to New Jersey for finishing. I flew to New Jersey to see it in its final stages of completion. I asked that a wound be placed in hand of Jesus, for though he rose and was glorified, he was still wounded. The first two versions of the cross failed; the vicar/bishop allowed us to try a third and final time. It worked. The cross was sent to Inverness; a big chunk of windows had to be temporarily removed to get the cross into the church. A number of engineers worked on hanging it over the sanctuary. The final cost was eight hundred thousand dollars—a lot of money for a shanty Irish guy from the southwest side of the city. I had trouble with that dollar amount, but I came to appreciate the cross because I saw the transformation it brought about in people. In artistic form, people could see the whole mystery: life, death, and resurrection. I was asked one day as pastor what I wanted to name the cross. I said, "The Cross of New Life." Paradoxically, that cross communicates the essence of what we are about this week—our belief that new life, and eventually eternal life, comes from the crosses that we experience in life.

The cross and crucifixion were the ultimate forms of punishment that the Roman government used to control and discipline people whom they had conquered and overtaken. Crucifixion usually involved preliminary scourging and abuse, followed by the prisoner carrying the cross to the place of execution. Nails, six to eight inches long, were hammered into the wrists of the crucified. Roman soldiers learned how to cut tendons in the wrists that made it impossible for the crucified to have any power in their arms. The crucified could only support themselves through the use of back muscles and feet, one foot nailed on top of the other. Eventually, the crucified died of suffocation, unable to breathe. If the person was slow in dying, the legs were broken, so that the person could no longer push up for gasps of air. Crucifixions took place close to the ground where dogs and other animals could get to the crucifieds' bloody bodies. Sometimes crucifixions would go on for more than a day. After death, the body was usually left on the cross so birds and other scavengers would destroy it, leaving nothing to bury. The fact that Jesus died in so short a time indicates that he was probably very abused before he was crucified. This brutal form of capital punishment has become the central symbol of our faith, and paradoxically, a symbol of hope.

The cross—the crucifix—takes different shapes and forms in religious art. My favorite cross was given to me by a teenager, about fifteen years old, in 1972. The teen's name was Jim. He made the cross with his dad. It is very simple, without a corpus on it, but on the back of the cross, Jim and his dad carved these words from Pauline theology: "If we die with him, we shall also rise with him." Wherever I have lived these past forty years, Jim's cross has had a prominent place. Many times through a day, I stop at the cross, stand before it, kneel before it, and venerate or kiss it. Jim's cross gives me a sense of Christ's presence especially if I am carrying any hurt or burden. This cross reminds me that, in different ways, I am sharing in the same mystery that Jesus experienced. Jim's cross gives me meaning and hope.

We possess so many crosses of different shapes and sizes. Having worked with the Franciscans for several years now, the San Damiano cross has become important for me. This cross is a replica of the cross that St. Francis of Assisi was praying near, when he heard Jesus calling him to deeper conversion, to rebuild his church. For Francis, the Greek letter *tau*, which resembles our "T," became an important crosslike symbol. Francis would use it to sign his name. A friend gave me a cross made of Irish crystal; this cross is in my bedroom. I kiss it or venerate it every morning and night. I have a Christmas ornament that is a small Irish crystal cross. I frequently feel a small cross in my pocket on my rosary; sometimes just holding that little cross gives me strength.

All of us have crosses of different shapes and sizes in our lives. The loved ones of seventeen-year-old Trayvon Martin grieve the loss of a young man to handgun violence, and the apparent injustice that his killer is not being held responsible for this violent act. Tom Schuman, an eighteen-year-old baseball player and golfer at Lincoln-Way Central High School in New Lenox, went home early last Friday, not feeling well. Saturday morning, his brother could not wake him. He passed away in his sleep. An autopsy as to why he died has been inconclusive. His family and his friends are grieving in confusion. What happened to this strong, charismatic young man?

Some of us deal with chronic illnesses. Some have acute pain in their lives. Some of us are dealing with disappointment and rejection. Many of us are dealing with grief from different kinds of losses. Many people suffer emotionally from anxiety, stress, worry, or depression. Some have financial concerns. Some of us are un- or underemployed. For some, aging is a difficult and painful experience. For some, there is the pain of relationships falling apart. Some people's lives have been seriously harmed by addictions of some kind. Some are worried and concerned about an unclear future. We all know the pain, the vulnerability involved in being human. These issues might not be as violent or bloody as Christ's crucifixion, but they are nonetheless shares in the mystery of his cross.

In the movie *The Passion of the Christ*, director Mel Gibson portrayed Jesus as kissing and embracing the cross when the Roman soldiers put it on his shoulder. Gibson presented Jesus as fully accepting the cross, believing that Abba/God was with him as he walked toward Golgotha, and that God would lead him through the cross to vindication and eternal life. When the cross came to Jesus, he venerated it, embraced it, and carried it. As the Scriptures teach us, he fell under it several times. He was so weak that finally he needed help to carry it. Good Friday calls us to take on Jesus's approach to the cross. Whenever and however the cross enters our lives, we are to venerate it, embrace it, and carry it. Sometimes we need to be humble enough to ask for help in carrying our crosses. If and when we see other people struggling with crosses, we should try to help them with theirs.

Let us keep in mind the seven last words of Jesus as he hung on the cross:

Father forgive them; for they know not what they are doing. (Luke 23:34)

I assure you: this day you will be with me in paradise. (Luke 23:43)

Woman, there is your son. . . . There is your mother (John 19:26–27)

I thirst. (John 19:20)

My God, my God . . . why have you forsaken me? (Matthew 25:46; Mark 15:34)

Father, into your hands, I commend my spirit. (Luke 23:46)
It is finished. (John 19:30)

I have shared with many of you how helpful that sixth word of Jesus has been for me. When Jesus said, "Father, into your hands I commend my spirit," he was praying Psalm 31:6. It was and is a statement of total surrender into and trust in God's love in the face of the pain of the cross. When the mystery of the cross enters our lives, we are to venerate it, embrace it, carry it, and live and pray: "Father, into your hands, I commend my spirit." That attitude, posture, and behavior of total trust and surrender will always lead to new life.

New Life . . . Eternal Life

Easter

My journey of adult conversion began in my early twenties. As some of you know, from things that I have written or talks that I have given,

I wrestled with problems with anxiety as a young adult. In fact, that tendency toward anxiety still exists; I am one of those people who has an anxious nature. This anxiety problem led me in my twenties to seek out counseling and spiritual direction. I was the first and only person in my family, that I know of, who had to seek out psychological and spiritual help. (Probably most of my family also should have done this. I took one for the team.) Those years of getting help surprised me a great deal: I grew in a kind of existential wisdom, and a deep trust in the power and love of God at work in my life. Psychological pain gave way to new life.

This psychological and spiritual growth helped me in my first assignment as a priest in St. Hubert's parish in Hoffman Estates, Illinois. Those early years in the 1970s were truly happy years spent in work in religious education and youth ministry. But after seven quick years, I had to move on. I remember on my last Sunday afternoon at St. Hubert's stopping at the home of a family with whom I was very close. We hugged and cried. I went on to start the Office for Chicago Catholic Evangelization, which led me to resource most of the parishes in the Archdiocese of Chicago in parish-based evangelization and parish renewal. I also went on to serve wonderful people at St. Albert the Great in Burbank, and St. Michael's in Orland Park. I began teaching at the Institute for Pastoral Studies and writing books. I began to travel to different parts of the country and the world to speak. Leaving St. Hubert's was a death for me; but it led to so much growth and new life.

In the early 1990s, my aging family began to leave me through death. I was responsible for the wakes, the funerals, the funeral homilies. Through it all I was strong and effective, but I was not in touch with what all this loss was doing to me internally. I began to find it difficult to go to work each day. I tried to get out of talks and responsibilities that I had assumed. I went back to my counselor and explained how I felt within, and he diagnosed me as suffering from dysthymia, an extended, subtle form of depression that does not completely stop you as major depression can. I resented the counselor's diagnosis and resisted it. Not too many days later, I had to ask Cardinal Bernardin for time off to deal with the depression. It took me weeks and months to get through this time, but I heard God's call in the midst of all this to become a new creation, to become new in and through Jesus Christ. God again blessed me with new life.

I began a full-time job after this at the Institute for Pastoral Studies at Loyola University, and I began working part-time with the Rite of Christian Initiation of Adults and Small Christian Communities at Holy Family Parish in Inverness, Illinois. Increasingly, I was becoming my mother's primary caregiver, which necessitated driving to her house in Tinley Park, Illinois, every day. My doctor convinced me that I had to get help in caring for her, that I would begin to have emotional problems again if I did not get help. Though my mother did not like the situation, having help caring for her greatly reduced my stress. Again, in the early 1990s, God blessed me with new life.

Disagreements led me to leave the Institute at Loyola. Thus, I was in my late forties and again an associate pastor. I loved my work at Holy Family and was graciously accepted on to the staff full-time. Then something unexpected happened: The pastor of Holy Family decided that it was time for him to step down. Because I was known and trusted by many people in the parish, I was encouraged to apply to be pastor. I did. Though Cardinal Bernardin knew of my previous emotional struggles, he and the priests' placement board appointed me pastor. I rose again, through the power of God, to new life. I began the happiest and most fulfilling years of my priesthood. I stayed at Holy Family for seventeen years—three years as an associate pastor, and fourteen years as pastor.

I always feared that I would not be able to face my mother's death. But with courage and conviction I was able to say over her as she was dying on Valentine's Day 2003, "Father, into your hands, I hand over Ma; into your hands, I hand over her life." With wonderful friends to help me, and a wonderful parish standing by me, I was able to navigate the weeks and months of grief. I still miss her. I speak with her regularly, and I look forward to being with her and all of my loved ones who have preceded me in death. I am convinced that all crosses—all death experiences, in whatever shape and form they come in—always lead to new life and eternal life on the other side of death.

I had to leave Holy Family in 2009. It was a truly great loss. The parish had indeed become my home and family. I again thought that I would not make it through this experience, but I did—because of the God who always invites us to new life, and because of faith-filled relationships that I shared with friends and three new communities where I began working.

I was blessed to be able to work at the Clare, a continuing care retirement community operated by the Franciscan Sisters of Chicago; for the last three years I have worked at starting a new kind of parish—an interdenominational community made up of Catholics, Protestants, Jews, and some who claim to be atheists—all in the pursuit of the meaning of life.

For almost three years I have also worked at St. Thomas the Apostle parish in Naperville, Illinois. This is a wonderful community with excellent ministries, excellent liturgies, and people who are true, humble servant-leaders.

At the urging of friends, though I was computer-illiterate at the time, I began the *National Center for Evangelization and Parish Renewal Newsletter*, which contains my weekend homilies. To receive the newsletter, people have to request it. Thousands of people have requested to receive this weekly reflection, and it has resulted in a virtual Internet community of people around the world with whom I communicate. It is amazing!

The Clare, St. Thomas, and the newsletter community have become new life for me.

With the exception of his female disciples and several other men, Jesus was more or less abandoned by those closest to him in the final hours of his life. But after his resurrection, these weak and diffident apostles and disciples became strong witnesses to his resurrection. In sharing parts of my life story with you this Easter, that is what I am trying to do. I have, as you have, lived and died and risen with Jesus Christ over and over again. We were baptized into this mystery. We know and live the paschal process—from life, through death, to new life. It is sloppy, in the sense that we can be in the middle of a new life experience and a death experience can happen. As followers of Jesus, we have come to trust this process. We know that this is not an experience of God doing everything for us. In growing into new life, we have to engage in effort, cooperating with God in moving toward new life. Having lived and died with Jesus multiple times over the years, and now celebrating Easter at sixty-five years of age, I believe that this process will continue over and over again. The day will come when we come to the end of our physical lives. Then the process will continue; we will be invited to eternal life with God and those who have gone before us.

Because we have lived, died, and risen with Jesus multiple times here on earth, by way of analogy it becomes reasonable to make that leap of faith that Jesus truly rose from the dead on that first Easter. Jesus lived and died to reveal the paschal nature of life—that he rose from the dead—and he invites us to do the same in small ways during our days on earth, and in a final, full way when we die.

The feast of Easter, the resurrection of Jesus, and the promise of our resurrection assure us that all of life has meaning and purpose; we can face and experience anything because of our faith in the risen Jesus and the paschal process. As Peter and the other first witnesses of the resurrection experienced, the message of Easter must be shared; as they were witnesses to the resurrection, so must we become. Especially to people who are struggling, who are doubting the meaning of life, we must tell them that all of life is good and meaningful because of the Easter event. Let us think about the people in our lives who need to hear about Jesus and resurrection. Let us become witnesses to them. Let us pass on the good news.

THE CLEANSING OF THE TEMPLE

The cleansing of the temple appears in all four of the Gospels, which suggests that an actual incident took place in which Jesus confronted the marketplace activity in the temple. Matthew, Mark, and Luke place this story in close proximity to the crucifixion of Jesus. John places it at the very beginning of Jesus's ministry. This confrontation in John's Gospel seems to have turned the religious leaders against Jesus early on in his ministry. Jesus seems to have become a kind of outlaw, constantly eluding the religious leaders with whom he was in conflict.

What troubled Jesus so much about what was going on in the temple? The priests and other religious leaders demanded that people pay tax or dues to offer sacrifice. In addition, people had to pay money to purchase an animal for sacrifice. Most poor Jews could only afford the doves mentioned in the Gospel. Most people would come with Roman coins; money changers would transform the Roman coins into Jewish currency. In effect, worship and sacrifice had become an institutionalized system, a business that abused poor people and made religious leaders wealthy.

Jesus was opposed to the whole sacrificial system as well as the lifestyle of the priests and other religious leaders. The cleansing of the temple was a strong, prophetic act against the status-quo religion of the day. Jesus, in cleansing the temple, was undermining the very identity of religious leaders. John suggests that these leaders decided early on that Jesus had to be taken out of the picture.

In his book *What Jesus Meant,* Garry Wills wrote that Jesus opposed religion as it was understood in his time. This is what led to his death; religion killed Jesus. Jesus opposed the sacrificial system, the Sabbath and eating codes, the priesthood, the rules of the Sadducees, Pharisees, and scribes. He called people to a spirituality of the heart. We never hear of any priests becoming followers of Jesus. Wills writes that religion today would look all too familiar to Jesus, perpetuating the very things he critiqued about the cleanliness code, the Sabbath rules, the sacrificial system, and the temple. Wills wrote,

What is the kind of religion that Jesus opposed? Any religion that is proud of its virtue like the boastful Pharisee. Any that is self-righteous, quick to judge and condemn, ready to impose

burdens rather than share or lift them. Any that exalts its own officers, proud of its trappings, building expensive monuments to itself. Any that neglects the poor and cultivates the rich, any that scorns outcasts and flatters the rulers of this world. If that sounds like just about every form of religion we know, we can see how far from religion Jesus stood.

The temple can serve as a metaphor for religion in our own day. If Jesus were to enter the temple of our Church today, I think he would have trouble with some of the language that we now use in the prayers of the mass, which makes God seem so distant from humanity. Jesus had a concept of a close, loving God who seeks spiritual intimacy with us. I think Jesus would cleanse our temple of a hierarchical approach to leadership. When Jesus taught his style of leadership, he washed his apostles' feet. He modeled servant leadership. I think Jesus would cleanse the temple of the clericalism that is connected to the priesthood. Again, Garry Wills says that Jesus had trouble with a separate caste system of priests. Any approach to religion that says a group of men is ontologically different from the rest of the people, and are to be treated with greater dignity or respect, would trouble Jesus. Jesus would critique the hierarchical and clerical leadership of the Church that makes so many people in the Church conforming sheep.

Jesus would cleanse our Church of any form of Church busyness that is not respectful of people's gifts. Jesus wants a Church where people discern their gifts and use them—where people are allowed to discover their voice. Jesus would cleanse the Church of a narrow understanding of vocation. Jesus would share another vision that speaks of all people being called by God to use their gifts for God's glory and the common good.

Jesus would cleanse the Church of its impoverished understanding of leadership. Jesus wants a Church in which all the baptized hear the call to leadership and respond to that call.

Jesus would cleanse the temple of our Church of its demeaning approach to women. He would cleanse the Church of its blocking women to assume greater leadership roles. Jesus would cleanse the Church of its celibate-only leadership. In examples from around the world, Jesus has already begun this process. Jesus would cleanse the temple of our Church of its jaundiced view of human sexuality.

As he did with the Jewish leaders, Jesus would critique and cleanse the temple of our Church of any antiquated laws and regulations that no longer serve any useful purpose. Jesus would cleanse our Church of religion that is not rooted in heartfelt spirituality and religious experience. This Jesus who called people to change their lives would cleanse the temple of religion without conversion and spiritual transformation. The mission of Jesus Christ was and is the reign of God. Jesus would cleanse the temple these days of any approach to religion that emphasizes Church or structure over the reign of God.

I believe that Jesus would cleanse the temple of our Church of boring liturgies, poor preaching, and liturgies that fail to provide religious experience. I think Jesus would critique and cleanse the temple of our Church of any leaders or authorities who participated in the covering up and moving around of pedophile priests. I think Jesus would cleanse the Church of people who emphasize religious devotions without a commitment to and action for social justice.

I think Jesus would enter the temple also of Evangelical Christianity and cleanse it of its vision that gospel living assures economic prosperity. Jesus would cleanse the temple of any world religion that emphasizes the differences among people rather than our commonality and unity, any religion that espouses violence in the name of God.

If Jesus were to return and get serious about cleansing our contemporary temple, he would devise a new kind of whip of cords, and he would be busy and need a long time to do his work. He would drive contemporary money changers out of the temple, and he would overturn many tables. As with the religious leaders of his day, Jesus in the present experience would be and is a threat to religious leadership. He would have to be assassinated. He would have to be gotten out of the way, as was attempted with his crucifixion.

But there is no getting Jesus out of the way. Yes, on one level in this gospel passage Jesus was predicting the fall of the temple in Jerusalem. But when he spoke of destroying the temple and raising it up again in three days, he was speaking of himself. He was predicting the victory of his resurrection. People will continue to pollute the temple of the Church, with banal realities far from the vision and lifestyle of the reign of God to which Jesus invites us. The victory of his resurrection and his prophetic challenge to continuously cleanse the temple will always prevail.

As Paul says in 1 Corinthians, "Christ [is] the power of God and the wisdom of God."

Jerusalem, Our Destiny

I have fixed my eyes on your hills, Jerusalem, my Destiny. Though I cannot see the end for me, I cannot turn away.
We have set our hearts for the way; this journey is our destiny. Let no one walk alone. The journey makes us one.

These beautiful words are the refrain from Rory Cooney's song "Jerusalem, My Destiny." The first two lines speak of the mind and heart of Jesus in the days before his death. St. Luke tells us in his Gospel, at least twice, that Jesus very deliberately moved toward Jerusalem. The implication is that he could have gone another way. He could have gone elsewhere, but he courageously embraced the confrontation that awaited him in Jerusalem. Cooney suggests that perhaps Jesus did not know completely what the end would look like. It seems clear that he knew he would be executed. It seems clear that he knew the Father would vindicate him and that death would not be the end for him. But all the details, all the struggle, all the pain that was awaiting him in Jerusalem—perhaps he was not conscious of all that. Nevertheless, Cooney portrays Jesus as saying, "I cannot turn away." He very deliberately went toward Jerusalem.

In the last two lines of the refrain, the speaker changes. The speaker seems to be all of us, the Body of Christ, disciples of Jesus. We have set our hearts for the way. We have used Lent, haven't we, to move toward this celebration—the death and resurrection that we mark during Holy Week? The refrain goes on: This journey is also our destiny. Jesus is the prototype, but we share in the same mystery he experienced.

I read a story recently by a man who was reflecting on Holy Week. The man said he never completely understood the relevance of Holy Week for him personally. It seemed to be a week that historically marked the death and resurrection of Jesus Christ. It was not until his three-year-old daughter developed a serious heart problem that required open-heart surgery that he began to gain insight into the paschal mystery and how not just Jesus but all of us share with him, over and over again, in the mystery of life, death, and resurrection. When the gentleman and his wife had to surrender their daughter to the surgeon, they knew what death was all about. As the little girl recovered, regained health, and began to grow to be a healthy young girl, they grew in understanding of what resurrection and new life here on earth is all about. Holy Week is a very meaningful celebration for this family now.

Jerusalem comes to each of us in different ways. Sometimes we choose Jerusalem when we willfully and intentionally choose patterns of feeling, thinking, and behaving to help us experience repentance, metanoia, conversion, and growth. Sometimes Jerusalems happen to us. We lose a job; we suffer financially; we lose a relationship; we go through a divorce; we move; we age. Something significantly changes the world or the lives of the people whom we love. When Jerusalems happen to us, we cannot hide from them. We must keep moving toward them as Jesus did.

Then there will be the final and full Jerusalem, the Jerusalem of physical death—our own deaths and the deaths of people whom we love. The words of my forty-eight-year-old friend Tim still stay with me. When I saw him in his apartment the last day I saw him alive, we hugged, he sat down, and he said, "I'm dying. I am dying from cancer."

I said, "I know, Tim, and we are all moving in the same direction."

He said, "Yeah, I am just getting there before all of you."

This week we go forth, not morbidly, but realistically focused on the ultimate Jerusalem of our physical deaths, trusting again as Jesus did that God calls us through death to eternal life.

"This [his] journey is our destiny. Let no one walk alone. The journey makes us one." The last line of Cooney's refrain reminds us that no matter how we feel, no matter the circumstances of our lives, all of us are in this mystery—the paschal mystery—together.

To understand Jesus's walk toward Jerusalem, we have to understand what his main mission in life was. In Luke 4:43 he says he has come to the world to reveal the nature of the reign of God. Jesus was a man of truth. That is how he describes himself several times in the Gospel of John. He had to continue to speak the truth of the reign of God. He could not allow either the religious leaders or the civil leaders to deter him from that mission. It was revealing the nature of the reign of God that necessitated him to speak and to engage in the behaviors that would reveal the truth of death leading to new life and eternal life. His mission would not be complete until he had engaged in this final revelation.

I asked the people down at the Clare what the promise of eternal life does for them each day. Several of them said, "It means everything to me. Everything in life has meaning because of Christ's life, death, and resurrection."

I recently gave two presentations at the Los Angeles Religious Education Congress. One was on transitions in life. Some people attending the conference were there because they were going through a career change themselves. Some had gone through divorce. Others were wrestling with the transition of pastors in their parishes. I used William Bridges's material on transition for a significant part of the presentation. Bridges writes that transition is really a way of life. We are in the midst of changes all the time. Change needs to involve transition. Change itself is situational. Transition is psychological, spiritual, and interpersonal. Without working a process of transition, we often are not successful with change.

Transition is a secular way of understanding the paschal mystery. In the mystery of life, death, and resurrection, to use Bridges's language, we must in our lifetimes endure many *endings*. We need to say good-bye to people. We need to let go of realities that we are losing. These endings propel us into what Bridges calls the *neutral zone*, a period of time characterized by moratorium. The neutral zone is almost more painful than the ending, for in the neutral zone we do not know where we are going. Perhaps we even have assumed new roles or new jobs, but we do not feel at home in the world. People want to skip the neutral zone or get through it quickly, but it must be passed through. In the neutral zone, the third phase of transition, *new beginnings*, has already started, but often it is imperceptible to those going through the transition.

Bridges used the decades-long wandering in the desert of the Jewish people as they were led by Moses as an example of a journey through the neutral zone. He says that the establishment of the covenant and the Ten Commandments at Mount Sinai did not happen in the promised land. Rather it happened in the neutral zone and was the initial experience of a new beginning for the Jewish people.

The paschal mystery, as we experience it with Jesus, is proceeding through endings, neutral zones, and new beginnings over and over again. To go through this process we must capture the trust and surrender that Jesus had as he walked toward his personal, final Jerusalem. We need to trust and hope that Jerusalems always lead to new life here on earth, and eternal life when our physical lives come to an end. Bridges says that a series of neutral zones experienced for a lifetime are what lead us to have wisdom for life. Daniel Levinson, another psychology writer reflecting on transitions in people's lives, says that transitions are what contribute to individuation, or each of us becoming the "self" that we are intended to be.

Let us watch and pray with Jesus this week, and let us be reminded of the truth of the Rory Cooney song. Let us become one with the experience of Jesus. "I have fixed my eyes on the hills, Jerusalem, my

Destiny. Though I cannot see the end for me, I cannot turn away." Let us also be reminded of the words of the refrain that speak about the Body of Christ, the disciples of Jesus. "We have set our hearts for the way. Let no one walk alone. The journey makes us one." Let us not be isolated these next days, but one with each other in a deep experience of the meaning of life.

Part 2

CONVERSION

Hate . . . Really?

For a few moments, try to see in your mind's eye the people whom you love the most: your spouse; your children; your grandchildren; your siblings; your parents, whether they are living or deceased; extended family; friends. As you visualize all of these wonderful people now, hear the message that Jesus delivers in the Gospel of Luke. We are to hate these people. Can Jesus really mean that? Jesus, who in other parts of the Gospels calls us to radical love of, service toward, and justice for other people? We are to hate the people whom we love?

At the end of this Gospel passage, we are told that we cannot be his disciples or followers if we are not willing to renounce all of our possessions. That is unsettling. Jesus never had to worry about a recession. He never had to worry about unemployment. He did not concern himself with getting kids through college. He did not worry whether his resources would last into his senior years. He did not face the difficult economic times that many of us are experiencing. We are to renounce possessions even as the economy stagnates and resources are dwindling?

I believe Jesus is using hyperbole in this particular teaching. He is exaggerating to get our attention and make a point. I think he is teaching us that no one or no thing should have the force or the role of God in our lives except God. Only God can be God. I think Jesus is teaching us that we must make our relationship with God, in and through Jesus and the Spirit, foundational in our lives. If we have this foundational relationship or first relationship, we are more empowered to share love and mercy and justice with other people. If we are not controlled by our possessions, we are in a better position to share our resources with those in need. I am sure that Jesus understands that we need to have enough to live relatively peaceful, happy lives, but he is teaching us to not be possessed by or controlled by the resources in our lives. Each of us will die, and we will not be able to take any of our things with us. Things need to be contextualized. The world's resources need to be shared more equitably.

In Adlerian psychology, we speak of the life tasks—the realities of life that people must confront, deal with, and get through to be healthy adults. There is the task of *healthy self-esteem*, the task of *forming friendships*, the task of *being intimate* with another person, and the task of *finding meaningful work*. As Adlerian thought developed, another task was added to these first four: the cosmological task, *coming to terms with the role of God* in their lives. People need to grow in a sense of meaning and purpose. I think that Jesus's challenge to us today is to work on the cosmological task now and throughout our lifetime.

Jesus offers himself to us as the foundation for our lives, the meaning for our lives. It is from this foundation, this center point, this still point, that we are to live, love, and have our being. Experiencing Jesus as our foundation necessitates that we make a deliberate, intentional decision for him. It is also necessary to have a lifelong, ever-growing, ever-deepening relationship with him. It is necessary to become a student of Jesus, a disciple of Jesus, always striving to grow in understanding and living what he meant by the reign of God.

Making Jesus our foundation is not something that we do alone. While there obviously are individual aspects, the experience of Jesus becoming our foundation happens in and through relationships, in and through community.

What I am describing here is the born-again experience, at least as I understand it. In being born again, the experience does not just happen once. Rather, decisions, relationships, learning, and communal dimensions of faith are realities in which we need to be constantly growing.

In the gospel, Jesus makes reference to someone building a tower and another person engaging in warfare. He talks about the importance of intentionality, or doing things with reflection and on purpose, if people are to succeed. So it is with the experience of making God—with Jesus, in the Spirit—the foundation of our lives. It requires moments each day, time each week, for us to be deliberate and intentional about faith and spirituality. We need to plan our spiritual lives. We need to develop a spiritual program in which we do things that place us in daily conscious contact with God, or abstain from doing certain things that inhibit that contact.

The Scriptures invite us to make a fundamental option for Jesus to be the Lord of our lives. The fundamental option needs to express itself in our living the attitudes and behaviors of the reign of God. This fundamental option must be deliberately and intentionally renewed on a regular basis. This decision for Christ also opens for us a share in what is talked about in the book of Wisdom, a share in God's wisdom, a share in God's Holy Spirit.

In Paul's short letter to Philemon, Paul writes from prison, and he writes about a slave, Onesimus, whom he met there. Through their shared time together, Paul used the opportunity to make a convert of Onesimus, helping him to make that decision for Jesus Christ. Onesimus was a runaway slave. He had run away from Philemon, who apparently was a convert of Paul's and the leader of a house church. Paul sends Onesimus back to Philemon and he asks Philemon, "Do not see Onesimus any longer as a slave." He says to Philemon, "I am sending you my heart, and I want you to accept him as a brother." Paul beautifully demonstrates the change in attitude, thinking, feeling, and behavior that results from making this fundamental decision for Jesus Christ. The slave was a commodity in Paul's day, a person who was treated like a thing. Paul calls Philemon to recognize Onesimus as a human being and a brother. He calls all of us to see each other as equals, brothers and sisters in the reign of God. Some scholars believe that this short letter was included in Paul's body of work because of its long-term challenge to the institution of slavery. Let us respond to Jesus's challenge this week to make him the foundation of our lives, our first, life-giving, spiritually empowering relationship.

I received a story this week about a little girl, a mom, and apparently an anonymous person working in the dead letter department of the U.S. Postal Service—all of whom are striving to make Jesus the foundation of their lives.

Story of Meredith and Abbey

Our 14-year-old dog, Abbey, died last month. The day after she died, my 4-year-old daughter Meredith was crying and talking about how much she missed Abbey. She asked if we could write a letter to God so that when Abbey got to heaven, God would recognize her. I told her that I thought we could, so she dictated these words:

Dear God,
Will you please take care of my dog? She died yesterday and is with you in heaven. I miss her very much. I am happy that you let me have her as my dog even though she got sick.

I hope you will play with her. She likes to play with balls and to swim. I am sending a picture of her so when you see her you will know that she is my dog. I really miss her.

Love, Meredith

We put the letter in an envelope with a picture of Abbey and Meredith and addressed it to God/Heaven. We put our return address on it. Then Meredith pasted several stamps on the front of the envelope because she said it would take lots of stamps to get the letter all the way to heaven. That afternoon she dropped it into the letter box at the post office.

A few days later, she asked if God had gotten the letter yet. I told her that I thought he had.

Yesterday, there was a package wrapped in gold paper on our front porch addressed "To Meredith" in an unfamiliar hand. Meredith opened it. Inside was a book by Mr. Rogers called When a Pet Dies. Taped to the inside front cover was the letter we had written to God in its opened envelope. On the opposite page was the picture of Abbey & Meredith and this note:

Dear Meredith,

Abbey arrived safely in heaven. Having the picture was a big help. I recognized Abbey right away.

Abbey isn't sick anymore. Her spirit is here with me just like it stays in your heart. Abbey loved being your dog.

Since we don't need our bodies in heaven, I don't have any pockets to keep your picture in, so I am sending it back to you in this little book for you to keep and have something to remember Abbey by.

Thank you for the beautiful letter and thank your mother for helping you write it and sending it to me. What a wonderful mother you have. I picked her especially for you.

I send my blessings every day, and remember that I love you very much. By the way, I'm easy to find. I am wherever there is love.

Love, God

TEMPTATION AND POTENTIAL

I have shared before an incident that occurred in my life that has remained a high-consciousness conversion moment. I was having a difficult time some fifteen or sixteen years ago. I was seeking one night a Catholic church to pray in, and I could not find one unlocked. So I drove to a Lutheran church, entered the church, and sat quietly reading the Scriptures and gazing at the Lutheran sanctuary. There were two banners hanging on the wall of the sanctuary, with Pauline theology. One read, "Become a new creation." Another read, "All things can be made new in Jesus Christ." That was a moment of high awareness for me. It struck me very powerfully that I could not handle the problems I was struggling to handle by myself. But the banners told me if I renewed my relationship with Christ, Christ would carry the burdens with me. Jesus Christ could keep me from sinking into a hole of depression and hopelessness.

The words of those banners come back to me as I prepare for Lent. I really want to use these 40 days to become a new creation, to allow all things to be made new within and around me, through Jesus Christ.

Genesis tells the story of the temptation of Adam and Eve. The Gospels remind us of the temptations of Christ. When we hear these temptation stories, we have a tendency to focus on the serpent in the Genesis story and Satan in the gospel story. The fact is that they are not main characters at all. The focus of these two stories is to reveal the inner life of the Adam and Eve figures, and the inner life of Jesus. The temptation stories are about *potential*, the potential within each of us to do God's will and do it God's way, or the potential to do our own will and go our own way.

The Scriptures remind each of us that we are constantly being put in situations of temptation, situations in which we have to make a choice as to how we are going to be in the world, what we are going to do in the world.

The focus during Lent is your inner life and my inner life: What do we give our minds and our hearts to? Interiorly, who are we? And based on who we are within, how do we act and interact? I know it is overly simplistic, but the experience of temptation is to choose that which is life-giving or that which is death-dealing—God's will and way, or my own will and way, which often can be quite flawed and misdirected.

What was the temptation of Adam and Eve? God had asked them to recognize some boundaries or limits. The serpent convinces them that they will become like God and won't need God. Their temptation was toward a kind of self-idolatry or self-will.

The temptations of Jesus? I think the temptation around bread or food was a temptation to focus his life too much on self-gratification or pleasure. The temptation to throw himself off the top of the temple was a temptation toward self-will, and we all know that Jesus always pursued not his own will, but God's will. The temptation of being offered all the kingdoms of the world was certainly a temptation toward basing his life on earthly, worldly power. The temptation of Jesus shows who he was and is: Abba-centered, seeking God's will, seeking wholeness, seeking justice and truth.

Let us consider temptations that we face each day.

- Each day we can choose patterns of health or nonhealth.
- We can be tempted to fall into patterns of anger, or choose inner peace.
- We can give in to worry and anxiety, or choose trust and sur-render in a power greater than ourselves.
- We can give in to depression, or reach for the hope that a rela-tionship with Jesus Christ offers us.
- We can remain in relationships or situations of abuse, or choose self-respect.
- We can become stuck in addictive ways, or choose freedom.
- We can stay in relationships or situations of domination, or choose to confront those who would seek to dominate.
- We can get stuck in patterns of narcissism, or choose self-sacrificial love.
- We can conform to the dominant culture around us, or practice what John Kavanaugh calls "spirituality of resistance."
- We can stay in American isolation and independence, or choose what is offered to our parish regularly—opportunities for com-munion and community.
- We can choose division and divisiveness, or reach for the whole-ness that comes from a relationship with God.

We are being tempted all the time, tempted in the sense of constantly being challenged to choose God's reign, God's way, and God's will as it manifests itself in many different ways; or we choose our own private-logic ways, or the ways of the dominant culture around us. We are constantly being challenged to choose between sin and grace.

"Become a new creation." "All things can be made new in Jesus Christ." Paul in Romans reminds us that the type of person epitomized by Adam is not to become our model and paradigm for the spiritual journey of Lent. Jesus Christ is our model. Jesus Christ is our paradigm. We have the potential within to be like Jesus. Let us, during the forty days of Lent, choose life, choose God's will, and choose Jesus Christ.

LOST AND FOUND

I have a fearful nature, and that fearful nature has led me to be somewhat obsessive-compulsive. I like to be in charge and in control of things happening around me and within me.

I had a very frightening evening many years ago that challenged my obsessive-compulsive tendencies. I was still in theology school before I was ordained, and I had been out to dinner with friends somewhere in Wheeling. I had to get back to the seminary in Mundelein, Illinois, so I started out. A heavy snowstorm developed—a blizzard. I got on an expressway that I thought would bring me back to the Mundelein area. As the snow got heavier, it became evident that I was far from my destination. I had no idea where I was. It was difficult to read signs. I finally stopped and asked a solitary man out in the snow where I was. He said, "Young man, you are out near Elgin. You are pretty far from Mundelein." He redirected my efforts and I started back in the direction that he had suggested. I eventually reached Mundelein and I practically kissed the ground when I got there. I had been lost, completely lost, but I finally found my way home.

I would like us on the Feast of the Epiphany to reflect on the experiences of being lost, and then finding our way, or being found. The Magi, spoken of in Matthew's Gospel, were probably priests of the Zoroastrian religion coming from the east, either from Babylon or Yemen, which is in the news these days. Some contend that these might have been Jews coming from Yemen, but their being called "magi" indicates that they probably were of this Zoroastrian priestly cult, who were very much into the study of stars. They thought the stars delivered divine messages and that following stars could lead them in important directions. (The word "magic" comes from the original word *magi*, meaning "sorcerer.")

When the early Christians studied some of the prophets, as we hear about in Isaiah 60, they elevated the status of the Magi from Zoroastrian priests and sorcerers to kings. Isaiah 60 reads, "Nations shall walk by your light and kings by your shining radiance." Isaiah is speaking to the exiles waiting to return from Babylon. He is promising the restoration of Jerusalem and the temple. He is also promising that, in the future, what once was a movement only for the Jews would become a movement open to the entire human family. A universal kingdom is coming.

Keep in mind that the Magi were seeking someone, and in their search they followed the stars. For years I worked very near Willow Creek Community Church in South Barrington, probably the biggest evangelical church in the country. Willow Creek refers to many people who come to their services on the weekends as "seekers." They are people who have come to worship because there is something missing in their lives. They want somehow to find this something, or someone, and in finding to discover meaning for their lives. The Magi were seekers. They were seeking someone. This newborn king ushered in a new kind of kingdom.

I believe that we are all seekers. We somehow need to find a picture frame for the portrait of our lives, and we need to reach some convictions about the nature of God. On the Feast of the Epiphany, we celebrate this fundamental spiritual seeking and searching that is part of being human.

In this feast, we also celebrate the mystery of revelation. We believe that in Jesus Christ, God has offered to us the One for whom we are seeking and searching. In our tradition we believe that Jesus Christ is both the model person and the revelation of the mystery of God. In Jesus, we discover who we are meant to become. In Jesus, we encounter the human face of God, or as one of the Christmas prefaces to the Eucharist Prayer says, "In Jesus, we encounter God made visible, and we are caught up in love of the God that we cannot see." God still remains a mystery, but we meet God in and through Jesus.

This feast celebrates another reality, certainly embodied in the figures of the Magi (most likely non-Jews) and made clear by Paul in Ephesians 3 when he highlights his special ministry, that of the evangelization and pastoral care of Gentiles or non-Jewish people. The Feast of the Epiphany celebrates that Jesus Christ is a Savior for all people. All people are invited to relationship, individually and communally, with Jesus Christ.

I think the themes of seeking and searching are beautiful images for us to reflect on as we all seek to grow in conversion. The journey of conversion, or greater oneness and intimacy with God, involves times when our felt experiences in life are similar to the one I had in the snowstorm. Sometimes we feel lost in life. The experience of conversion is the experience of finding that divine Someone, in and through Jesus. However, another way of looking at conversion is not so much finding, but rather God, through Jesus, finding us. The song "Amazing Grace" states, "I once was lost, but now am found." The metaphor of the hound of heaven chasing us down is another way of understanding conversion.

Many people understand the experience of conversion as turning to God. Others would say that before we ever turn, we are grasped. The theologian James Loder in his book *The Transforming Moment* spoke of the felt experience of conversion as swimming ashore after an experience of waters of chaos. Loder suggested that perhaps a more accurate description of conversion is that from the waters of chaos and confusion we are washed ashore. Perhaps the most holistic and accurate description of conversion is as a dialogical experience. We turn *and* are grasped. We swim *and* are washed ashore.

In each of our lives, conversion takes on different tones and shapes. Early in the spiritual journey some people simply awaken to mystery, but other times people awaken to mystery and call the experience

"God." This is *theistic conversion.* There are other different types of conversion. Sometimes the conversion is directly to Christ, or *Christic conversion.* Sometimes the conversion experience involves a definite church experience or the need for community. This is *ecclesial conversion.* Sometimes the experience is a call to live our lives in more loving, merciful ways. This is *moral conversion.*

A theme I speak on frequently is that conversion happens through human experiences. The process of being lost and finding, or being found, happens through the ordinary human experiences of life. My major conversion experiences have been protracted, lengthy in time and space. They involved dealing with realities like anxiety and stress; dysthymia, a low-grade depression; struggling with the occasional loneliness of celibacy; loss of and grieving for loved ones; leaving the faith community that I felt wedded to after seventeen years. In this last experience, there have been many days, weeks, and months of feeling lost. But then, through the goodness of God and the people of the Clare and St. Thomas the Apostle in Naperville, I've experienced finding God through Jesus and community again and being found anew.

In conversion experiences, status-quo and secure aspects of our lives fall apart. In our apparent weakness and the shambles of our lives, we find a new strength. That renewed strength is a new bond, a new communion with God and with other people, and a new call to service. These have been some of the major turning experiences, or being-grasped experiences, of my life. I am sure you could share many more arising from marriage, family life, parenting, grandparenting, work, and so on.

The major experiences of being lost, finding, and being found need to be joined to a term I borrow from Jim Collins's book *Good to Great.* The term is a *culture of discipline.* The major conversion experiences of our lives require a discipline of prayer, worship, spirituality, mercy, service, and justice that keeps us on the journey of conversion. This journey involves the development of one's own personal spiritual life, one's own spiritual program, what one does or does not do each day to maintain daily conscious contact with God.

Our yearlong theme at St. Thomas the Apostle in Naperville is "Companions on the Journey." You and I are companions on the journey with the original Magi. We are all journeying to Bethlehem to experience the mystery of incarnation or God with us. We are all journeying to Jerusalem to experience the deepest dimension of the mystery of life, which is life, death, and resurrection—new life and eternal life coming from struggle and death.

Let us be people who come to the new, renewed Jerusalem like those spoken of in Isaiah 60, who are bearing gold and frankincense. Let us offer to Christ this new year the gift of our lives. When the Magi open their treasures for the child Jesus they offer the gifts of gold, frankincense, and myrrh. The gold seems to point to Jesus's role as king; the frankincense underscores his role as a priest; the myrrh, which is used for embalming, speaks of his impending crucifixion. Research says that myrrh came from Yemen and was very hard to obtain. We experienced an act of terrorism that almost took hundreds of lives on Christmas day by a young man who seemingly trained for terrorism in the country of Yemen. We are hearing of hundreds of young men being trained for multiple acts of terrorism in the future.

Let us pray as we celebrate the Epiphany, the Manifestation, the Revelation of the mystery of God, and the ideals of humanity in the person of Jesus that more and more people of all different cultures and faith expressions will hear Jesus's fundamental call to respect, peace, love, mercy, and justice.

DECISIONS, DECISIONS

I am part of community of managers that directs the efforts of the Clare, a fifty-three-story senior care facility in downtown Chicago. A personnel issue arose, and I was invited in by the executive director to help make a decision regarding the issue. I was informed that the Franciscan Sisters of Chicago, who run the Clare and other senior communities around the county, in fact have a decision-making model that they engage in when important decisions have to be made. While many of us perhaps unconsciously also employ elements of this model, I found it striking, and perhaps it would be helpful to look at it together.

We are all about the business of decision making. We have to make moral decisions. We need to make vocational decisions about our future and our work. We need to make decisions about relationships and decisions about physiological and psychological health. We need to make decisions about our own spiritual growth. Sometimes we need to make decisions individually; sometimes, as in the presenting issue at the Clare, we need to make decisions together. One of the greatest gifts we can pass on to children and to teens is teaching them how to engage in effective decision making, which helps us to avoid simply reacting to things or acting on impulse.

In the Franciscan decision-making model, decisions are always made against the Franciscan Sisters' mission, values, and vision. Our shared mission in Franciscan work is *to honor the dignity of life by serving as a compassionate community*. Our values are *respect, stewardship, joy, dedication, and service*. Our vision is *to be the optimal means that frees individuals up to experience the fullness of their lives*. All decisions must be made relative to mission, values, and vision. Maybe each of us as individuals, and any of us who work together, should articulate our mission, values, and vision and use them as a foundation for decision making.

Step one in the Franciscan decision-making model is *defining the issue*. In this step, the facts of the issue are identified: who, what, where, when, why, and how. Relevant factors are identified: social, political, economic, financial, and legal. At this step also, people need to identify any secondary or intangible implications of the decision.

Step two is *framing the perspectives*. Here people identify their own perspectives and solicit the perspectives of others. Clarifying perspectives involves asking, "How do you see the issue?" It also includes reviewing the perspectives of various stakeholders.

The third step in decision making is *analyzing the values involved and determining their impact on mission and vision,* as explained earlier. People discern what values are at stake, what values are being affirmed, and what values are being negated.

Step four of the process involves *identifying the alternatives.* In this step, people identify all possible alternatives and values at stake. They ask about the pros and cons of each option, including doing nothing.

The fifth step is *making or affirming a decision.* Here people choose a path among the possible alternatives. People ask which option best achieves the clarified mission, values, and core strategies.

The sixth step involves *implementing the decision.* The process needs to be identified for carrying out the decision. Questions asked include, "Who will implement the decision?" and "How and when will the decision be communicated to all stakeholders?"

A very important concluding step, the seventh, is *evaluating whether the solution addresses the defined problem.* What process and criteria that can be measured will be used to evaluate the decision and its outcomes?

I find great clarity in the Franciscan model for individual as well as shared decision making. But I think this week's Scripture readings add important steps to the Franciscan model. In the first reading, from the book of Wisdom, Solomon is presented as praying for wisdom, praying for God's wisdom. Sometimes in making decisions we can seek too much—our own counsel or the counsel of other people—but not spend enough time turning to God, praying that God reveal God's will to us. In all the decisions that face us, major and minor ones, I think it is important to pray, so that we operate not just out of our own wisdom but also God's wisdom. The book of Wisdom says, "I prayed, and prudence was given to me."

In the Letter to the Hebrews, we pick up another important piece in decision making, and that is to turn to God's Word for help. The author of Hebrews tells us that the Word of God is living and effective. God's word certainly comes to us in the form of Scripture. God's word comes to us also in the insights, thoughts, feelings, and intuitions that God sometimes places within us—and for which we need to be attentive—if we are going to connect with God's word.

Mark 10 gives us another guideline in the process of decision making: We are to be very cautious about our valuing and using of wealth and material resources. Wealth and material resources can indeed be a block to happiness here on earth, and a block to spiritual development. As we practice caution about our acquisition and use of wealth and material resources, Jesus gives us another horizon that we should include in decision making: a concern for the poor, the hungry, the homeless, and others lacking in wealth and resources.

So far, in addition to all the fine Franciscan steps in making decisions, we are to pray for God's wisdom, seek out God's word, be cautious about our need for and use of material things, and be concerned about those less fortunate than we are. These last two concerns are constitutive pieces of the mission, values, and vision of the reign of God as Jesus preached it.

As we make decisions, I think we need to tap into two other resources. One is the tradition of the Church. We have centuries of teaching on various issues related to human life. I think it is important to be in touch with what the wisdom of Christians down through the centuries might have to say about a given decision. In addition, the Church does not possess all the wisdom there is in the world. Other academic and professional disciplines—philosophy, sociology, psychology, and medicine, among others—offer us much material that can factor into our decision making.

The Franciscan tradition and the Word of God remind us of what a great gift God has given us in allowing us to make decisions. God has given us freedom to direct the course of our lives. When we have to make individual decisions, let us put aside our pride and seek help from other people. And when a decision should be truly shared, let us avoid the pride that sometimes occurs when an individual, or a few, make a top-down decision in a situation when others—spouse, family, or work associates—should be involved in the process.

I know some important decisions are awaiting me about the future, as I am sure you have important decisions pending in your life. Let us be reminded today that when we need to decide, let us work a spiritual process.

DIRT . . . OR DOWN TO EARTH

Miles Levin was diagnosed with a rare form of cancer in 2005 when he was sixteen years old. He died last week. He and his family live near Detroit, Michigan. Reflecting on his impending death, Miles said, "Death doesn't scare me. What scares me is dying and having no impact, dying and not having made a contribution to the world."

Miles did something to make sure he made an impact, so that he made a contribution before he left the earth. He had a daily blog entry on the journey through sickness and chemotherapy, and toward death. He invited people to reflect with him on the most profound mystery, moving toward that horizon of death, believing in another side, but not knowing exactly what is on the other side. In one entry he wrote, "I've tried to show what it is to persevere and what it means to be strong."

In his final entry he said, "I have just been told that there is no chemotherapy combination that will work for me, and so I am going to discontinue my entries now. This is a time for my family and me. Thank you for all the love and support that you've shown me."

Miles had a great impact on the many people who connected with him daily. He appeared internationally on CNN. He did not live to be a successful anything or anyone, but he accepted the reality of his life, did the best with the reality of his life, and tried to be generative with the reality of his life, even though that reality was sickness and death.

Another story struck me recently. It is the story of Don Hayen, a seventy-three-year-old retired dermatologist. Some months ago his wife started to notice significant memory losses on the part of her husband. After significant testing, he was diagnosed with having Alzheimer's disease. Don now carries a notebook and a recorder with him to help him live with his memory loss. He also has started a blog to help people understand the journey of a declining Alzheimer's patient. He invests his retirement time in working for the Alzheimer's Foundation. He also is an example of a man who has accepted the reality of his life and taken that reality, though it be aging and mental decline, and invested it for the well-being of others. Truly, he is what Erik Erikson would call a generative man, invested in the lives of other people.

The book of Sirach and the Gospel of Luke call us to be people of humility. Humility is a challenging virtue. Many of us who grew up in a certain era of Catholicism tried to be humble, but really suffered from poor self-esteem or even humiliation at the hands of others.

I have begun to understand a little bit what humility is all about. It is accepting the reality of oneself. It is being totally honest about oneself—with the self, with others, and with God. Humility is the honest realization that all of us have strengths, all of us have gifts. Humility is the honest realization also that all of us have limits. In confronting those limits, we perhaps can develop certain qualities that are underdeveloped in us, because we have not been intentional about growing. But it is okay to be able to look at ourselves and say, "I am not good at that. I'm not gifted at that. That's not one of my strengths. I could use your help in that."

Humble people do not seek or wield power over other people. They do not seek power through position or wealth or resources. They, nonetheless, can be powerful people. Someone once told me, "Don't ever seek to be a person of power, but continue to be a powerful person." One can be humble and hold a position of great influence in an organization, but that position does not go to the head of a humble person.

In line with this aversion to power, humble people are deliberate, as Jesus teaches in the Gospels, in seeking out, associating with, and caring for the broken people of the world. Robert Putnam has a study out on how contemporary people are now avoiding diversity, trying to not associate themselves with people who are different from themselves. Humble people break out of that tendency to seek out those who are similar to themselves. In so doing they really live out what Jesus meant by his new social order of the reign of God.

I think humble people are honest about their own sinfulness. They strive to engage in repentance from those patterns of sin. Humble people realize that they have hurt others and have been forgiven, and therefore they should always be forgiving. Humble people always seek reconciliation in any of their relationships that have become troubled or estranged.

Humility comes from the Latin word *humus*, which means soil, earth, or dirt. I think some of us, in striving to be humble, thought of ourselves as dirt. We suffered from poor self-esteem. Again, perhaps we allowed ourselves to be humiliated by others. I prefer to interpret the *humus* component of humility not as being like dirt, but being *down to earth*, being real, honest, and comfortable in one's own skin.

In the 1980s I worked somewhat with the famous youth minister and religious educator James DiGiacomo and the Maryknoll missioner John Walsh. They popularized a theory at that time in which they coined two phrases that they believed spoke of true spiritual growth. To be spiritually growing, to be converting, DiGiacomo and Walsh said, you have to experience the primal cry for more and the primal cry for help.

The *primal cry for more* refers to people's realization that they need a higher power, that they need God. This cry does not have to do so much with doctrinal clarity as much as an emotional and relational bond with God. We believe that this happens for us as Christians in a relationship with Abba, our Creator/Parent; and Jesus, his Son and our Lord; and the Holy Spirit, our daily companion.

The *primal cry for help* refers to the growing realization that each of us should have a need for other people, a need for healthy dependency on others. We need to be dependent on others for friendship, intimacy, support, and sometimes help in the given tasks of life. Humble people are not afraid of engaging in that primal cry for more and the primal cry for help.

Many of us who have struggled with self-esteem issues have had to adopt certain disciplines to help us grow in humility and self-esteem. Frequently, if I feel like avoiding an area of growth because of fear or anxiety, I deliberately place myself in that situation, so that I might learn courage for life and self-confidence.

Many Sundays before I preach, I am quite anxious and do not feel like I have the strength to stand before such a large assembly. But I stop before the altar before I preach, and I pray. I pray three things: *God, help me to feel good about myself.* I don't say that out of pride or power. It is a real plea. Sometimes I don't feel very good about myself. What I mean by the prayer is, "Please, God, help me to get rid of those feelings so that they don't get in the way of my preaching and proclaiming Your truth." Second, I pray, *Help me to love these people.* When I speak or preach I don't want to impress. I simply want to use words to care for people, and try to offer them meaning and direction based on my own struggle with God's word. Finally, I pray, *Help me to give witness to You.* I really want to share with people that God is a living and life-giving reality, who can make a beautiful, wonderful difference in each of our daily lives.

Help me to feel good about me. Help me to love them. Help me to give witness to You. When I say those prayerful words, and mean them, I am blessed with a courage for life that I do not have on my own.

Let us strive to be humble people. It simply means totally being ourselves, living connected lives with others and with God, and realizing how much we need both other people and God. Let us also do our best to never humiliate another person. Humility is good. Even being humbled by certain situations or awareness of one's inadequacies in certain situations are good. Humiliation—being humiliated—is never good.

And, if ever you find yourself in a situation of humiliation, let each of us pray, *God, help me to feel good about myself,* and assertively tell the humiliating person that such a relational style is totally unacceptable. Let us be humble.

THIS TOO SHALL PASS

I received a message on my voicemail recently from Monsignor Ken Velo, my classmate and friend. He said, "Pat, I am giving a mission in Orland Park and I thought of you. I thought of all the great work you did in the southwest suburbs, as well as the great work you've done at Holy Family and St. Hubert's in the northwest suburbs. I know that this must be a hard time for you. Hang in there. This too shall pass." I tried to reach Ken in response, to thank him for his words of encouragement and consolation.

"This too shall pass." Those words offer a perspective for me and for others who are experiencing struggle or difficult times. What seems insurmountable can be faced and passed through. When we face a struggle or a challenge, we have to use our memories. We have faced struggle and challenge before, and we have gotten through those experiences—and doing so has resulted in growth, conversion, and a new and better life for many of us. "This too shall pass."

Are any of you facing experiences or moments that you dread or fear? Is something coming your way that you would prefer to not experience? Sacred Scripture supports Ken Velo's insight: "This too shall pass." Nonetheless, for something difficult to pass, *we have to pass through it.*

The Letter to the Hebrews tells us that as Jesus faced his confrontation in Jerusalem with Jewish and Roman leaders, he engaged in "loud cries and tears . . . he learned" as he awaited his crucifixion and death.

We hear a hint of Jesus's apprehension about what is to happen to him when he says in Luke's Gospel, "I am troubled now," yet he goes on to say that passing through the crucible of crucifixion is the very reason he came to the world, to reveal to the world the truth of eternal life on the other side of death. Jesus is presented to us as having very human reactions to the struggle he is about to experience; yet his human reactions are joined to a strong, convictional faith that Abba, his loving parent, will pass through the mystery of the cross with him and lead him to glorification. Jesus accepts the pain of the upcoming event with the hope of the new and eternal life that awaits him after "this too passes."

Jesus turns to nature to explain the mystery of spiritual growth and transformation. If a grain of wheat is never planted, it remains just a grain of wheat, but if it goes to the earth and dies to its former identity, through the miracle of nature it gives new life to stalks of wheat. Just so, when we face struggles here on earth, a grain of wheat is falling to the earth and dying to produce much fruit. When we face the mystery of death in ourselves or in the lives of people whom we love, the grain of wheat is falling to the earth and dying, producing the fruit of eternal life.

"This too shall pass." But the mystery of the cross only passes by us passing through it. *Through it.* That is the challenge before us. When we approach the cross in its various forms, we are called to go through it, trusting in the grace of God.

Jeremiah offers support to this conviction about passing through struggles and crosses with convictional faith. Jeremiah tried to prevent the fall of Jerusalem by encouraging the Jewish king to surrender to the Babylonians without violence. After the fall of Jerusalem, Jeremiah promised the Jewish people who would be exiled that something better would come. Jeremiah believed that God would use the fall of Jerusalem and the Babylonian exile as a purification of the people. He would change the people and enter into a *new covenant* of intimacy with them. Not only would the people know *about* God, they would *know God* in a personal relationship.

So it is when you and I have "This too shall pass" moments, and experiences when the only way through it is through it. Our faith tradition promises that a new covenant awaits us, a new bond of closeness with God, a new experience of knowing God personally. God is with us in the mystery of the cross. He is the change agent that produces the new life, the new covenant that awaits us.

"This too shall pass"—only when we pass through it. The only way through it is through it, with God at our side, moving into an ever closer relationship with us, moving within us, so that we know him in our hearts.

Let us be reminded that cries and tears are okay when we are facing the cross, and the cross promises the bottom line of our faith: "this too shall pass."

HELP!

I can remember being in grade school, perhaps sixth grade, when we were covering as a class some rather complicated math, at least for me. I remember feeling lost. The guy sitting next to me, Eddie Haggerty, offered to help me. Eddie was a cool, popular kid, and I was not. So, as he leaned toward me to try to explain some of what I was not getting, I pushed him away and told him that I did not need his help. I did not want to feel dependent or inferior in the eyes of one of my classmates.

In high school, however, I started a tutoring program at Quigley South called Student Aid. I was in advanced classes in high school. I did pretty well. So I lined up a lot of other guys who did pretty well to tutor other young teens who were struggling with their grades. Student Aid had sessions running after classes throughout the Quigley South building.

However, I remember in my junior year of high school being in advanced trigonometry. I was off for some days with the flu. I came back and had no idea what the instructor was talking about relative to trigonometry. I was reluctant again to ask for help, and it is only through the grace of God and the generosity of that priest instructor that I even passed that course.

So I notice a tendency in myself. It is easy for me to reach out and help others. It is difficult for me to be vulnerable and have to ask for help. Yet several times in my adulthood, I have had to turn to colleagues, friends, and psychotherapists and seek their assistance and guidance.

The fact is, as in the gospel story of the wedding feast at Cana, we all reach times when we "run out of wine," times when we just run out.

Our resources, our wisdom, our strength perhaps become depleted. We face challenges for which we are not equipped. Sometimes we just break down. It has been important for me to learn the importance of humility, the humility that is needed to ask for help. As St. Paul teaches us in 1 Corinthians, we are all gifted. We have all been given gifts for the common good, but no one of us has all the gifts. We complement each other in our giftedness. Complementing each other is what makes us community. It is what makes us church. We need each other.

Mary, in John's Gospel, is humble enough to go to her son Jesus and intercede for help for the family whose wedding they are attending. Initially Jesus resists, saying that his hour has not come. His hour seems to refer to his death, resurrection, and glorification. Perhaps what Mary was signaling to her son was that the beginning of that hour had dawned, and he was to begin his public ministry with this first sign worked at the wedding at Cana. Mary was humble enough to say, "Help." You and I need to develop a similar humility.

I started a custom at Holy Family Parish in Inverness, where I was pastor, regarding the washing of the feet on Holy Thursday night. Rather than having twelve representatives from the parish, representing the twelve apostles, have their feet washed by the presider, when it came time for the washing of feet, we had multiple stations around the church. Everyone was encouraged to assume the chair at one of the stations and have their feet washed. The person who just had his or her feet washed would in turn wash the feet of the person who washed his or her feet. Holy Thursday foot washing was probably my least favorite ritual. Again, it is not so much that I have a disdain for washing someone's feet. I am okay with that. I did not like to have my feet washed and let people see my arthritic joints. But it was one of those "will to discomfort" circumstances that I thought was important for the congregation and me to experience. Indeed, we need to help each other, but we also need to ask for help.

Two books that I have been recommending recently are *Bowling Alone: The Collapse and Revival of American Community* by Robert Putnam and *Better Together: Restoring the American Community* by Robert Putnam, Lewis Feldstein, and Don Cohen. Both books are about the decline of social capital or social connectedness in American culture. Putnam and his associates see contemporary people becoming increasingly isolated and independent, contributing to greater anxiety, stress, and depression in our culture. The Internet and the remarkable technologies that we now have at our fingertips, while contributing to greater social connection, can also contribute to people being further away from each other emotionally and physically. Putnam feels that one of the greatest contributions that religious congregations and communities can provide for the society and culture around us is to remind each other of the great need that we have for each other and that we have for each other's help. Parishes especially should offer people opportunities for connection and sharing of resources on many different levels. We were not made for social isolation. We were made for communion and connection.

Mary's example for us is to not be afraid to ask for help. I think that we should be willing to ask for help in different ways. We need to grow in humility and ask each other for help, but we also need to retrieve a sense of dependency on God. Mary expresses this dependency on the divine in going to her son. Isaiah 62 reveals to us a dimension of God that we need to embrace with greater frequency. In Isaiah 62, God is portrayed as a bridegroom in love with his bride. The bride, in this particular passage, is God's people, you and I. God refers to us as "my delight; my espoused." The authors tell us that "the Lord delights in you; God rejoices in you." The great love of God for each of and all of us is being presented for our prayerful consideration. Sometimes we can become prayer-less; we can be living our life on spiritual fumes. We need to turn to God and say to God, "Ouch . . . Help" daily, with regularity.

Let us briefly reflect on the theology of John's Gospel. Unlike the other three Gospels, the Synoptic Gospels, John's Gospel is highly stylized, very symbolic. It has a number of theological themes running under the story line. In John 1 and 2, we hear of the first week of Jesus's public life. Moving into chapter 2, we are told that Jesus's call to his disciples and his connection with John the Baptist all unfold in seven days. What John is symbolizing here is that the beginning of the ministry of Jesus is the beginning of a new creation, a new creation that Jesus is ushering in. As the Gospel unfolds, the first main section after the prologue is called the book of Signs, extending from 1:19 to 12:50.

In John, there are seven miraculous events that are called "signs." In Hebrew literature and tradition, signs refer to events that reveal the power of God at work in the human story. In John's Gospel the first of the seven signs is the transformation of water into wine in the story of the wedding at Cana (John 2). This sign seems to speak of the replacement of Jewish ceremonial washings and symbolizes the entire creative transforming work of Jesus.

The second sign, the cure of the royal official's son in John 4, signifies the power of Jesus's life-giving word. We are told that the man's son recovered at the seventh hour, another reference to the seven days of creation and Jesus ushering in a new creation.

The third sign, the cure of the paralytic at the pool of Bethesda, continues the theme of water offering newness of life. Connected to the story of the woman at the well, there are sacramental references to Baptism in these passages.

John 6 contains two signs, the multiplication of the loaves and the walking on the waters of the Sea of Galilee. These signs seem connected with the blessing of the manna and the crossing of the Red Sea. They symbolize a new exodus for the human family. The multiplication of the loaves is followed by the bread-of-life discourse in which Jesus invites us to come to him in a personal relationship, and then to ritualize that personal relationship in the celebration of the Eucharist.

The sixth sign is in John 9, the healing of the man born blind. While again having hints of baptismal theology, Jesus is also proclaimed here as Light for the world.

The seventh sign, the climax of the signs, is the raising of Lazarus in John 11. Jesus calls Lazarus back to life. Jesus is the Resurrection and the Life, who ironically will be put to death because of his gift of life to Lazarus. All who believe in Jesus as the Resurrection and the Life are promised eternal life.

The book of Signs in John is followed by the book of Glory, 13:1–20:31. These chapters tell of the growing conflict that Jesus has with the religious leaders of his time, resulting in his crucifixion and death, but the book of Signs ultimately points to the empty tomb of John 20, the appearance of the risen Jesus to Mary Magdalene and to the disciples, and the resurrection appearance of Jesus in Galilee in John 21.

The book of Signs and the book of Glory all lead up to the resurrection and glorification of Jesus and the inherent promise, in his glorification, that we are invited with him to eternal glory.

I began this reflection on the human need for asking for help. The death, resurrection, and glorification of Jesus offer ultimate help to us as we face the most difficult mystery of each of our lives, the mystery of death. Jesus invites us to put our faith in him, to rest secure in the deep meaning and the purpose that are contained in the good news of his death, resurrection, and glorification. In the face of suffering and death, Jesus extends to us the ultimate help.

Changed Minds, Changed Hearts, Changed Behavior

It is Tuesday, August 25, early in the morning. This is when typically I compose an article—in the past for Holy Family's bulletin, and now for this *National Center for Evangelization and Parish Renewal Newsletter*. I am feeling very edgy this morning, so I have to force myself to ask that question that Eugene Gendlin encourages people to ask in his movement and book called *Focusing*. The question is, "What is this really?" Gendlin found that often people have psychological and physiological symptoms and discomfort because they are not in touch with what is going on inside of them. Gendlin encourages people to take time each day to name thoughts and feelings, and even to go back over thoughts and feelings, to gain greater precision—to gain what Carl Rogers called "congruency with the self."

From a feminist perspective, Anne Wilson Schaef encourages

women and all people to do "deep process work" to get in touch with thoughts and feelings and memories and dreams. If we do not do what Gendlin, Rogers, and Schaef recommend, we run the risk of repressing feelings, which can cause many kinds of psychological and physiological discomforts.

What is this really on Tuesday, August 25? It is the twentieth anniversary of my father's funeral. I had lost touch with that. I sometimes am confused about what day he died and what day was his funeral. Today is the anniversary of his funeral. I have many feelings about my father. I miss him; I love him; he hurt me, very significantly at times. Sometimes I feel I am still angry at him.

What is this really on Tuesday, August 25? It is the first day of school, not just generically; it is the first day of school at Holy Family Academy in Inverness. I helped many people found that school. I was the recipient of a lot of criticism because some families felt, and I agreed, that a parochial school was the next outgrowth of our method of family-based religious education. Some people disagreed with this. I love all the children at Holy Family Parish; I had special love for the children of the academy because I saw them with greater frequency than the other children. I would also always do the opening Mass for the school year. I did all school Masses at 9:00 a.m. on Wednesdays. I would do classroom Masses and Reconciliation services. I feel strangely separated from those children and their parents. I feel like I should be there, but someone else has made a decision that I cannot. I'm hurt; I'm angry. That is also why I feel edgy today.

People who know me know of my love of both psychology and theology. I have always found that psychology is a great tool for understanding the dynamics not only of psychological but also spiritual growth. To be people of spirituality and psychological health, we need to have an interior life. We need to take time out of the busyness and complexity of our day to get in touch with ourselves. We need to take the time also to deliberately and intentionally connect with the Holy Spirit of God and how God might be at work in our lives.

In the book of Deuteronomy, great emphasis is placed on the law.

Moses taught the nation Israel to keep the law, and by doing so they would be close to God. Centuries later, Jesus offered a different perspective on the law. He confronted the Pharisees and others who were trying to trap him regarding his nonpractice of some aspects of Jewish law. He accused them of externalized religion. He challenged them to become people of greater interiority. In other parts of the gospel, he tells these religious people that all 613 of the Jewish laws are summarized in the statement, "Love God, love your neighbor, love yourself." Jesus challenges us in the gospel to become people of interior inventory, not only on a psychological level, but also on spiritual and moral levels. We are to be in touch with ourselves; we are to be critical of ourselves; we are to challenge ourselves to live what Jesus taught by the reign of God.

Not just the Pharisees of old, but all of us have a tendency to be nonreflective, to not be in touch with ourselves psychologically and spiritually, to not be in touch with God. Becoming people of the reign of God is truly an inside job. We need to engage in deliberate, interior work, often changing our thoughts and changing our feelings so that—to use an image from Jesus—our "hearts" are close to God.

But in psychotherapy we know that being in touch with the self is not enough for true growth. It is important to be in touch with thoughts and feelings and to often change thoughts and feelings; it is important to change thoughts and feelings toward greater congruency with Jesus and the reign of God, but we really do not grow until we *change behavior*. That is what the letter to James emphasizes when the author encourages his readers and encourages us to become "doers" of the Word. I find it challenging that he connects doing the Word with deeds of mercy toward those who are victimized by impoverishment or injustice. What behavior do we need to confront and change to be true doers of the Word?

On a psychological level, we grow when we change thoughts, feelings, and behavior. On a spiritual level, we also grow when we change thoughts, feelings, and behavior, more toward the ideal of Jesus's teaching and preaching about the reign of God. This work of spiritual conversion cannot happen if we do not develop interior lives.

Again, we see in the Scripture readings a radical change in perspective. We hear of Moses's valuing of the Jewish law and we hear Jesus's warning against the preoccupation with the minutiae of Jewish law. Again, Jesus saw in the Pharisees and some of the other contemporary religious groups of his day a people who were going through the motions of religion, a people who talked a religious game but failed to live God's will. Jesus critiques what Leonardo Boff called some years ago the traditionalist dimension of religion, a preoccupation with ritual, rules, and laws and a failure to attend to what might be God's will, God's expectations, and God's laws.

That temptation toward traditionalism is certainly present in the Catholic Church today. There are people who are drawn to a pre–Vatican II image of the Church and a preoccupation with devotional ritualistic, legalistic minutiae, all the while being completely unconscious of the calling and the demand of the gospel and the reign of God.

God's word today calls us to a holistic understanding of the spiritual life. Engaging in the externals of organized religion is not enough. The metanoia needed for ongoing conversion involves an ongoing change of cognition, emotion, and behavior. Psychological growth and relationships demand these three changes also.

In the name of God's word this week, I challenge us to avoid getting lost in the emptiness of externalized religion and traditionalism. Let us make a commitment to be people of true interiority and action for behavior change.

SPIRITUAL INTELLIGENCE

Decades ago, scientists began to develop instruments that measure human intelligence. In the field of psychology, intelligence testing has become one of the standard tests that therapists use in assessing personalities and emotional difficulties. Intelligence has an influence on how we view the world and how we live. IQ is an important indicator of a person's holistic approach to life.

Some years ago, psychologists introduced another concept: emotional intelligence. EQ has to do with a person's self-understanding, congruence with one's feelings, effectiveness in relating to other people, and capacity for significant relationships.

The book of Proverbs and also the letter to the Ephesians speak of the reality of wisdom. Wisdom is another kind of intelligence. Perhaps we can equate wisdom with spiritual intelligence. Much like emotional intelligence and IQ, spiritual intelligence is something in which we can be highly developed, somewhat developed, or not very developed at all, yet all of us have the capacity for spiritual intelligence. As followers of Jesus, we ought to take seriously the importance of developing spiritual intelligence. Spiritual intelligence is approaching the world, other people, and God through a lens of faith and spirituality.

Proverbs says that Wisdom has built herself a house and that the house is set on seven columns; the author of this Proverbs passage sees women as possessing great wisdom, given that Wisdom is characterized in the feminine. Let's equate wisdom with spiritual intelligence, and perhaps using the imagery of the passage, let's try to identify what might be the seven columns that make up Wisdom's house.

The first column of spiritual intelligence, or wisdom, is highlighted in the passage from Proverbs. Inviting people into her house, Wisdom says, "Let whoever is simple, turn in here." One characteristic of wise people is *simplicity*. Sometimes we fill our lives with too much activity, unneeded resources, roles, and responsibilities. Life becomes too cluttered. Sometimes we can have a feeling of no more room, which is connected with the stress we sometimes feel in life. Wise people, spiritually intelligent people, try to keep their lives relatively uncluttered and simple.

The second column of Wisdom's house, I believe, is *empathy*. Empathy is a proactive effort to feel with other people, to gain insight into other people, to walk in their shoes, to get into their skin.

Empathy leads to Wisdom's third column, *understanding*. We can be quick to judge, quick to criticize, and quick to diminish other people. Wise people make an effort to understand the inner workings and also the circumstances of other people's lives.

The fourth column of Wisdom's house is *love and compassion*. If we practice empathy and understanding of others, we will be more willing to extend unconditional love, self-sacrificial love, and compassion, or feeling with other people. Love and compassion have various degrees of involvement and commitment. Love and compassion, however, are really key ingredients of a worldview, or a whole approach that wise and spiritually intelligent people have. Related to compassion is justice. Part of being a wise, spiritually intelligent person involves valuing justice. In Catholic tradition, we have divided justice into three categories, as mentioned earlier—commutative justice, which has to do with practicing honesty in all of our affairs; distributive justice, which is concerned about the fair, equal distribution of the world's resources among all people; and social justice, which seeks to change structures that hold people in unjust situations of abuse or impoverishment.

The fifth column of Wisdom is spoken of in the Gospel of John. Jesus, in the bread of life discourse—speaking about the Eucharist and taking into ourselves his body and bread—talks of remaining in him, as he, Jesus, remains in the Father. Wise, spiritually intelligent people live with the *felt experience of dwelling in the presence of God*. This incarnational way of life, living in and with the presence of God, gives people feelings of peace, hope, comfort, and at times, challenge. Jesus reminds us that, as his disciples, we have a tremendous gift in the Eucharist, which helps us to experience this in-dwelling of his Spirit in us. Remaining in God demands a life, a schedule of prayerfulness, in which we deliberately attend to the presence of God multiple times throughout our days. This prayerfulness also involves attending to God together with other people in worship, specifically as taught by John 6, in and through the Eucharist.

The sixth column of Wisdom's house is *recognizing our need for other people and recognizing our need for community*. We were not made for all the isolation and independence that characterizes contemporary life. Human beings have been made for communion with each other and with God. Wise, spiritually intelligent people, recognize their need for others. They gladly come to large group experiences of community, and some choose, in many faith communities, to be part of Small Christian Communities, which help people experience communion and connection on a close, more intimate level. Wise people know that they need community.

The seventh column of Wisdom is spoken of in the letter to the Ephesians—*understanding the will of the Lord*. Wise people pursue not just their own will or the approval of other people. Rather, they search out—they discern—what they believe to be God's will, God's truth, what God would ideally have us become or do. Related to the will of God is the reign of God. The reign of God was and is the mission of Jesus Christ, and therefore should become the mission of each of us, and all of us. People living the reign of God place God at the center of their lives, and then try to do life and live life according to the standards they believe God would want for each of us, and all of us.

To be a wise person, a spiritually intelligent person, is to strive to be a person of holiness. Holiness is not a way of life that is very popular in this culture, but holiness is a path to inner peace, oneness, and reconciliation with our fellow person.

Jesus reminds us, if we eat his body and drink his blood, if we remain in him through the Eucharist, if we are wise and spiritually intelligent people, we already have, in part, the gift of eternal life. We have begun eternal life, and he promises us that eternal life—which we have partially here on earth—will become a full gift for us on the other side of death.

Let us strive to not just be smart or intelligent. Let us be reminded by the Scriptures this week that what is most important is that we try to be people of wisdom, or spiritual intelligence. Spiritual intelligence is a way of approaching and knowing life, other people, and God.

THE POWER OF SURRENDER

I have been reflecting somewhat on dealing with painful emotions: anxiety, depression, grief, loss. I suffered from anxiety problems in my twenties and required some help for that condition. I still have an anxious nature, though over the years I have learned to tame it somewhat.

The counselor whom I met with for a long period of time mentored me in an approach to symptoms of emotional pain. He used to say that symptoms are only smoke, and therapy was for addressing the fire. By the "fire" he meant the lifestyle, the worldview, the convictions, the pattern of thinking that produced the smokelike symptoms of fear or panic. In anxiety disorders, one of the things that you have to beware of is secondary fear. Secondary fear refers to fear of your symptoms, or fear of being afraid, fear of feelings of panic. Thus, I had to learn over the years to grit my teeth and pass through painful symptoms, always striving to better understand the fire, or the cognitions and values that made me feel the way I felt.

As a counselor now, I tend to be rather direct in counseling people to stand through the storm of their symptoms, to better understand their patterns of thinking, their worldview that might be producing the symptoms. Trained in Adlerian psychology, I have never been overly enthused about psychological medication. Don't get me wrong; I know that sometimes people need it. But I think sometimes medication can excuse us from the hard work of self-understanding and life change.

One of the techniques that I have employed over the years, and I also encourage other people to try it, is paradoxical intention. Victor Frankl introduced the notion of paradoxical intention to psychotherapy. In paradoxical intention, a person tries to experience and feel that which one fears most. Thus, if the person does not want the feeling of fear or panic, the person is encouraged, paradoxically, to try to feel fear and panic. If a person is suffering from obsessive thoughts or behavior, the person is encouraged to try to have obsessive thoughts and obsessive behavior. With paradoxical intention, one is encouraged to face, or to try and make happen, that which one most fears; in so doing, the fear is robbed of energy or power. The person is freed to get beyond symptoms to examine those larger issues of vision, lifestyle, cognitive patterns, values, and behavioral patterns, some of which may need to be changed.

There is a reality that has helped me penetrate the power of psychological symptoms. That reality is faith. In psychological growth, especially if someone is trying to grow out of severe psychological pain, there needs to be a will to discomfort. Whether it is using paradoxical intention or some other technique, a person has to be willing to experience discomfort in order to grow. Part of this will to discomfort is a gradual desensitization regarding symptoms. One begins to be able to embrace pain for the greater benefit of learning, liberation, and growth.

Throughout my adulthood, faith has been the firm foundation that I can stand on when I am trying to grow. I can practice the will to discomfort. I can practice paradoxical intention because I believe so strongly in what Paul writes about in Romans, that there is a God of unconditional love who is with us. As Paul said, God is always working all things for our benefit. The mystery of life, death, and resurrection is going on in small ways in each of us throughout our lifetime. We need to experience moments of death that we might pass through to moments of resurrection and new life.

Isaiah tried to express this conviction more poetically when he invited the beleaguered people, returning to Jerusalem after the Babylonian captivity, to allow God to comfort them with water, milk, and other symbols of God's love. They were returning not to a lovely homeland but a trashed city that had been robbed of its beauty and glory. Isaiah challenges the people to see beyond appearances to the God at work in them, leading them to new life.

When Jesus heard of the death of John the Baptist, his cousin, we are told that he went off to a solitary place. Jesus is portrayed as doing this many times in the gospel. He seeks solitude—from the crowd, from activity. I think he did that to get in touch with this unconditional love that God gives each of us if we open ourselves to it. Jesus was such a strong person—strong enough to walk directly to the cross—because he believed in the love that Abba had for him, and he believed in the process of life, death, and resurrection. He needed to root himself in these spiritual realities with moments of solitude.

But then Jesus offers us another example of how to deal with our own pain and struggle. Still in grief over the death of John the Baptist, he rises above his disciples' protests that the people should be dismissed to attend to their own hunger. He performs the miracle of the multiplication of the loaves and the fish, feeding thousands of people, the gospel tells us. Jesus demonstrates that we need to rise from our own pain to minister to the needs of others, and in so doing not only do we help others but we contribute to our own healing.

I was reading Eckhart Tolle's book *The Power of Now*. In the book he has a section on the way of the cross. He says that people frequently say they found God through their suffering. He challenges several things about that statement. In a way, you cannot find God because God can never be lost. God is. Perhaps we are not attentive to God at times, but God is always available. Tolle portrays God as present in each of us. There is an imminence about God. He dwells within each of us and all around us.

He goes on to say it is not suffering that leads us to God. Suffering, at times, can be symptomatic of our resistance to God. It is surrender to God that leads us to God. Surrender is letting go into God's presence. Surrender is letting go into God's unconditional love for us. Surrender is letting go into the process that we are convicted about—of life, death, and resurrection. Surrender is conviction that God draws new life from any struggle that we are experiencing. Surrender is the conviction that Paul speaks of, that nothing—not life, not death, not principalities or angels—can separate us from the love of God that comes to us through Jesus Christ.

Let us surrender anew into the unconditional love of God for us. Whatever our symptoms may be, whatever the situation is that we might be in, we will discover a new experience of *exousia*, or power—the power of rising with Christ.

THE END

It was the week after Christmas four years ago. I was on a day off, and I decided to go to Lake Geneva, Wisconsin, where my brother and I own a small place. Sometimes I go there just to rest, read, and walk. I came to a four-way stop and stopped; then I proceeded into the intersection. I was on a country road in Wisconsin, sort of a back way into Lake Geneva. As I looked out of the corner of my eye to the right, I saw an SUV coming my way. The SUV was blowing the stop sign and was coming directly at the passenger-side door of my car. I had one simple thought. *I am dead.* The woman driving the SUV had to be going forty-five, fifty, fifty-five miles per hour. I had the instinct to turn my wheels sharply to the left, hoping that perhaps she would miss me and pass me by. No such luck, but I do think the turn helped me a great deal. She plowed into the right side of the car near the right front wheel. As I sat there in the driver's seat, the seatbelt grabbed me around the chest. I watched my windshield shatter. I saw her drive past me, and I saw my front bumper fly into the air. I had another simple thought at this point. *I am not dead.*

Two simple, but profound thoughts: *I am dead; I am not dead.* All of a sudden, all of the cars around the two vehicles involved in the accident came to a stop. People ran to my car. I tried to open the door, but the frame of the car was so badly damaged, the door would not open. A woman familiar with health issues came to the car and cautioned me to not move. She did not want me to do any further damage if I were injured. Eventually, the fire department arrived. They told me that they would have to cut me out of the car. They asked me where the battery was because they were afraid of an explosion or a fire. When the fire department used the Jaws of Life to get me out of the car, I was immediately transported to the satellite of a hospital where the medical people discovered, thank God, that I was not seriously hurt. The car was totaled. I subsequently had to get a new car.

That day in Lake Geneva has stayed with me these past several years, and I think about it. I do not think about it in a panicky, horrific sort of way. I think, rather, that I got up that day with the thought of taking a day off. I had no concept, whatsoever, that it possibly could be the last day of my life. I had no inkling that I would be in a traffic accident in which my car would be totaled. But that day has taught me to always live with that consciousness—that today could be the last day of my life. If it is, what do I want this day to look like? If it may be, what do I want my life to look like? The victims of the shootings in Fort Hood, Texas, and Orlando last week had no idea when they woke up those days that, for some of them, it would be the last day of their lives or, for others, a day on which they would be seriously injured.

The book of Daniel is an apocalyptic book that speaks of a time of ending and transformation. Inherent in this book is a promise that God is going to end the status quo of things and bring his kingdom, his reign, to fulfillment. We hear a similar theme in the Gospel of Mark, in which Jesus engages in apocalyptic, eschatological talk. He is talking about the end of time as we know it and the establishment of God's reign in its fullness.

The end, the end of time—many people have been frightened by the popularization of a belief from an ancient culture, the Mayan culture, which populated Mexico and other parts of Latin America from the third to the ninth centuries A.D. The Mayan calendar comes to an end on December 21, 2012. The Mayans believed that there would be the end of time as we know it and a new world order would begin. Many who have read popularized versions of these assertions have become convinced themselves that the world as we know it is indeed going to end in December 2012. Scientists say that there is no reason scientifically to believe this. Nonetheless, popular culture is challenging us to bear down on a theme that some of us find discomforting—the end of time. The world is going to end in December 2012. A movie starring John Cusack tells the story of the end of the world in 2012 with tremendous special effects.

There are several ways to look at the end of time. First of all, time for all of us comes to an end eventually. We all have to face the inevitability of our own deaths. We are not adult, we are not mature until we have looked at this issue squarely and developed some beliefs or convictions about what happens in and through this great passage. In the book of Daniel there is an Old Testament foreshadowing of what has become the Christian belief of the resurrection. Daniel speaks of those who have fallen asleep waking up, and some living forever; others live in everlasting disgrace. Though the Jewish people did have a belief in an experience after death called Sheol—a place of shadows where both good and evil people went in some form after death—they did not have a developed belief in the afterlife. However, for some Jewish people, some belief in the afterlife gradually evolved. Belief in life after death would later develop among the Pharisees. Jesus's death, his resurrection, and the first Christians' experience of him as risen from the dead made belief and hope in life after death the foundational conviction of Christian faith. We can look at the end of personal time with courage and hope because of the life, death, and resurrection of Jesus.

Another way to look at the end of time was popularized by the church father Irenaeus, and in more contemporary times popularized by the paleontologist and theologian Teilhard de Chardin. These two great thinkers believed in evolution, but they did not so much emphasize the descent of human beings from primates; rather they believed that human beings were evolving toward the experience of the *homo futurus*—the future man, the future person. They saw the goal of human history to be the evolution of the human family to conform more and more to the lifestyle and teaching of Jesus. This is the positive understanding we have of eschatology or the end of time, that hopefully there will be time when the human family achieves and experiences the fullness of God's reign.

With the fear that we have of nuclear proliferation, we know that the end of time could be much more of a disaster than the positive scenario just discussed. Human beings have the capacity to end the world with the weapons of mass destruction that we now possess. Similarly, each and any of us can bring about the end of our own personal time by living lives that are misguided, misdirected, steeped in sin, and contrary to God's will. We need to work and pray that the end of time never happens in such painful, destructive, misguided ways.

Another kind of end we all must deal with throughout our lifetimes is change or transition. We age, we go through developmental stages of life, we change roles, and we lose people to death. These and other human experiences all involve endings. In his book *Transitions: Making Sense of Life's Changes*, William Bridges writes that all of life's transitions can be broken down into three phases: endings, the neutral zone, and new beginnings. He further discusses five aspects of the ending experience: disengagement, dismantling, disidentification, disenchantment, and disorientation. Transition or real change begins with letting go of something—something that one has believed or assumed, some way that someone has always been or seen oneself, or some outlook on the world or attitude toward others. Bridges has an optimistic view of transitions, saying that endings are the first, not the last, act of the play.

Another expert on psychology, Daniel Levinson, in *Seasons of a Man's Life* and other writings, has spoken of the inevitability of transitions. He says that life structures are not permanent, and that they must change over and over again as new life structures are established. Before a new life structure can be established, though, there is a necessary period of transition. Levinson says that a transitional period involves three main developmental tasks: termination of one's life structure, the experience of individuation (or the experience of a person gaining a clearer sense of who he or she is, becoming more autonomous), and initiation. In transition there is both an ending and a beginning. In the initiation phase, the person explores new possibilities and makes new choices. These choices mark the beginning of the new life structure.

The end: Jesus says in the Gospel of Mark that we know not the day or the hour. Only the Father knows that day and hour of our physical end. As I listened to the news this week and heard of the execution of John Allen Muhammad, and heard also about the jury struggling to decide whether Brian Dugan of the Chicago area should be executed, it struck me that capital punishment is really an attempt to rob God of God's proper role. I believe God decides on the day and the hour when we die. Even though Allen Muhammad and Dugan have done awful things, I do not believe that capital punishment, or death for death, is an effective response to a crime.

Something is not quite right when a person sentenced to death is given a meal of choice four hours before the execution, accompanied by alcohol if desired. The condemned is asked to take a shower two hours before death, and then the person administering the lethal injection (in this case) swabs the person's arm with alcohol before injecting the prisoner with the fatal injection that will end life. In Allen Muhammad's case, as in many cases of execution, about thirty people stood behind glass watching this person breathe his last, some rejoicing in revenge as he got what he deserved. I do not think such a response, even to great crime, is of God or of the gospel. Only God should know the day and the hour.

One of the principles of Stephen Covey's popular book several years ago, *The 7 Habits of Highly Effective People*, is "always begin with the end in mind." Covey gives a positive spin to the notion of *the end*. He understands the end as a sense of personal goals and a sense of direction—where we want to go and where we want to be. This is our end or our purpose, our reason for being alive. Covey teaches that each of us should have a sense of a personal end, and that our lives ought to be directed by this sense of purpose. We should be teleological or purpose-filled people. Let us not have a negative, fearful understanding of the end. Let us rather have a sense of the end as something that directs us, something that moves and nudges us toward a positive future.

REPENTANCE

I was conducting a seminar recently at the Clare, the senior care facility where I work. The seminar was on the book of Job. We were discussing why bad things happen to good people, as happens in the storyline of Job. One participant, a Jewish lady, asked a question. She said, "When people hurt other people, is it really morally wrong or could it be, from what we are discovering through science, that a lot of the bad things that happen to people are the result of people's brain chemistry being off? People cause hurt in the lives of others because of the misfiring of chemicals in the brain." My response was that it was a "both and" rather than an "either or." I do think that sometimes objective wrongs and crimes are committed by people who have mental disease. Having said that, though, I would not want to discount the possibility of wrongdoing or sin. I still hold to the old Catholic tradition that sin is knowing that something is wrong, but willing it and doing it anyway. There is grave sin that is very harmful to us and potentially to others. There is less than grave sin or venial sin, but sin is a reality of life. We have a tendency to rationalize or euphemize when we talk about our sinfulness. But sin is a fact, a human reality.

In the Gospel of Luke, we are taken on a journey through the political and religious time of John the Baptist and Jesus. Luke names all those who are in authority, both politically and religiously; after going through that history, Luke then introduces the character of John the Baptist. The message of John the Baptist that strikes me this week is his call to repentance. We are told that he engaged in a baptism of repentance for the forgiveness of sin.

Let us focus on repentance and forgiveness. What is repentance? The Greek word for repentance is *metanoia*, or changed mind. In cognitive behavioral therapy, we emphasize that changing thoughts or changing minds frequently must be joined to a change of behavior if there truly is going to be a change in a person's life. Repentance is a change of mind, heart, and behavior. The change comes after the recognition that one has engaged somehow in sin.

A phrase in the letter to the Philippians is constitutive to the repentance process. Paul called his readers and us to "discern what is of value." An important step in the process of repentance is discernment. *Discernment* refers to "sifting through" or "sorting through." As we sift and sort through what is of value in our lives, as Paul encourages us, we also should focus on those aspects of our lives that are, perhaps, morally wrong.

I am rather traditional in my discernment. I think the Ten Commandments still have legs as we look at patterns of sin in our lives. I think it is important to discern around Jesus's three commandments: Love God, love neighbor, and love self. I think it is important also to be attentive to what it means to be a practicing Catholic Christian in the world today. We ought to be conscious of communal expectations that are put on us because we are followers of Jesus in terms of a faith life, prayer and worship life, a life of service, ministry, mercy, and justice. In twelve-step work, people call such a discernment process a "moral inventory." People recovering from addiction or who have a connection to someone who is addicted are encouraged to take a moral inventory on a regular basis. Discernment and a moral inventory lead to repentance, change of mind, and a change of behavior.

Luke tells us that John's call to repentance was also an invitation to forgiveness—God's forgiveness of our sins. An image flowing from the prophet Baruch I think helps us understand sin. Baruch is writing to the Jewish people, who were led into exile away from their homes to Babylon around the year 587 B.C. Think of the image of *exile*. Exile speaks of us being cut off from our best selves. Exile speaks of alienation in relationships. Exile speaks of feelings of separation from God. When we sin, we voluntarily place ourselves in a kind of existential exile. Experiencing God's forgiveness is being called from exile to come home again.

We celebrate the reality of God's forgiveness as Catholic Christians in many ways: in the Penitential Rite of our Mass, in private prayers of contrition, but also in the Sacrament of Reconciliation. The Sacrament of Reconciliation started in the early church as a pastoral response to the reality of sin in people's lives. In essence, people violated their Baptism by sinning. Church leaders wrestled with the issue of what to do with people who had sinned seriously. The pastoral response was that the Church ought to have a process similar to how people came into the Church, a process of reconversion that came to be known as the Order of Penitents. The Rite of Christian Initiation of Adults emerged for people joining the Church. The Order of Penitents was a process for people to return to the Church or return to God after sin. Key to the process was a Greek word—*exomologesis*, which means *confession*. A confession in this process did not just mean the admission of sin. Confession also meant profession, a profession of faith. The early Christians in the ancient Order of Penitents professed faith in a God of love who forgave them. The words of absolution in this process were a proclamation over the returning penitent of God's love, mercy, and forgiveness.

I think we need to recapture some of the spirit and steps of the ancient Order of Penitents around our own engaging in the Sacrament of Reconciliation. The Sacrament of Reconciliation ought to be a rich, full experience of moral inventory, repentance, admission of sin, and profession of faith in God's forgiveness. God's forgiveness should temper the pain of guilt that occurs when we sin, although I believe that guilt, in some ways, is a healthy experience. It is an alarm clock going off, warning us that we have stepped into morally dangerous territory. I encourage people to celebrate the Sacrament of Reconciliation, but I always add another dimension in talking about forgiveness and reconciliation. I think it is important for us to do forgiveness, contrition, and reconciliation work in real life. What value is the Sacrament of Reconciliation if we go home to broken relationships or continued patterns of sin or hurting each other?

I wrote a book some years ago, *The Way of Forgiveness*, in which I emphasized steps that are involved in forgiving another person. We need to get in touch with our own hurt and how we have been hurt and not deny it, but we need to then practice empathy, trying to understand what was going on in the life of the person who hurt us. We need to get in touch with the fact that we ourselves are people who sometimes hurt others and are in need of forgiveness ourselves. We need to make a decision to forgive, to work a process in which we let go of the need to hurt back; then, whether it is done face to face, in written form, or perhaps just intrapsychically, we need to decide to forgive people.

The writing of Baruch contains an attitude of joy, despite the fact that the people are in exile. I think the process of forgiveness should end in joy and thanksgiving, for when we forgive, we share in Christ's victory over evil in his life, death, and resurrection.

I think we need to work on a similar process of contrition. We need to say that we are sorry, because we have hurt other people; wherever, whenever possible, when there is brokenness in our relationships, we need to work a process of reconciliation, sometimes calling on the help of a spiritual director, counselor, or life coach in trying to bring healing to relationships that are hurt or broken. Two writers who have done extensive research on these matters of forgiveness, sorrow, and reconciliation are Robert Enright and Everett Worthington. I encourage you to look into my research in *The Way of Forgiveness* and the research of these other two men.

The prophet Baruch uses the words "take off" and "put on," alluding to the taking off and putting on of clothes. I would like to suggest that those are important words in this process of repentance. Repentance involves the doing of penance. The doing of penance requires that we abstain from some things and do certain other things. "Putting on" has levels of meaning. One level of meaning for me is that of practice. To do penance, we need to practice new, healthier, happier, holier ways of doing our lives.

John the Baptist encourages us to "prepare the way of the Lord." One way we prepare a way for the Lord in our lives is by getting serious about repentance: discerning sin; doing moral inventory; admitting sin; professing faith in God's mercy; accepting God's forgiveness; living in a spirit of thanksgiving for God's forgiveness; trying to practice forgiveness, contrition, and reconciliation in real life and relationships; doing penance; or "taking off and putting on." I think it would be good if each of us and all of us found time for repentance.

PRODIGAL SON, COMPASSIONATE FATHER, RESENTFUL BROTHER

Recent news has told bloodcurdling stories of real-life events. We heard about the murder of three family members in Darien, Illinois, over a child custody battle. We heard of a family being wiped out by a fire arranged by the landlord of the building who wanted to gain the insurance money. We have heard of the sexual abuse and murder of two young women in the San Diego area, perhaps by a serial abuser who was living in the area.

Reflecting on the story of the prodigal son, someone asked me recently, "Do you think God, Jesus, really expects the family and friends of people who have been killed to forgive those who took the lives of their loved one?" I responded hesitantly. I said, "I know emotions and feelings of the families and friends of the people who lost their lives are raw and perhaps they cannot forgive at this time, but I believe Jesus would say that eventually even people involved in these situations have to get to forgiveness."

Forgiveness is a gospel mandate. We always must forgive. I have found in my research that forgiveness also contributes to psychological and physical health for the person who forgives.

I am reminded of the psychologist Everett Worthington, one of the foremost writers on the psychology of forgiveness. Worthington's mother was killed on a New Year's Eve some years back. He describes his immediate reaction as one of violence and vengeance. He wanted to hurt the two young men who took his mother's life. He decided that he—as a teacher of forgiveness, if he were to have integrity—had to work a process of forgiving the men who killed his mother. He said he has worked such a process. He does forgive them.

The great story of the prodigal son introduces us to three spiritual values: sorrow or contrition, forgiveness, and reconciliation. Let us look at each of these values through the lens of the characters in the prodigal son story.

The prodigal son, asking his father for his share of the inheritance before the father died, was equivalent to saying, "I can't wait for you to die! Drop dead!" Narcissistically, the young man wanted what he wanted *now*. In love, the father divides the property between the two sons with immediacy. The younger son goes and literally wastes and destroys all that the father has earned and given him in love. Finding himself poor, hungry, and homeless, the younger son decides that he is going to return to the father to express sorrow for what he has done. He hopes that the father will take him back as perhaps one of his workers. The prodigal son does not have true contrition. His apparent sorrow is motivated by his own needs. He nonetheless displays some steps in the process of contrition.

I have talked about some of these steps in a book I wrote a few years ago, *The Way of Forgiveness*. To be a person of contrition, we need to take moral inventory of ourselves on a regular basis, assessing how we may have hurt other people. Contrition requires empathy, putting ourselves in the shoes or in the skin of the people we have hurt, trying to understand how we made them feel. Contrition is part of a larger process that we call repentance. Contrition cries out for prayer and requires a decision. We need to decide to say "I'm sorry" to someone we have hurt. As the prodigal son exemplifies, contrition requires rehearsal, trying to prepare in a good sense for what and how we will say to the person we have hurt. Contrition requires action. Either face to face or in some other fashion, we need to connect with the person we have hurt. We need to engage in a nonrationalizing expression of sorrow. If it seems appropriate, it might be helpful to pray with the person toward whom we are expressing sorrow. If we have been able to work some of these steps, we certainly ought to praise God for the grace and the courage that he has provided us with to be able to express sorrow. Contrition demands that we repent and remember other people we might have hurt to whom we should be expressing sorrow.

Everett Worthington, whom I spoke of earlier, uses an acronym, CONFESS, to help people learn how to express contrition or sorrow:

Confess without excuses.

Offer a specific apology.

Note the other person's pain verbally.

Forever value—let the person harmed know that he or she is
   of great value.

Equalize by offering restitution to balance the injustice caused
   by the hurt.

Say you will try to make sure that the hurt will not happen
   again.

Seek forgiveness. Ask clearly for forgiveness. Acknowledge
   that you did wrong.

The prodigal son, while expressing imperfect contrition, gives us some hints of some of these steps.

The father figure, on the other hand, is an example of someone who forgives. In *The Way of Forgiveness*, I talk about steps in the forgiveness process. They are similar to the steps of contrition. To forgive, we need to name the pain. We need to listen for the hurt and name it and name the people who have caused it. We have to pray for the grace and the courage to forgive. Forgiveness also calls for a decision to work a process toward forgiveness. Rehearsal might also be needed here. We might need to think through how we are going to express forgiveness. In the process of forgiveness, we need to take action and connect with the person whom we are going to forgive. In a spirit of kindness and hospitality, then, we need to grant forgiveness as a free gift. If praying with each other is helpful, we could or should do that. If we truly have been able to forgive someone, we ought to praise God for the help he has given us in reaching that point. And here also, we should not forgive and forget, but forgive and remember. We should remember to whom else we should be granting either sorrow or forgiveness.

Robert Enright is another psychologist who has given his life to the study of forgiveness. Enright feels that forgiveness is a process that unfolds in four phases. He calls the first phase the *uncovering phase*. He says that many people who have been hurt deny that they have been hurt. It is only gradually that the nature and the depth of the hurt begins to emerge in a person's consciousness. The person moves on to almost obsessing about the hurt, replaying and reliving it over and over again. The person grows in feelings of resentment or hatred. The person becomes upset that the one who has done the hurting is doing very well while the hurt person is miserable. In this phase, the person begins to see how unfair life can be.

The second phase is the *decision phase*, in which a person comes to terms with not wanting to stay in the negative energy. While the person is not at the point of forgiveness yet, the person makes a decision: "I am going to work a process of forgiveness."

That leads to the third phase which is the *work phase*. The work phase is quite difficult. It largely involves practicing empathy toward the person who caused the hurt. The hurt person needs to try to discern what was going on in the person's current life or perhaps past history that caused him or her to hurt the hurting person. The empathy and understanding are not condoning the hurt. The hurt person can still name the hurting behavior as wrong, but the person is trying to understand the wrongdoer. In the work phase, the person continues to decide, "I am not going to hurt back. I am going to absorb this pain like a sponge absorbs water." Then the person grants forgiveness face to face or intrapsychically, or both, as a free gift, a gratuitous gift.

Having granted forgiveness, the person moves into the *deepening phase*, in which a person may experience the psychological, physical, and spiritual benefits that come with forgiveness. For example, many people who forgive report lessening of anxiety, depression, and aggression. In this phase, the person who has forgiven another realizes that he or she has hurt people, too, and has been forgiven. In this phase the person may begin to build forgiveness into one's own vision or philosophy of life.

Worthington has another acronym for teaching the phenomenon of forgiveness. It is in the word REACH.

Recall the hurt.

Empathize with the person who has hurt us.

A stands for forgiveness as an Altruistic gift.

Commit publicly to forgive. Worthington believes there has to be some sort of public ritual or a conversation with another person to externalize the reality of the forgiveness process.

Hold onto forgiveness.

Worthington feels that perhaps this REACH process has to be used a number of times for one hurt to actually hold oneself in forgiveness.

The father figure in the prodigal son story represents both human forgiveness and divine forgiveness. In other words, the father can be a model for us on the human level, but the father is also an image or a metaphor that Jesus uses to reveal the nature of God. Jesus does not use a word we have used frequently—empathy. Rather, Jesus says at the sight of his returning son that the father was filled with compassion. He ran toward the son and hugged and embraced him. From what I have heard from Scripture scholars, a patriarchal, hierarchical Jewish father would never run toward a son with compassion. Jesus is trying to give us a revolutionary glimpse of who and how God is. He passionately welcomes us back and forgives us when we sin. The father is a model of forgiveness.

The image in the prodigal son story of the model of nonforgiveness is the older son, who resents what the father is doing in celebrating the younger son's return. The older son's reaction also leads us into the third topic I would like to focus on: reconciliation. The older son will not reconcile with his brother. He will not go into the party. In the unfolding of this parabolic story, who knows what would have happened to the older son if he would have forgiven, if he would have reconciled? In the posture of nonforgiveness, though, he is filled with anger, resentment, competitiveness, and aggression—none of which are good for the human soul. The father, on the other hand, seems to have worked a process of reconciliation with the younger son already, a process to which the older son is not even close.

Reconciliation and forgiveness are not the same thing. Forgiveness can lead to reconciliation. In some cases, we can forgive and we ought not to reconcile because of the dangerous, abusive nature of a relationship. Reconciliation is an attempt to rebuild trust where trust has been broken, an attempt to rebuild and heal a broken relationship. There needs to be a mutuality of commitment on the part of all parties involved if there is to be reconciliation. Reconciliation is almost building a bridge toward one another. It necessitates detoxifying a relationship, removing the toxins or the poisons of frequent criticism, feelings of contempt, defensiveness, stonewalling, and deadening oneself to each other. Reconciliation is hard work.

Let this wonderful story of the prodigal son remind us of the gospel mandates for contrition, forgiveness, and reconciliation. All are processes. In all three cases, we need to be careful about pseudo-contrition, pseudo-forgiveness, and pseudo-reconciliation. We all would be healthier and holier people, and have sounder relationships, if we worked at these three spiritual realities.

JOHN 3:16

Occasionally, watching sporting events on TV, we can see someone raise a sign that simply says "John 3:16." The sign holder is using the opportunity of the camera being on to deliver one of the most beautiful passages in the New Testament and the *kerygma*, or the core of our faith: "God so loved the world that he sent his only son, so that whoever believes in him may not perish, but may have eternal life."

The reason for Jesus's coming to the earth is revealed in this passage. Certainly Jesus came to reveal all that he meant by the reign of God, but at the core of his reign-of-God preaching and teaching is the good news about eternal life. If we believe in him, we have eternal life. Death has been conquered. Suffering has been conquered. All of life has meaning and purpose, because of the life, death, and resurrection of Jesus.

Jesus says in this famous John 3 passage that he will be lifted up so that whoever believes in him may have eternal life. The lifting up seems to have several connotations. Lifting up obviously refers to Jesus being lifted up on the cross, but it also refers to his being lifted up on Easter Sunday, in and through his resurrection. The lifting up also seems to refer to his ascension, or his glorification with Abba and the Spirit in heaven.

Throughout John's Gospel there are references to "the world," and John seems to send mixed messages about this topic. Jesus says in parts of John that we are not to be of the world, we are not to assume and live the world's standards. Some of the mores and practices of cultures down through history have been contrary to the reign-of-God preaching and teaching of Jesus. But the world in and of itself is not evil. Jesus goes on to say in the Gospel that he did not come to condemn the world, but to save it. One of the original meanings of salvation is *healing*. Jesus came to heal the world.

So we have discovered a couple of truths already in the Gospel: Jesus came to offer us eternal life through belief in him; in his death on the cross, his resurrection, and his glorification he has come to heal us. Maybe we might ponder where the world needs healing and ask Jesus to enter those dimensions of life.

Certainly the tension between nations, and the anger and violence of terrorism cry out for healing. The reality of chosen sin cries out for healing and forgiveness. People and nations ravaged by poverty and hunger are in need of healing. Sick people among our primary relationships and in our parish are in need of healing. World economies are in need of healing. Wherever there are brokenness, division, and alienation between and among people, there is a need for Christ's healing.

At the Eucharist and in our personal prayer, let us be aware of where the world needs healing. Let us be aware of where we personally need healing, and invite the healing power of Jesus into those situations and into our lives.

In Ephesians, Paul speaks of this notion of salvation also. We are reminded that the salvation, the healing that comes to us through Jesus Christ is not a result of our work, but it comes as grace or free gift. All that we can do is place faith in the saving power of Jesus and in the grace of God.

The second book of Chronicles tells us about the sinfulness of the Jewish people at a given period in their lives and their history, and how their sin punishes itself. Punishment often is inherent in the sin in which we engage. In the case of the Jewish people, their nation collapsed. Jerusalem and the temple were destroyed, and many of the people were led into Babylonian exile for decades.

Second Chronicles reminds us that God can use anyone to mediate his grace and accomplish his will. He uses the pagan king of Persia, Cyrus, to liberate the Jewish people from Babylon and to send them home to Judah, to Jerusalem, to rebuild their city, their temple, and their lives. The liberation from Babylonian captivity is a precursor—a sign—of the liberation and healing that Jesus brought and brings to the world.

Let us go back to an idea that we began with—the love of God for the world, the love of God for us. Believing in God's unconditional love for me has changed my life, transforming me from being a fearful, anxious person to a person who, sometimes reluctantly, places my total trust in and surrender into God's unconditional love for me. This is a foundational conviction of my life.

I want to remind you that God has the same unconditional love for each of us. He wants us to trust in that love. He wants us to surrender into that love.

I am really talking here about vertical love—"vertical" in the sense of connecting with a divine, spiritual love that comes to us in the Spirit. Plugging into this love can give us courage, hope, meaning, and purpose despite any of the circumstances of our lives.

I encourage anyone experiencing any kind of pain to emotionally, spiritually, and physically open yourself to God's unconditional love, mediated in and through the Holy Spirit. God's love can change us.

I want to remind us also that in addition to vertical love there needs to be horizontal love, the love that is expressed from person to person. So many people in the world are starved for human touch, a kind word, a verbal expression of love and affection. When we share love with each other we also are mediating divine love. Divine love is immanent in and present in the words and deeds of love that we share with each other. Such horizontal love further manifests itself in acts of mercy, charity, and a concern for involvement in justice.

Jesus came to save the world, which means Jesus came to heal the world, and he wants all of us to work with him in healing the broken world by being people of greater love.

I ask us to reflect on when and how we have felt love from other human beings throughout our lifetime. What lovers have encouraged us and given us life? Let us praise God for them. When and how have we encountered and do we encounter God's unconditional love? For all the love that has been given to us, by God and by others, let us be thankful, and let us be challenged to be more deliberate and more intentional in sharing love with others. If God does not condemn and judge us, we should be less judgmental and critical, kinder and gentler with one another.

Finally, please keep in mind the context from which the Gospel exchange with Nicodemus comes. Nicodemus has just come to Jesus in the dark of night, reluctant to be known publicly as his disciple. Jesus gives the famous teaching to Nicodemus on the importance of being born again or born from above. Nicodemus does not understand Jesus's notion of spiritual rebirth. He thinks that Jesus is referring to grown people somehow returning to their mothers' wombs. Jesus further clarifies: Unless you are born again, through water and the Spirit, you cannot enter the reign of God.

All of us, through baptism, are called to be born again, and if and when we are deliberately and intentionally born again, we live lives permanently and significantly influenced by God's unconditional love.

WOMEN AND SALVATION

Two strong women stand out in the Scriptures for me: Mary and Elizabeth. From what we know and understand, Mary was an adolescent girl of about fourteen, betrothed to a man named Joseph. She is mysteriously pregnant. The child she carries is not Joseph's. She has to tell her betrothed that the child is from God. Try to get a feeling of the challenge that Mary faced in the Jewish culture that she was part of—an unexpected pregnancy, father unknown. Yet, in the midst of all this mystery, Mary trusts. She is involved in something much bigger than herself, something that involves the salvation of the world—the child who is coming is from God. Take note that although Mary is pregnant, she makes the effort to visit Elizabeth, whom she knows is in need of assistance. We are told that Mary went in haste through the difficult hill country. Mary's concern was not herself, but for Elizabeth.

Elizabeth, her kinswoman, we are told, was an older lady. Perhaps in those days, in that culture, an older lady might have been forty-plus. She was perceived to be barren. She had never had a child, a social stigma in Jewish culture. Now this older woman was blessed with a child, John the Baptist, whom she was carrying when Mary arrived to greet her. Older women would perhaps look upon an expected pregnancy in later years as a burden. Elizabeth looked on her pregnancy and her coming child as a blessing, a gift from God.

Some years ago, the psychologist Erik Erikson gave us the epigenetic theory of human development. Erikson said that human beings pass through eight stages of development. At every stage, there is a crisis that one must resolve, ideally positively, so that one can go on to the next stage. One of the stages is middle adulthood, generally from forty to sixty-five. Erikson said the crisis at this stage is generativity versus stagnation. *Generativity* refers to making a positive contribution to the world around us, influencing the future, and working with those younger to help shape a new future. The opposite of generativity that people can fall into is *stagnation*, becoming focused too much on the self, a kind of frozen narcissism.

Carol Gilligan, the feminist thinker and writer, wrote some years ago that she felt Erikson's stages were male skewed. As we understand generativity, Gilligan said, women do not wait until their forties or fifties to be generative. Women are generative throughout their lives. Mary and Elizabeth strike me in their femininity to be truly generative women, concerned about others, concerned about the young, concerned about the world, concerned about the future. Let the generativity, kindness, compassion, generosity, and profound faith of Mary and Elizabeth be ideals that we strive to imitate.

Mary and Elizabeth remind me of three of the Franciscan values we live out at the Clare: respect, or seeing the face of God in those whom we serve; service, responding to the needs of others before our own; and joy, giving from the heart. As Elizabeth is described in Luke, let us try to be filled with the Holy Spirit.

In our busy times, times of many expectations and pressures, times of joy and sadness and struggle, let us turn to Mary and Elizabeth for their guidance. Let us celebrate the roles that women have played in salvation history. Let us show appreciation and admiration to the women in our lives, who have been and are so generative.

Now let's consider the prophet Micah. The Jewish people are up against a new enemy, Assyria. Micah warns of much struggle for the Jewish people for the foreseeable future. He does an interesting thing. Micah promises that the nation Judah will survive, but he adds that Judah's survival is not going to come through the big city of Jerusalem, but rather through the smaller town of Bethlehem where David was born. A new king will emerge from Bethlehem, Micah prophesies, and he describes that coming king as peace, saying, "He shall be peace."

What is our personal Bethlehem this year; or where do we need peace? Let us invite the Spirit of Jesus into our contemporary personal Bethlehems, where we need peace. What is Bethlehem for you this year? Is it a relationship? Is it a hurt? Is it a pattern of sin? Is it emotional pain? Is it job related? Is it a financial concern? Where do you need greater peace? Name your Bethlehem so you can truly have a felt sense of a new kind of inner peace that comes from our relationship with Christ.

In the letter to the Hebrews, the author reminds us that the multiple rituals and sacrifices of the old law are no longer to be the center of faith. The center of faith is Jesus. We are to invite him into our lives in a new way. The author of Hebrews describes Jesus as the one who gave himself for the human family in an attempt to follow and fulfill God's will.

Let Christmas be connected with Easter in our consciousness. Our faith in Jesus cannot be based on an infant of historical memory. Our faith is in the Lord and Savior who indeed was born as a child in Bethlehem and gave himself in sacrifice to reveal the reign of God and the truth of eternal life. As he always pursued God's will, let us pray for the fulfillment of God's will in our lives.

Generativity; our personal Bethlehems; peace; a rebirth of the living, dying, rising, saving Jesus—let these realities be in our thoughts and prayers.

LOOK IN THE MIRROR

I always experience Holy Week as a kind of mirror of the human condition. By that I mean as we look at and listen to the stories of Holy Week, we get a glimpse of many things that we ourselves experience as human beings, and we are blessed with a shared belief system that a loving God is at work in all that we experience in this human condition. So let us look into the mirror of Holy Week and find ourselves, and find God with us.

Holy Week is a story of domination systems abusing people. There is the domination system of the military and the government representing Rome, and the domination system of corrupt religious leaders using struggling people for their own profit. In Holy Week we see the conflicts between empty religion and faith-filled spirituality. In Holy Week we see the strong prophetic action of Jesus, who organizes a parade at the beginning of the week, that is juxtaposed to the huge military parade that Pontius Pilate organized. Pilate was proclaiming that Caesar was God. In his parade, Jesus was proclaiming that God reigns. As we look into the mirror, we get a growing sense of the price that Jesus will pay for his prophetic truth.

Looking at the first Holy Week, we see a man of great integrity and wholeness, Jesus, who spoke truth, healed broken people, and revealed the nature of the reign of God. We see a man of profound faith who, despite his knowledge of what would happen to him soon, continued his ministry in the midst of his foes. In Jesus we see a man who did not run from the inevitable conflict that awaited him, but walked toward it.

Holy Week is a story of human nature. It is a story about how fickle people can be. Disciples lauded him and praised him as he entered Jerusalem, and called for his execution just a few days later. Holy Week is a story of mortality. It is a story of the horizon of death that we all must face, regarding our own lives and the lives of the people whom we love. But Holy Week, in the face of death, again is a story about faith in an emerging conviction that God can transform death into new life and eternal life. As we look at mortality in the mirror of Holy Week, we see not only death, we see sickness, we see suffering, and we see the faith of Jesus telling us that God can transform all that is painful and hurting into something new, something eternal.

Looking at the first Holy Week, we see a unjustly convicted victim of capital punishment. We see a man of terrible desolation and isolation, abandoned by almost all who said they were committed to him. In the face of this abandonment, we see and hear a man who can nonetheless surrender his total self, body and soul, into the loving care of a Creator/Parent that he believed to be always with him and for him.

Looking into the mirror of Holy Week, we see patterns of sin into which we all fall. We see the avarice or greed of Judas, who would betray a friend for material resources. We see the spinelessness of Peter, who denies that he knows his friend. We see so many broken relationships—apostles and disciples who abandoned him. We see the loneliness of the abandoned Jesus.

Looking into the mirror of Holy Week, we see the human story. We see the story of life, death, and resurrection that is unfolding in each of our lives. Perhaps some of us can identify with different aspects of the Holy Week story. Place yourself in this story, find yourself in this story, and be one with Jesus in the unfolding of the story. The story is about you, and me, and life. The story is about God, who never abandons us, and ultimately always works all things for our benefit.

Look into the mirror. Let us see ourselves, and let us try to grow in the great trust and hope that Jesus exhibits in the Holy Week story. Let us especially be attentive and prayerful around the Holy Thursday meal that he gave us as gift. Let us watch with him and embrace the mystery of the cross. And then let us wait for the glimmers of sunlight, new life, and eternal life that always come with the Easter vigil and Easter Sunday morning.

Don't waste Holy Week. Let us take it very seriously. Look in the mirror.

JOB MOMENTS

An old friend of mine, someone who was a leader in a youth group I started at St. Hubert's thirty-six years ago, asked to see me last week. I took him over to Durty Nellie's in Palatine and we had lunch together. He brought me up to date on all that has happened to him in the last five or six years. He married, and had a child. His wife and child are the joys of his life. But he also went through a terrible bout with leukemia. Through a lot of chemotherapy and medical treatments, that has gone into remission, but since he has developed skin cancer—and now a full-blown cancer in one of his glands—he is in chemotherapy again. He has developed the shingles, a very painful inflammation of nerve endings. He cannot work much. Money is very tight.

This relatively young man always led a very good life. He was athletic, didn't drink, do drugs, or smoke. He has lost over thirty pounds. As I looked at him and listened to his story—listened to the strong emotions that he is feeling of anger, confusion, and fear—that difficult question loomed in my mind: Why? Why does this man have so much suffering in his life? Why will his lifespan probably be much shorter than those of his peers? Why do such bad things happen to good people?

I appreciate the book of Job. We hear some of Job's despondency at the loss and suffering he experienced. In the book of Job, Satan goes to God and gets a green light to bring suffering into Job's life to test him. God claims that Job will never waver in faith. Job loses family, resources, his own health, and by chapter 3 he is crying, "Cursed be the day that I was born. Why didn't I die?"

Three friends visit Job to offer him some consolation. They also offer him sort of a quick-fix understanding of what is happening to him and why. Many people in Jewish culture believed in divine retribution. The reason for suffering in a person's life had to do with punishment for some sin or evil that the person engaged in at some time in his or her lifetime. In this theology, God always gets his person and gives that person what he or she might deserve as a result of evil attitudes or actions.

Job resists the three friends' interpretation of the situation. He claims that he has been a good man, that he has done nothing to deserve what he is experiencing. This drama concludes with a young man, Elihu, coming on the scene to tell Job and his three friends that none of them truly understand what is going on with Job. The young man challenges the four, saying that they are essentially dealing with mystery that cannot be easily explained by their mechanistic understanding of God and life.

Why do bad things happen to good people? We do not know. It is mysterious. The book of Job seems to suggest, however, that suffering is a form of evil that enters into a person's life. It is not something that people choose or deserve. In the mystery of things, evil and suffering happen to good people.

In Job 42, the story reaches completion. Job says, "I have been meddling in things that are beyond my understanding. Before this suffering I only knew God by hearsay, but now I have come to know him face to face." I think Job's comment is one of the most beautiful statements about suffering in the Scriptures. Suffering can be a crucible in which we move from empty religion to a living faith that comes to know God personally. I think that is happening with my friend who is suffering so greatly. He is being called to a new kind of faith that many people will never know or experience. As he hangs on in faith, as Job hung on in faith, such people become teachers to the rest of us about trusting, hoping in, and surrendering into God, in the face of affliction, when we do not completely understand what is going on or what is happening to us.

One portrait of Jesus painted in Mark's Gospel is that of healer. People come to Jesus because they are sick, hurt, or broken in some way, and he brings healing to them. The same is true in our own day. Jesus is a healer. Perhaps Jesus will not heal the cancer of my friend or give a specific healing that we want in given circumstances, but turning to Jesus in faith and asking for help always brings some kind of healing.

In the miracles of Jesus, the two dynamics at work are the power of Jesus and faith. When needy people approach Jesus in faith and they connect with his divine power, something more than human always happens. Some kind of healing enters our lives. It might be a healing that involves blessing us with more courage, blessing us with hope, blessing us with a new kind of trust and surrender into divine providence.

If any of us are experiencing the Job experience in some way, if any of us are hurting in some way, let us turn to Jesus and pray for healing. If we go to Jesus in the midst of hurt and suffering, he can lead us beyond a tired, outmoded, overused image of God to a new, fresh, living experience of God. He can heal us so that we can say with Job, even if the pain and suffering do not leave us, "Before this struggle, I only knew God by hearsay, but now I know him personally. . . . Now I know him face to face. . . . Now I have a closer walk with him, because of the healing that Jesus has brought to my life."

THE DANGERS OF RELIGION

A Reflection on the Readings for January 22, 2012

I have wept over the laxity of the church. But be assured that my tears have been tears of love. There can be no deep disappointment where there is not deep love. Yes, I love the church. . . . There was a time when the church was very powerful—in the time when the early Christians rejoiced at being deemed worthy to suffer for what they believe. In those days the church was not merely a thermometer that recorded the ideas and principles of popular opinion; it was a thermostat that transformed the mores of society. Whenever the early Christians entered a town, the people in power became disturbed and immediately sought to convict the Christians for being disturbers of the peace and outside agitators. . . . So often the contemporary church is a weak, ineffectual voice with an uncertain sound. So often it is an archdefender of the status quo. Far from being disturbed by the presence of the church, the power structure of the average community is consoled by the church's silent—and often even vocal—sanction of things as they are. But the judgment of God is upon the church as never before. If today's church does not recapture the sacrificial spirit of the early church, it will lose its authenticity, forfeit the loyalty of millions, and be dismissed as an irrelevant social club with no meaning for the 20th century. Every day I meet young people whose disappointment with the church has turned into outright disgust.

Martin Luther King Jr.
Good Friday 1963

I came across King's "Letter from a Birmingham Jail" on the occasion of his eighty-third birthday this week. He wrote the letter to white clergymen who critiqued him for his nonviolent demonstrations against racism in Birmingham. These clergy spoke of King as an outsider and demeaned his strategies as inappropriate for a Christian minister. Obviously Dr. King had a broader understanding of the message of the Scriptures and strategies for living the message than his critics had. King critiqued them for distorting Christianity to maintain the status quo of a racist society.

Some years ago I began reading some theologians who warned about the dangers of religion. Their insights sounded true to me. Some extremely religious people act as if they completely understand God. They are lacking in a sense of God's mystery. None of us can completely know or understand God. Some religious people act as if they control God by their fundamentalist approach to Scripture and prayer. Religious people can become authoritarian, judging, and ostracizing people who do not completely conform to their understanding or ideology. Religious people can become arrogant and elitist. They can be lacking in critical thinking, and have a very superficial, dogmatic understanding of Scripture and tradition.

Some religious people have a very mechanical understanding of

God; they think that if people act in a certain way, God is going to respond in a certain way. This is a dynamic critiqued in the book of Job, in which Job's three friends tell him that he is suffering because of some wrong that he did. Job responds that he did not sin, but Job nonetheless believes that God acts in such a way. He cannot understand why God is punishing him.

Some religious people can be extremely pious, but have little concern for mercy, compassion, and justice. Acting out of self-righteousness, religious people can run the risk of being nonforgiving. Religion, in some cases, has morphed into hierarchical triumphalism. Religion has been used to justify war and terrorism. In my research into evangelization over the years, I have heard many stories of people who have felt screened out of their parish or the church in general because of who and how they are. In the name of God, some religious people have done and do very hurtful things to people. Religion seems to enable some people to feel very good about themselves, while looking down on others. Some religious people even convey that they have "arrived," and that there is no need for repentance or conversion in their lives.

This is what the book of Jonah is about. Jonah is not history; it is a parable about the dangers of religion. God calls Jonah to go to Nineveh and call the people to repentance, threatening them with destruction if they fail to change their lives. Nineveh seems to represent Babylon, Persia, and other countries that overran and abused the Jewish people. Because of what these countries have done to his people, Jonah refuses to take on the mission to the Ninevites. He tries to escape to Tarshish in a ship. The men working on the ship do not share the same faith as Jonah. A terrible storm blows up, and the men on the ship are frightened and want to know the source of the storm. They intuit that Jonah is somehow running from his God. Jonah confirms their suspicion and tells the men to throw him overboard. They do, and the storm dies down.

Jonah is swallowed by a whale, and he lives in the whale's belly for three days. He is spit out on dry land, and God issues the mission again to go and preach repentance to the Ninevites. This time Jonah reluctantly goes. He believes that he has a three-day mission ahead of him, traveling throughout Nineveh. However, at Jonah's first call to repentance, the king of Nineveh repents and along with him all the people of Nineveh.

At the end of the parable, God finds Jonah angry and unhappy that he was successful in his mission. Jonah felt that, in justice, the Ninevites should have been destroyed. He is upset with God's mercy. In fact, Jonah tells God that he tried to escape from the first mission, because he knew that God would be merciful to the Ninevites, if they repented. Jonah wanted a God of revenge and strict justice. He did not want God to be compassionate toward his enemies. Jonah's anger is abated somewhat when God gives him a plant to provide him with shade. The next day God allows a worm to get within the plant and destroy it. Jonah is angry and depressed anew. God explains to Jonah that he is angry over a plant that he lost, that he really did not deserve. If Jonah is upset about a plant, how could God not care for the 120,000 people of Nineveh?

The paradox of the story is that it was not just the Ninevites who needed to repent. Jonah needed to repent; he was filled with some of the dangers of religion. He believed that God should have been loving and kind to him and his people alone. He judged the Ninevites to be sinners to be punished. Jonah was angry at the expansive love, mercy, and forgiveness that God extends to all people.

The story of Jonah reminds us of the dangers of religion. We are challenged to assess how much those dangers influence us as individuals and as a church. The Jonah passage connects beautifully with the Gospel of Mark. We hear Jesus's first spoken words in Mark: "This is the time of fulfillment. The kingdom of God is at hand. Repent and believe. . . . "

The reign of God is that vision of life and way of life that Jesus lived, taught, and embodied. Jesus lived and died for the reign of God. The reign of God is a God-centered life, characterized by vigilance, prayerfulness, mercy, kindness, compassion, and forgiveness. The reign of God is anchored in conviction about the paschal nature of life—that life is about living, dying, and rising over and over again, until we are fully blessed with eternal life. The price we pay for life in the reign of God is repentance, over and over again. We are never done with repentance; we never completely arrive in the reign of God until and unless we are blessed with the gift of heaven.

The work of the Christian religions is to call people to a lifelong journey of repentance. All of us are flawed; we are all sinners. We are all in need of ongoing conversion, repentance, and spiritual transformation. We are a community of equals on a common journey. No one of us should use religion or faith to create a caste system in which some people are better than others. Are we comfortable with the God who forgave the Ninevites? Are we comfortable with the God, Abba, revealed by Jesus? Do we realize that the Church and religion exist as servants to the greater reality that is the reign of God? All Jonahs, repent!

Do Not Be Afraid

The December 5, 2011, issue of *Time* magazine had an interesting cover story titled, "Why Anxiety Is Good for You." The subtitle was, "As Long You Know How to Use It." The article did not go into a lot of theories regarding the origins of anxiety. Rather it focused on what happens to the body when we are anxious. I would like to mention one school of thought that always made me feel better about my anxious nature. It is the existential school, with thinkers like Søren Kierkegaard and Rollo May. This school basically says that life is tough; we must face limits, freedom, mortality, ambiguity, and not knowing—a lot. Kierkegaard said the greater the anxiety, the greater the person. He contended that the only way to respond to anxiety was through lives of passion and conviction.

The *Time* article said that anxiety in extreme forms can be paralyzing and take on the shape and form of disorders. Alice Park, the author of the article, also said that there are positive dimensions to anxiety. We must learn from anxiety and learn how to manage it. She distinguishes between threat anxiety and challenge anxiety. With threat anxiety, we can fall into the fight-or-flight syndrome. This is the kind of anxiety in which we perceive danger that must be resisted or from which we must escape. The goal of anxiety management is to transform threat anxiety into challenge anxiety. With challenge anxiety, we use the heightened physical and cognitive states that anxiety places us in to accomplish things. Many artists, performers, athletes, and leaders have learned to transform threat anxiety into challenge anxiety, going on to accomplish things that perhaps they initially felt that they could not do.

Many characters in the Scriptures confront threat anxiety and turn it into challenge anxiety. Mary was such a person. Initially, she is greatly troubled by Gabriel's Annunciation visit. The angel tells her, "Do not be afraid, Mary. You have found favor with God." Earlier he told Mary that she was full of grace and ". . . the Lord is with you." Gabriel goes on to reassure Mary, "The Holy Spirit will come upon you, and the power of the Most High will overshadow you. . . . " In explaining the pregnancy of Elizabeth in her old age, Gabriel says, "Nothing will be impossible with God."

It appears that Mary began with Gabriel in a state of threat anxiety. But in a very spiritual and historical way, Mary was able to transform all threat into challenge. She responds to Gabriel with these sentiments: "Let it be. . . . Though I do not completely understand what is going to happen to me, I trust in the power and love of God." Gabriel had reassured Mary that she was filled with the presence of God, that the Lord was with her. He reassured her that the Holy Spirit was working and would work in the future in her life. He convinced her of the possibilities that awaited her if only she would place her trust in God.

The words spoken to Mary are words that apply to us also as we try to transform threat anxiety into challenge anxiety. Grace surrounds us. The presence of God is in us and around us. The Holy Spirit is with us. That which threatens us can be transformed. We can transform threat into challenge. We can do much more than we ever thought we could. For all of us, nothing is impossible with God. We have to say with Mary, "Let it be." We need to learn how to let go into grace, into Spirit, into God's presence.

I grew up to be a pretty anxious, guilt-ridden Irish Catholic. Not until my mid-twenties was I introduced to a God of unconditional love. I began to change my consciousness by praying Psalm 31 and Luke 23. The latter passage depicts Jesus dying on the cross, praying Psalm 31: "Abba, into your hands I commend my spirit; into your hands I hand over my life." Praying those words and living the spirit of the words has transformed so much threat anxiety into challenge anxiety for me. I am not 100 percent into challenge anxiety; there are times when I vacillate back and forth. But faith, trust, letting go, and letting God have made me a much more convictional and courageous person.

The spirit of Mary's religious experience with Gabriel is apparent in 2 Samuel. David tells Nathan that he wants to build a house for the Ark of the Covenant. Nathan tells David, "Go do whatever you have in mind; for the Lord is with you." Then God tells Nathan to go and remind David: "I have been with you wherever you went." The passage speaks of the many enemies David had to confront in his leadership of the people. It was his emotional, convictional trust in Yahweh that transformed David's threat anxiety into challenge anxiety.

Second Samuel and the Gospel of Luke are filled with promise and anticipation. God promises David that he will raise up an heir who will establish a kingdom that will endure forever. This heir will be God's son; God will be father to him. Gabriel assures Mary that she will have a son named Jesus, who will be in the line of David. The kingdom of Jesus will have no end. Jesus and the reign of God that he revealed and which he calls us to is the fulfillment of the promise made to David.

Tim Tebow was the well-known quarterback for the Denver Broncos and now the New York Jets. I am not an avid football fan, though I do enjoy watching the Chicago Bears and Notre Dame occasionally. Some sportswriters say that Tebow is not a great quarterback, although his 2011 season was a surprising success. During games, Tebow regularly drops to one knee and puts his hand to his forehead. He pauses for a moment and prays—prayers of thanks and sometimes prayers of petition. Some people criticize him for being so public about his faith, but he maintains that Jesus is the Lord of his life; it helps him to connect with Jesus. He is not ashamed to show how important his relationship with Jesus is. I do not know the exact nature of his praying, but maybe he is an example of how practicing the presence of God can transform threat anxiety into challenge anxiety. His pausing for prayer has become known as Tebowing. Now other people are engaging in Tebowing, dropping to one knee and spending a moment in prayer.

The days before Christmas are an opportune time to practice spiritual surrender into the love, grace, presence, and Spirit of God. The power of God can have a transformative effect in our lives, similar to what happened to David and Mary. Back to Kierkegaard: Life presents us with experiences that seem overwhelming, threatening. Truly great people realize that life presents apparent threats, and they transform those threats into challenges through lives of passion and conviction. We all need to do more regular Tebowing. Hear these words spoken to you and to me today: Do not be afraid. Let us pray with Paul: ". . . To the only wise God through Jesus Christ be glory forever and ever. Amen."

DISCIPLESHIP SHOULD COST

Dietrich Bonhoeffer was born in 1906. He came from a prosperous German family and decided to be a Lutheran pastor. He was very successful in his studies. He seemed destined for an idyllic life, but along came Adolf Hitler and his vision and strategy of national socialism and the Nazi movement, including the Nazi subjugation of churches and the Nazi persecution of Jews. Bonhoeffer felt compelled to develop a kind of Christianity different from the Christianity he had been raised in or had studied in theology. It became clear to him that Hitler was the evil one, the enemy. His faith compelled him to fight Hitler directly. He helped Jews escape to Switzerland. Bonhoeffer himself engaged in an attempt to assassinate Hitler, thinking that such an action would be a greater good than allowing Hitler to continue in his savage ways. Bonhoeffer was arrested, imprisoned, and offered liberation if he would verbally renounce his former ways and behaviors, but Bonhoeffer would not relent. Just days before the fall of Germany, he was hanged at the Flossenburg concentration camp on April 9, 1945.

Some notions became important to Bonhoeffer in his attempt to liberate people from Hitler's hold. His overarching concern became discipleship. Jesus calls us to discipleship in the Gospels. He says that his disciples in the future will be recognized by the quality of their love. Bonhoeffer interpreted Jesus's call to love as self-sacrificial, suffering love. Bonhoeffer began to equate discipleship with suffering, thus the title of his classic book, *The Cost of Discipleship.* To be a follower of Jesus, Bonhoeffer taught, we must embrace the mystery of the cross and live the cross. We cannot be above our master, Jesus, who gave his life for liberation and redemption. In embracing the mystery of the cross, Bonhoeffer taught we become truly and totally human. We also experience the mystery of the Incarnation, or the Spirit of the living Jesus alive in us.

Bonhoeffer warned against what he called "cheap grace." *Cheap grace* became his term for watered-down Christianity: the Christianity that allows us to be comfortable, the Christianity that can be in alliance with the forces of evil. He called people, rather, to live "costly grace." *Costly grace* is the whole and true gospel of Jesus Christ, which necessitates suffering for the reign of God.

In the Acts of the Apostles, we read that Paul and Barnabas return to the town of Lystra, one among the many towns that they visit. In Lystra, Paul, who participated in the stoning death of Stephen, was himself stoned and left to die. Paul goes back there convinced of the truth of what he and Barnabas teach in Acts 14: "It is necessary for us to undergo many hardships to enter the kingdom of God." Paul and Barnabas lived Bonhoeffer's concept of costly grace, discipleship that costs.

Bonhoeffer warned against a Christianity that makes us feel warm, fuzzy, and happy. While the message of Jesus can bring some of those elements to us, the core message of Jesus is a countercultural message that threatens the status quo of both organized religion and society. As Ronald Heifetz has taught in his books on leadership, true leaders intimidate people because they call people to change. People like to maintain the status quo. Thus, there often is a movement to assassinate those who would be leaders. Bonhoeffer warned that both Catholics and Protestants can hide behind ritual, hide behind sacraments, and pretend that we are doing the work of Jesus, all the while avoiding true conversion and tough discipleship. He said that Hitler could take over significant parts of the world because so many Christians failed to lead; so many Christians were and are trapped in cheap-grace religion.

Discipleship costs. Are we truly disciples? Bonhoeffer suggested that many people never embrace this identity of being a disciple, of being a learner of Jesus and his ways. We rest comfortably in our denominational titles of Catholic, Lutheran, Episcopalian, and so on. Few in organized Christianity would identify themselves as disciples or know what lies at the heart of discipleship.

The Cost of Discipleship was written in 1937. More recently, a Jesuit priest by the name of John Kavanaugh has published several editions of *Following Christ in a Consumer Society*. Kavanaugh challenges us to confront forces in our world that are perhaps more subtle and subversive than was Hitler's movement. Kavanaugh warns us about consumerism and capitalism, and the dehumanization that results when we give ourselves over too much to what he calls "commodity form living." He contrasts commodity form living with "personal form living." Personal form living, with great emphasis on the dignity of each human person, is closer to what Jesus intended in preaching and teaching about the reign of God.

Kavanaugh says that each of us must make a fundamental decision. Do we want to live the commodity form living of materialism or the personal form living of the reign of God?

In Revelation 21, John glimpses a new heaven and a new earth. The former heaven and the former earth have passed away. He speaks of a loud voice coming from the throne in a new Jerusalem. The voice says, "Behold, God's dwelling is with the human race. He will dwell with them; and they will be his people; and God himself will always be with them as their God. He will wipe every tear from their eyes, and there shall be no more death or mourning, wailing or pain, for the old order has passed away." The One who sat on the throne said, "Behold, I make all things new."

Jesus Christ calls us to new life. This new life is a life of a transformed world order, a transformed vision, and a transformed way of doing our lives. New life in Christ transcends the cult and regulations of organized religion. New life in Christ is discipleship that throws off the superficiality of cheap grace and embraces and lives in costly grace.

In John 13, Judas leaves the room on the night of the Last Supper. As Judas leaves, Jesus begins to speak of his glorification, saying, "Now is the Son of Man glorified, and God is glorified in him. If God is glorified in him, God will also glorify him in himself, and God will glorify him at once." In the mind of Jesus, the impending suffering that he is about to endure on Good Friday is going to give way to new life, eternal life, and glory. The conviction of Jesus is the conviction of all of us who say we want to be disciples. In many different situations, we know that discipleship costs. Bonhoeffer wrote that when Christ calls a person, he bids the person to come and die. Bonhoeffer believed that sacrifice was an essential component of faith. He also believed that through fellowship and communion with the Lord, we recover our true humanity. We are delivered from individualism, which is the consequence of sin, and receive solidarity with the whole human race. In addition, we are promised to share in the eternal life and glory that Jesus experienced.

In a beautiful reflection on the Sermon on the Mount, Bonhoeffer reminds us that in his vision of costly discipleship, the kingdom—the reign of God—is not just worldly bound. Bonhoeffer encourages those who read this reflection to keep their eyes fixed on the bottom line of costly discipleship. "Rejoice and be exceedingly glad, for great is your reward in heaven."

SEARCHIN'

For the last thirty-one years, religious educator Dawn Mayer and I have cohosted a radio program that has come to be known as *Horizons*. The theme song that we have used these many years is *Searchin' So Long* by Chicago. One of the lines of the song sings about "searchin' for an answer." We thought the words of that secular song captured the essence of faith. With faith we do not have scientific knowledge. Rather, faith largely deals with mystery. Mystery invites us to an ongoing, ever-deepening search. On the Epiphany, I think it is appropriate to think and pray about whom or what many believers are searching for.

Let us look for a moment at the story of the first Epiphany. Three men from the east—presumably Persia, Syria, or Arabia—journey in search of the newborn king of the Jews. They first go to a place of power, Jerusalem, and speak to the current king of the Jews, Herod—causing him to become quite intimidated that someone may be attempting to usurp his role. They go on to a more humble city, Bethlehem. There they find Jesus. These three wise men have come to be known as Casper, Balthasar, and Melchior. The common understanding now is that they were some kind of astrologists. At the time, astrologists took special note of new stars appearing, as they possibly indicated the birth of a great person. Scripture scholars debate whether this star is a literary development of Numbers 24:17, which refers to a star advancing from Jacob, a reference to the coming Messiah. If it was an actual historical occurrence, some suggest the star was a supernova or a comet. The motif of the story is that the three men were searching for and seeking out Jesus. When they found him, they gave him gold, signifying he was a king. They gave him incense, which pointed to his divinity. They also presented him with myrrh, a substance used for burial, prefiguring his death. The three wise men were *seekers*.

For a number of years I lived and worked in geographical proximity to Willow Creek Church, a nondenominational, evangelical church in

South Barrington, Illinois. Part of this church's evangelical strategy is to see all people as spiritual seekers. Everyone is hungry and thirsty for God. The congregation is encouraged to always be in a posture of inviting unchurched friends and family members to weekend services. These services are in fact called "seeker services," oriented toward people just awakening to their spiritual needs and the influence that God can and should have in daily life. Each week, tens of thousands of people attend services and educational opportunities at Willow Creek. Willow Creek has contributed to the birth of the "seeker-friendly / purpose-driven congregation." Seeker-friendly churches believe that all people are seeking for and searching for God, incarnated in Jesus. Many people are not yet conscious that they even are seekers. A huge number of people attending these churches are former Roman Catholics.

If we are seekers, what are we seeking? Three Viennese schools of psychotherapy address the question. Sigmund Freud's approach was that we are all in pursuit of pleasure, with aggression thrown in. Alfred Adler's approach was that social interest motivates us; we want to be connected to our fellow person, though we allow mistaken notions to keep us from that connection. Victor Frankl's school is known as logotherapy, which holds that what we are most in pursuit of is meaning. With meaning in our lives we can endure anything, even great suffering. Meaning refers to purpose, happiness, fulfillment, connection with others, and connection with a power that we perceive to be ultimate. Frankl believed that three forces—affluence, hedonism, and materialism—keep people from finding meaning.

For me, the feast of the Epiphany is about reminding us that we are all spiritual seekers in pursuit of meaning for our lives. Our conviction is that we find this meaning in a personal and communal relationship with Jesus Christ. Some people, like the geneticist Dean Hamer, postulate that our brain has a God gene or genes that hardwire into us the need for God. If we do not attend to our genuine spiritual needs, there will be some felt experience of deprivation.

How does Jesus bring meaning into our lives? Jesus reveals the ideals of what it means to be a person, a human being: the way he is, we should strive to become. Jesus has given us a vision and strategy for living; it is called the "reign of God." Jesus reveals to us the way God is; he is the human face of God. Jesus has also revealed to us the paschal mystery, which teaches us that struggle and suffering can lead to growth and transformation here on earth, and death can lead us to eternal life on the other side of death. Jesus is the embodiment of meaning for life. What we most need and want can be found in a relationship with Jesus.

Wade Clark Roof is a professor of religion and society at the University of California, Santa Barbara. Among his interesting books are two: *A Generation of Seekers* and *Spiritual Marketplace*. Roof's research has largely focused on the religious practices of baby boomers. He has found that people in this age group are profoundly spiritual and indeed are seekers. The generations younger than baby boomers have followed a similar pattern of seeking. People in America, indeed around the world, are spiritual seekers. Some have stayed with Catholicism and other forms of organized religion. But many people today are seeking God, seeking Jesus in ways not affiliated with traditional religious institutions.

My experience has been that whatever the denomination or theological underpinnings of a church, what attracts people to a church is the following: worship that more often than not is religious experience, preaching that offers people livable spirituality, warm and welcoming congregations, and ministries that address real-life needs.

Bishop Howard Hubbard of Albany, New York, wrote an article titled "Failings of the Church" that appeared in the November 17, 2011, issue of *Origins*. The bishop analyzes why one in ten American Catholics have left the Catholic Church, making them the second largest congregation in the country behind the Catholic Church. These statistics are from the Pew Forum on Religion and Public Life. Bishop Hubbard offers the following issues: the sex abuse scandal in the priesthood and its cover-up by the bishops and other Catholic leaders; insensitivity in parish closures and mergers; anemic parish life, lacking in inclusivity and hospitality; pastoral insensitivity on the part of members of parish staffs to parishioners; poor liturgies and homilies; inattention to youth and young adults; and parishes screening out certain subgroups of people.

Realizing that we are all seekers, let us strive to become seeker-friendly, purpose-driven faith communities. I am reminded of the passage from the first chapter of John. Two disciples are physically following Jesus. He turns to them and asks, "What are you looking for?" They answer, "Where do you stay?" He answers, "Come and see." We are told by John that they then went and stayed with him. Jesus asks us today, "What are you looking for?" He knows that we are seekers. He says to us also, "Come and see."

PAYING ATTENTION

I have a routine when I come home after work. I give the dog a treat, and then I go downstairs and watch the news for a moment. I come back upstairs, hoping that Bingo is sleeping on his chair because I like to read the paper. Frequently he does snooze on his chair, but sometimes he gets off the chair and comes right over to me and demands that he sit on my lap. As he is sitting on my lap, he sometimes will jump up and run to the window. And even though I have the shade pulled very low, he looks through this little bit of space at the bottom of the shade and barks with a lot of passion. Even if it is dark at night, Bingo can see and sense things that I cannot see or sense.

During the day, Bingo has different barks as he looks through his TV screen, the window next to his chair. There is a bark for a squirrel and a different kind of bark for a bird. There is a bark for a person walking down the street and a strong bark for a person walking another dog. Even when I walk Bingo in the morning and at night, he stops and looks around him, because he either sees or senses something that I do not see or sense. Sometimes when he barks, I try to see what he is seeing. I ask him, "What are you barking at?" Eventually, I will see what he is upset about, perhaps a half block away. Bingo is a schnauzer, a terrier. Terriers are high-energy, hyper dogs. He is a very vigilant animal, as most dogs and most animals are. He often is trying to protect himself, protect me, protect the house, and defend his turf.

Vigilance. That is the theme we find in Matthew's Gospel, in the famous story of the ten virgins, five of whom were foolish and five who were wise. The foolish ones took no oil for their lamps, but the wise ones took oil. The story line goes that the bridegroom was delayed in coming, and all the women grew drowsy and fell asleep. Then there was a cry at midnight: "Behold the bridegroom. Come out to meet him." Jesus said that the foolish women said to the wise, "Give us some of your oil, for our lamps are going out." The wise women replied, "No." The foolish women went off to buy oil. The bridegroom came, and those who were ready went into the wedding feast and the door was locked. When the five foolish women tried to enter the wedding feast, the bridegroom replied, "I do not know you." Jesus concludes the Gospel, "Stay awake, for you know neither the day nor the hour."

This Gospel passage calls us to vigilance. Vigilance is a confusing term. It is sometimes used to describe people who are prone to anxiety. People with anxiety problems are described frequently as being "hypervigilant" or overly sensitized to the realities of life, which often they perceive to be dangerous or frightening. But there is also healthy vigilance, and that is what Jesus calls us to in the gospel this weekend. Healthy vigilance involves being aware, paying attention to what matters in life.

The oil symbol in the Gospel of Matthew speaks of vigilance and preparedness. One reality that we ought to be vigilant about and prepared for is knowing God, knowing the Lord. Note what Jesus says to the five foolish women: "I do not know you." Part of being a vigilant person in a healthy sense is attending to and being intentional about our relationship with God, God's presence in our lives. That relationship with God should lead us also to a vigilance about our own moral principles, the quality of our lives, how we live our lives.

For the last couple of years at the Clare, all who work there have had to engage in health risk assessments—blood tests that reveal possible areas of concern regarding health. I think health is something that many of us take for granted. Throughout the life cycle, we should be vigilant about caring for our physical, emotional, and spiritual health.

As disciples of Jesus Christ, we ought to be vigilant about the well-being of others. We need to be concerned about the health and happiness of the people in our lives. Similarly, we should be vigilant about the quality of our relationships. Most often, when I have done relationship counseling, the people whom I have tried to help are people who have allowed certain relationships to get away from them through inattention. We need to be vigilant about the gifts that God has blessed us with and do our best to develop those gifts and use them for God's glory and the good of others.

As all of us pass through the different seasons of human development, we need to be vigilant about and attentive to God's call. What is God calling us to? What is God's will for us as we age, as we grow? We need to be vigilant about justice, what seems to be the right thing in God's eyes. During election times, we need to be vigilant about candidates who are seeking public office, vigilant about the well-being of our country and the world.

Certain themes run through the parables of Jesus. One theme is how God is active and present in our lives. Another is that God's ways are not our ways. Another theme is about the end or eschatology: our personal ends, the end of the world, the end of time. Related to that theme, Jesus implies that, in many ways, the end has already begun. Another disturbing theme in the parables is that perhaps, for some people, it is too late for redemption or salvation. The end of personal time, the end of time, and maybe it is too late are themes that seem to run through the passage from Matthew 25. Jesus warns us that we know neither the day nor the hour. Thus, one reality we need to be vigilant about is the horizon of personal death.

Steve Jobs was asked before his death why he consented to having a biography written about him since he was such a private person. He said that in his career, he had been away from home a great deal. He wanted his children to know who he was and why he did the things he did. In his years battling cancer, Jobs had to come to terms with the horizon of his own personal death. He became vigilant about it. But he also became aware of where he had not been vigilant—the quality of his relationships with his children. As he neared death and agreed to the biography, he was trying to rectify his lack of vigilance.

I have spoken of and written before about a contemporary theme in positive psychology. It is called *mindfulness*, becoming more and more aware of what is going on within us, what is going on around us, what is going on in the world. Mindfulness is another term not for hypervigilance but for healthy vigilance. In the years I have engaged in psychotherapy, both for my own benefit and in trying to help others, I have come to understand psychotherapy as a process of growing in awareness and vigilance. To the degree we are not aware and vigilant, we tend to engage in *suppression*, that is, setting aside realities that we need to attend to, or *repression*, an attempt to bury things that need our attention.

The first reading from Wisdom 6 calls us to wisdom. We are encouraged to keep vigil for wisdom. Part of being a wise person involves being vigilant. We need to pay attention to that which really matters in life.

MORAL COURAGE

I just completed a discussion series on the book *Moral Courage*, by Rushworth Kidder. Kidder feels that moral courage is becoming rare in contemporary culture. He explains moral courage as an attempt to live with a set of moral principles. Living such moral principles brings danger into a person's midst—danger because the principles threaten the status quo of the culture in which a morally courageous person lives. Despite the danger, the person endures in living the moral principles. Principles plus danger plus endurance equals moral courage. In one chapter Kidder talks about moral courage and its contraries. Among the fakes, frauds, and foibles of moral courage are timidity (a fear of the danger involved in moral courage), foolhardiness (a failure to reflect on the danger involved in moral courage), and physical courage (heroism that can endure danger, but which has little to do with moral principles).

Kidder goes on to describe other distortions of moral courage. He speaks of *groupthink*, a tendency on the part of a group of people to hold to certain convictions and behaviors without individual reflection and moral searching. An example of such mass mindedness was the German people being swept up by Hitler and the Nazi movement, with its horrific anti-Semitic attitudes and behaviors. Groupthink contributed also to the American endorsement of and engagement in slavery, leading up to our Civil War. Groupthink is present in our own day when groups of people become convinced of their own ideology, while often becoming hostile to the convictions and lifestyles of other people.

Another antithesis to moral courage is *deviancy becoming normal*. Kidder quotes Daniel Patrick Moynihan who wrote in 1993 about "defining deviancy down." Moynihan lamented that society currently accepts a lot of values, attitudes, and behaviors that would have been unacceptable some years ago. This includes dress codes among adolescents and young adults, differing shapes and versions of family life, sexual morality, and other realities. Kidder warns that as deviancy becomes more normal, the need for or interest in moral courage drops away.

In presenting another mirage of moral courage, Kidder shares a true story. Raphael was a high school senior from a developing country who was awarded the opportunity to study in the United States for his final year of high school. An affluent couple offered their home to the young man as a place of residence. The couple had a son, who was disabled on a number of levels. They loved their son, but he brought little parental pride or satisfaction to them. In his first months in the United States, Raphael was extremely successful academically and in gaining positions of leadership. One day the couple called Raphael in and asked to have a conversation with him. They offered to adopt him as their own son. The provision for the adoption was that it had to be immediate, and he was not to return to his native country or his family of origin. If Raphael did not agree to the immediate adoption, he would have to leave and return to his native land. This threw Raphael into a moral crisis. He knew if he went through with the adoption, he would have a comfortable and successful life. If he went home, he would return as a failure. Yet he could not bring himself to divorce from his family of origin or his native land. In an act of true moral courage, Raphael refused the adoption and returned home.

Kidder offers this story not only as a story of moral courage but also a story of the fake moral courage of the potential adoptive parents. Adding to groupthink and deviancy becoming normal, Kidder warns against *misguided altruism* or *misguided generosity*, which appears to be moral courage, but really is generosity rooted in self-interest. Kidder analyzes the would-be parents as people who were trying to gain a healthy, successful son, which they never had in the disabled son to whom they gave birth.

This misguided altruism reminds me of people whom I have encountered in pastoral settings, who have been very generous in supporting various campaigns, but in the end appeared to have attempted to buy or control those in authority for their own position and advantage. We can see this same tendency in American politics, in which ideological groups attempt to control candidates through the various kinds of support they provide. In misguided altruism or generosity, it appears that the altruistic, generous benefactors are concerned about another, others, or the common good, but their motivation is actually self-centered.

Kidder reflects on how people grow in morality. He agrees with Robert Coles, who wrote *The Moral Life of Children* some years ago. Both Kidder and Coles talk about the importance of moral conversations for growth in morality. These conversations can be coupled with reading and the study of situations, and the conversations can be held with people of all ages, for we can always be growing morally. To grow morally, people also need mentors, role models with whom they can experience and interact. In such mentoring relationships, the morality of the mentor can begin to rub off on the person being mentored. Finally, people simply need practice in being moral. Aristotle said: "We become . . . brave by doing brave acts."

A very interesting section of Kidder's *Moral Courage* is on sexually abusive priests and the right way to handle wrongdoing. I disagree with Kidder, who says that Cardinal Bernard Law lost his career over the cover-ups he engaged in regarding sexually abusive priests. Rather than losing his career, Law was kicked upstairs to an influential and lucrative position in the Vatican, saved from the American justice system that would have prosecuted him. What Cardinal Law did for abusive priests, someone in the Vatican did for him. Kidder laments that the abusive activity of some priests took place, but he adds that this activity is present in many professions. He is not justifying it. Rather, he is saying that the most stunning immorality was done by Catholic hierarchy, who moved priests around, paid people off, and attempted to cover up these misdeeds to save the persona of the Church—to save the institution. He says the fundamental problem facing the Catholic Church was not just sexual abuse but rather the absence of crisis management. He calls it "spiritual wickedness in high places." The people with moral courage were those who were abused, and who stepped forward and spoke out. The people with moral courage are the people who continue to speak out and act on hierarchical misdeeds and abuses. It is shocking that we currently have a bishop in the United States who has been indicted because he failed to report a situation of sexual abuse by a priest in a timely fashion.

Why, you might ask, am I giving so much time and space to *Moral Courage*? Because I think Kidder states positively what Jesus is getting at in Matthew 23. Jesus says,

The scribes and the Pharisees have taken the chair of Moses. Therefore, do and observe all things whatsoever they tell you, but do not follow their example. For they preach, but they do not practice. They tie up heavy burdens hard to carry and lay them on people's shoulders, but they will not lift a finger to move them. . . . They love places of honor at banquets, seats of honor in synagogues, greetings in marketplaces, and the salutation, Rabbi. . . . The greatest among you must be your servant.

Whoever exalts himself will be humbled, but whoever humbles himself will be exalted.

What Jesus saw in the religious leaders of his time were what Kidder calls fakes, frauds, and foibles—what moral courage is not. In Jesus's time and in our own age, moral courage can be confused with timidity, bystander apathy, physical courage, groupthink, the deviant becoming normal, and misguided altruism and generosity. Jesus knew and he reminds us that we cannot always look to obviously religious people for moral courage. Again, the reign of God is surprising and reverses our expectations. Moral courage is seen in a high school senior who cannot deny his family and homeland for a self-centered future. Moral courage is seen in victims of sexual abuse who stood up and stand up to hierarchy to speak the truth. We are called to become, as disciples of Jesus Christ, people of moral truth and moral courage. We need not look to any contemporary Pharisees to gain this. Moral truth and moral courage are always waiting to be born in us anew, as we journey in mentoring communities that help us learn and help us practice.

Turning

As I look forward to turning sixty-five, I am struck by the amount of attention I am getting in the mail and on the phone. In the mail, I have been encouraged to take out life insurance. There also was an invitation to subscribe to accidental death insurance. Several times I have been invited to restaurants for luncheons at which there will be presentations on financial planning for retirement. I asked one of the Irish ladies who walks my dog, Bingo, during the day to pick up some prescriptions from Walgreen's. Afterward, she told me, "Pat, they want to have a consultation with you about your future with Medicare and Medicaid." I really felt old when I heard that. Then I picked up a voice message from Blue Cross / Blue Shield that said, "Mr. Brennan, this is Blue Cross / Blue Shield. We would like to have a meeting with you about your future relationship with Medicare and Medicaid." Oh brother! Why don't these people just leave me alone? Probably the most dramatic letter came from an organization inviting me to prepare a prepaid cremation: "Why put your loved ones through all that hassle when you die? Take care of your own arrangements while you can."

Through it all I continue to receive multiple mailings from AARP, formerly known as the American Association for Retired People. You start receiving AARP materials at age fifty, but at ages sixty-four and sixty-five, you have entered the fullness of AARPdom; I hear from them now almost every day. They have become among my closest associates.

I am beginning to sense that turning sixty-five is going to be an emotional, major turning for me. When I was ordained a priest, my mother and father were sixty-four and sixty-five. I thought they were ancient, and I was always looking out for them, trying to protect them. Here I am at that same turning point. How terribly strange!

"Since he has turned away from . . . sins . . . he shall surely live," God said, speaking through the prophet Ezekiel. The notion of turning struck me in that passage. "Turning" is a beautiful word to express the essence of conversion. Conversion is turning away from sin, habits, compulsions, faulty thinking, and mistaken notions to more fully move toward God and the way of life Jesus calls us to in his reign-of-God preaching and teaching. I see turning sixty-five as a wonderful opportunity for deepening conversion. Many years ago, Erik Erikson spoke of the senior years, the years of maturity, as an opportunity for growth in integrity. Integrity certainly has moral connotations, but it is more than just a concern with morality. Integrity speaks of wholeness, trying to live a life in which all the pieces connect in a seamless sort of way. Integrity is a life of balance, congruency with one's self (as Carl Rogers described healthy self-awareness), and transparency—in which one's inner life is reflected in how one lives. Movement into the senior years ought to be a movement into renewed faith, which Iris Ford described in *Life Spiral: The Faith Journey* as including both suffering faith and resurrection faith.

Conversion toward integrity and transparency is dramatized in a story from the Gospel of Matthew. The father in the story asked one son to go and work in the vineyard. This first son said no, but he changed his mind and changed his behavior and went and worked in the vineyard. The man came to his second son and asked him to go work in the vineyard. The second son responded with immediacy that he would go, but he did not act on his words. He did not go and work in the vineyard. Jesus asked the chief priests and the elders of the people which of the two sons did his father's will. The religious leaders responded that the first son did the father's will. Jesus uses this parabolic story to teach people of his own day and us about turning toward integrity. The first son who refused to go to the vineyard, but who changed his mind and behavior, is an example of turning, conversion. The vineyard represents life in the reign of God. Jesus teaches that apparently nonspiritual, nonreligious people, like tax collectors and prostitutes, are turning toward the reign of God. So-called religious leaders, like the chief priests and elders, were and are going through the external motions of religion, but they are not experiencing true turning or conversion. Jesus says that the "religious" failed to turn toward John the Baptist's *way of righteousness*, and also failed to turn to the reign of God.

Part of turning and converting to greater integrity involves achieving a better balance between what we say and what we do. In the person of the second son, Jesus draws a portrait of a person who talks and speaks ideals, but then fails to act on them. The second son challenges us to reflect on how we might not always live what we say is important to us. If we speak about mercy and justice as values, but then do nothing to act on mercy and justice, then mercy and justice are not true values. If we say prayer and worship are important, but then give little time to prayer and worship, then they in fact are not true values. If we speak about the importance of love and relationships, but make little time for love and relationships, there is a disparity between our words and our behavior.

Back in the 1970s a movement toward values clarification was very prevalent in both secular and religious education. The leaders in this movement taught that you do not pick up on a person's values by what they say. Rather, people's actions reveal their values. The values clarification movement said that a person's values are found in what they say, what they emotionally prize, what they say and do publicly, and what they say and do consistently. Turning toward integrity, conversion to the reign of God involves a balance between what we say and what we do.

Jesus is the paradigm of integrity, transparency, and balance. In Paul's letter to the Philippians we have a beautiful, poetic reflection on the inner and outer life of Jesus. This is the famous *kenosis* passage. *Kenosis* is a Greek word for self-emptying. Paul writes,

> *Have in you the same attitude that is also in Christ Jesus, who, though he was in the form of God, did not regard equality with God as something to be grasped. Rather, he emptied himself, taking the form of a slave, coming in human likeness; and found human in appearance, he humbled himself, becoming obedient to the point of death, even death on a cross. Because of this, God greatly exalted him. . . . Jesus Christ is Lord, to the Glory of God the Father. . . ."*

When I first began to study psychology at the graduate level, I was struck by the classical distinction between insight therapy and behavior change therapy. *Insight therapy* helps people understand themselves—their attitudes, values, strengths, and mistaken notions about life. *Behavior therapy* is a discipline that helps people change their behavior toward healthier, more holistic living. I have become convinced of the value of an eclectic approach to psychotherapy. Real growth involves changing our minds and hearts, as well as changing our behavior. Psychology says in secular terms what Jesus says in calling us to turning and conversion to greater integrity. Conversion involves changed thinking, feeling, and behavior—all toward a more holistic and integral living of the reign of God. I hope to make this my focus as I move toward sixty-five. I encourage you to do the same, whatever your age.

In 1989, when my father died, my family went to Holy Sepulcher Cemetery on the southwest side to buy our family plots, or graves. As we interacted with the archdiocesan cemetery personnel, I received a discount on my grave, because I was and am a priest. Therefore, I am not going to take advantage of the special deal on a prepaid cremation.

NEVER FORGET

I am old-fashioned. I do not find great enjoyment on the Internet or other media devices. I enjoy watching the news. But one of my greatest enjoyments or relaxations is reading the newspaper. My father used to read four newspapers a day, when Chicago published four daily—the *Sun Times*, the *Chicago Tribune*, the *Chicago American*, and the *Chicago Daily News*. He would sit in the kitchen with his papers strewn across the kitchen table and the White Sox game on the radio. That was his enjoyment. After my day is done, I relax on a chair with several papers with my dog, Bingo, sitting on what has become his chair—two old guys.

One of the papers was quite disturbing this week. The *Sun Times* had a picture and an article titled *"The Falling Man." "The Falling Man"* is a rather famous snapshot of a man falling from one of the World Trade Center towers. What was disturbing was that the man was not just falling. He, along with many others, had jumped to escape the explosion, the heat, the fire caused by a jet airplane that had plowed into the tower. Many of us have seen other news footage, videotape footage of multiple people jumping to their deaths. The man in *"The Falling Man"* was hurtling head first onto the concrete below.

My goddaughter, Anna Mayer, asked her mother, Dawn, and me a question at breakfast recently. She asked, "Why did people jump from the burning buildings?" Dawn explained that perhaps some people got to the roofs of the buildings in the hope that helicopters would rescue them. I explained that I felt death seemed inevitable to many of them, and they chose to jump to their deaths rather than awaiting being incinerated. I do not think any of us can comprehend the horror and the terror of the people who were still living after the impact of those planes and before the buildings collapsed. Some people could not get out of the buildings, so some of them either jumped or were buried when the buildings fell.

Another paper this week had a front-page picture of six-year-old twins, a boy and a girl. They were holding up two signs that read "Never Forget 9/11" and "Never Forget!" How could any of us ever forget the horror of that morning? Where were you? What were you doing when you first heard about and saw the horror of those impacted buildings and then their falling? I was out jogging in those days when my arthritis was not so crippling. I was at my mother's house in Tinley Park getting ready to leave for the parish where I was the pastor. When I got inside the house, Matt Lauer and Katie Couric were reporting that a plane had flown into one of the towers. At first I thought it must have been some small plane that somehow failed or made a mistake and ended up crashing into the building, but then as I watched the news, another jet plowed into the second tower on live television. I still was incredulous. I thought somehow a mistake was made and the second pilot was following the lead of the first pilot. It was only later that it dawned on me, as I listened to and watched the news, that people had deliberately flown two jets into those buildings in an act of terrorism. I tried to explain to my mother what was happening. I talked to Dawn Mayer and other staff members from the parish on the phone. As I drove to the parish that day, it was a surreal ride. What I had seen, what I had experienced, as you did, stunned me. I was in shock. To not see any planes flying in the air was surreal.

That experience would continue for several days. Forget? How could we ever forget? Two wars. The pursuit and the execution of Osama bin Laden, strident security procedures at airports, and other events flowing from September 11, 2001, have etched into our consciousness those terrible events. It is a day like the black days of October 1929, when the stock market crashed. It is like the bombing of Pearl Harbor; the first use of nuclear bombs to end the Second World War; and the assassinations of John Kennedy, Robert Kennedy, and Martin Luther King Jr. These and other events have been etched into our collective consciousness.

In the face of 9/11 and its tenth anniversary, we hear some challenging words from Scripture. Sirach 27 teaches us that we cannot stay in response to 9/11 with wrath, anger, and revenge. Rather, Sirach teaches that we are to forgive our neighbors' injustice toward us. We are to pray that our sins will be forgiven. We are not to nourish anger against people who have hurt us. We are to see our own death as a horizon that we are moving toward and try to prepare ourselves inwardly for that transition. Revenge and resentment need to be left behind as we move toward the fulfillment of our lives.

Jesus reinforces these themes in Matthew 18. Jesus teaches Peter and us that we are to forgive people who have hurt us and to forgive innumerable times. He tells the famous parable of the servant who owed his master a considerable debt. The king, the master, forgave the servant his debt after the servant pleaded with him. But that same forgiven servant would not offer the same gift of forgiveness to a fellow servant who owed a debt to him. Jesus's parable teaches us that as God forgives us innumerable times for our sins and our failures, we also are to forgive each other "from the heart."

Some people have expressed to me the difficulty they have in loving and forgiving Islamic people, because it was Islamic people who were involved in the planning and execution of the 9/11 tragedy. Does Jesus really expect us to develop interior dispositions of forgiveness and reconciliation toward people involved in the first 9/11 and toward people who share a common spirituality or ideology with those original terrorists? The answer in the ideal order is yes: we are called to that ideal. We are called to let go of resentment and revenge and try to develop forgiveness and openness to reconciliation. We live in tension. The tension is the reality of what has happened to our country and the ideals of the reign of God that Jesus preached.

I would like to say that all religions speak to these ideals. There are great similarities among the world religions, be it Judaism, Islam, Christianity, or others. Most of us believe in a loving, caring, creator/parent figure who is the creator and parent of us all. These ideals of love, forgiveness, and reconciliation are ideals that the entire world and all the world's religions should move toward and embrace. We were not created for the violence, hatred, and division that are so present in our world, in our countries, in our cities, on our streets. We were made for loving connection, communion, and service toward our fellow person. We are all brothers and sisters. The tenth anniversary of 9/11 challenges all human beings to embrace better and more what Jesus meant by God's reign.

We Catholics sometimes have funny, convoluted, esoteric ways of saying things. Many of you are probably familiar with the word "anamnesis." Anamnesis is really made up of two Greek words: the Greek word for without, *ana*, and the Greek word for amnesia, *amnesis*. The translation for those two words put together is "without amnesia." "Without amnesia" is a primitive way of saying "never forget." The word "anamnesis" is used to describe that part of the Catholic Eucharist in which we essentially say, "On the night before Jesus died, he took bread and said, 'This is my body.' Then he took the cup of wine and said, 'This is my blood. Do this in memory of me.' " That is the anamnesis. We used to call it the consecration. It really is an act of remembering. In the Jewish-Christian tradition we believe that when we remember or memorialize, past, sacred events become present to us and we can become one with them mysteriously. So at the Eucharist we never forget. We remember Jesus in the movement of his life, death, and resurrection, and we become one with him in the mystery of life, death, and resurrection.

The life, death, and resurrection of Jesus have been etched into the consciousness of all Christian disciples. We can never forget him. We can never forget the Christ event, the paschal mystery. And as we remember, we are not filled with resentment or vengeance or anger about the people who crucified Jesus. Rather, we become one with and celebrate the great meaning for life that being one with his living, dying, and rising brings to our lives.

The life, death, and resurrection of Jesus even conquer and transform the tragedy of 9/11. As we get in touch with the power of anamnesis, never forgetting, let us remember the good people who died in New York City, at the Pentagon, on the field in Pennsylvania. As we remember them, let us realize that they are still alive, still present in their heroism, their love, their courage, their self-sacrifice. They live on. Anamnesis. 9/11. Never forget.

NEW BEGINNINGS

This past year has been like a 365-day-long Good Friday. It will be a year this June that I left a parish where I had served for seventeen years. I was pastor there for fourteen. Jackson Carroll, in his book *God's Potters*, speaks of the importance of what he calls a good fit between a pastor and a congregation. I have derived great meaning and joy from all of my assignments as a priest, but being pastor of Holy Family was a great fit for me and, I think, many of the parishioners.

Several times last year I went to Archdiocesan officials and asked for a little more time to finish a building project that we were in the midst of and, perhaps, to help break in the new pastor, but everyone in authority was united in the mandate that I had to leave. Although men my age had been allowed to stay on beyond their term limits, I eventually had to accept the reality of the situation, and I began to do anticipatory grief for months. I would count off the weeks and the days that I had left. I would look around the church at people I had grown to love and wondered what life would be like without them. I would look at children, teens, and young adults, many of whom were growing up and had grown up during my time at the parish. My heart would ache, for I knew the reality of the situation—that many of these relationships would no longer continue.

The Archdiocese did not approach me to take another parish. I began a conversation with the Franciscan Sisters of Chicago to consider work in health care at the Clare, a continuing care retirement community downtown. I said yes to their offer because it gave me a safe place for service; then I began a process of seeking a residence or a parish where I could help out. I must have sent about thirty letters out, most of them to Archdiocesan pastors. None of them responded positively. One pastor in the Diocese of Joliet did, and that is where I have ended up helping out, at St. Thomas the Apostle in Naperville.

As the time for my leaving the parish neared, things became very painful. In some cases, I was leaving working relationships that I had for years, one that I had for over thirty years. Though 74 percent of parishioners surveyed wanted me to stay on, at the end there was little fight on my behalf. People whom I considered friends began to distance themselves from me personally. They became more advocates for the change and transition than concerned about me. Some gossiped and made accusations about my poor style of leadership. I got through the final Mass, the party, the turbulent ordeal of cleaning out after seventeen years, and moving to two new locations for ministry.

I had thought the ending or the departure was going to be the hard part, but as William Bridges says in his work on transition, the neutral zone or the moratorium period that follows an ending can be more painful than the ending. I would sit during the summer of 2009 in a small office that I had at the Clare feeling lost and lonely. I had been accustomed to working with a big staff. I had become a department of one. I had worked with thirty-eight hundred households. Now I was ministering to fewer than one hundred people. Though I have an additional responsibility to also minister to the staff at the Clare, I could feel myself losing confidence. I looked ahead at speaking and teaching engagements that were coming up, and I felt that I could not do them—that I had nothing to say. Yet for each of them I diligently prepared and prayed for courage, and remarkably most of them were very effective and successful.

This experience has been the loneliest and most painful of my lifetime. It has involved a lot of grieving. I have lost almost everything that gave my life joy and fulfillment: my role as pastor of Holy Family, the faith home and the faith community that I had with the people there, the creative position that I had in leading adult evangelization and catechesis, acquaintances and friendships that gave me a sense of connection, friends whom I just do not see as frequently as I once did. There were times when I felt that I did not think I would get through this, but through faith and prayer, I pulled through.

They say that the experience of grief is resolved when you can "remember with less pain"; I think that is where I am at now. I can remember this past year now, and it does not hurt as much, but it still hurts. A book I read many years ago by the theologian Gregory Baum has greatly influenced me. The title is *Man Becoming*. In this book, Baum speaks of the whole human family as in a process of evolution and development down through the ages, growing in consciousness and morality. He speaks of each individual person in each of our lives as a process of becoming—becoming the self each is meant to be, as do all of us. In a very intense way, that is what this year has been for me. I have been a man becoming, a person becoming. And I can see now in hindsight, not only was I growing in the experience of remembering with less pain as I describe the resolution of grief, I have been becoming new. I have been rising. I have been being transformed.

I can see in many ways that I had lost myself in my role as pastor and in the flurry of activity of that big parish. I have begun to discover a lost self. I have begun to dig out a buried self. I have, through faith, discovered what Paul Tillich calls *courage to be*, or what Baum and I might call the *courage to become*. Tillich speaks of faith in Jesus Christ as the experience of Jesus as the New Being and, for all of us who believe, becoming new beings in Christ. Tillich looks on the human family as, in many ways, being estranged from each other, from God, and from the self each of us is meant to be. Through faith in the risen Jesus, this estrangement, alienation, and division begin to be healed. We grow in the experience of oneness and integrity with ourselves, others, and God. That has been my experience this last year. I am becoming. I have been becoming and am becoming a new self. I live each day with the words of Jesus on the cross, "Into your hands I commend my spirit. Into your hands, I hand over my life." This disposition of trust and surrender into God is transforming me and making me new.

In the last year I have developed skills that I did not have before now. I have been able to do research that I did not have time for in the past. I have been learning anew, facing new challenges and new responsibilities, developing new relationships while holding on to cherished ones. I am much more God-dependent than I have been in a long time. I am much more aware of my need for my fellow person. I appreciate the occasional moments of friendship with some people. I appreciate prayer and the Eucharist more than ever. I trust the paschal process—that we constantly are moving from life through death to new life—and that the process will continue through our actual physical deaths when we are blessed with eternal life.

Going to back to his work on transitions, Bridges suggests that new beginnings often start in that neutral or moratorium zone when we are in the midst of transition. Sometimes the person or people in the transition cannot see or understand the new beginnings. I believe that. I believe that in my life, and in all of our lives, the seeds of new beginnings are already at work. The cross that hangs in Holy Family Parish is called the Cross of New Life. It mysteriously presents Jesus as rising to resurrection and eternal life in the midst of the experience of his cross. The artist was trying to say that death and resurrection are not two separate events, but are intermingled. Resurrection flows from the experience of the cross. That has been my experience. Throughout my life and especially this year, I believe that I am rising with Jesus to new life. I believe, through the mercy of God, that someday I will rise with Jesus to eternal life.

I do not mean to overpersonalize this Easter message. I am trying to give witness to my belief in the paschal process and in the Christ event. I am trying to say that I find the Christ event, the resurrection, believable because I sense the same kind of process going on in and through me. But I know that resurrection is much bigger than Pat Brennan.

St. Paul, in Corinthians and elsewhere, speaks of Jesus having engaged in the one perfect sacrifice. Sacrifice was a ritual that Jewish people and other people engaged in to enter more fully into the realm of God, more fully into the presence of God. Jesus has once and for all united the human family with each other and with God. It just takes time for the human family to fully appreciate and understand the experience. Irenaeus, one of the fathers of the Church, spoke of Jesus as the *homo futurus*. Irenaeus looked on the risen, glorified Jesus as the fulfillment of all human development and evolution. He saw us not descending from apes, but all of us striving to ascend to the risen Christ. I have already mentioned Paul Tillich's reference to Jesus as the New Being, in whom all of us become new beings alive in the Spirit, alive in the reign of God.

Let us try to keep in mind some of the essentials of the death and resurrection experience that the Scriptures present to us. The Scriptures of these holy days tell us that part of the paschal mystery is painful Good Friday endings. There will also be fearful, lonely, lacking-in-hope, neutral-zone, moratorium-like Holy Saturdays. And then there will be Easter Sundays of new beginnings—beginnings of new life here on earth, and the beginning of eternal life after death. As with Jesus, as we pass through this paschal process, when we get to the new beginning, we are the same. Our identity is intact, but we are changed. We are transformed—growing and converting here on earth, and glorified with Jesus in eternal life after death.

Let Easter be a celebration of the profound hope and deep meaning for life that the good news of resurrection brings to each of us and all of us.

BURDENS AND KATE SMITH

Many years ago I had a priest friend who was a missionary in foreign lands. His work took him into nations and cultures that were not Christian. In his work, he experienced many people intentionally converting to Christianity. He explained to a number of us that working with non-Christians becoming Christian was quite different from working with people who are Catholic or Christian from birth.

He found conventional Catholics and Christians to be accepting of a faith tradition that basically was handed on to them by family or culture. The people he worked with in his missionary activity engaged in much more searching and seeking regarding Jesus and Christianity. He said that converts to Christianity actually experienced a coefficient of anxiety in letting go of one way of life to embrace a life of Christian discipleship. He also said that he noticed two events in the life of a true convert. He said converting people utter two primal cries. He called the first the *primal cry for more*: there must be more to life than meets the eye. This is equivalent to a primal cry for God. The second he called the *primal cry for help*: people had the experience of "I cannot get through life by myself. I need help—God's help and the help of other people." Two significant steps in conversion are the experience of needing God and the experience of needing community.

This language seems almost incongruous to our culture, which puts so much emphasis on individualism and independence. This vision encourages us to get in touch with our healthy need for dependency on God and others.

In Matthew's Gospel, we hear a beautiful, familiar teaching from Jesus in which he endorses healthy dependency. All of us to some degree or another are burdened. Perhaps some of us are burdened now. We become burdened by worry, anxiety, and depression. We become burdened with financial concerns, relational problems, and health problems. We become burdened with aging or taking care of people whom we love. Jesus encourages us today, if and when we become burdened, to not carry that burden by ourselves, but to share it with him. We are to take our burdens and prayerfully speak of them, expose them, and hand them over to Jesus. We have to truly act as if we do not carry burdens alone, but rather that he carries them with us. With that feeling of Jesus carrying burdens with us, we experience what Jesus calls in the gospel "his rest." The rest of Jesus is to be at peace, to be content, to be hopeful, to not be weighed down, and to live with a sense of buoyancy.

Paul, in his letter to the Romans, distinguishes between life according to the flesh and life according to the spirit. Many people mistake Paul's reference to the flesh as being too involved with sexuality. Rather, the flesh refers to too much self-reliance, an unhealthy independence that does not recognize one's need especially for God. Life in the Spirit is the recognition that ultimately we are not alone in life, that we are Spirit-dependent—and indeed the Spirit is present with us to give us courage, to give us strength that we do not have on our own. This weekend's Scriptures encourage us to live in the Spirit.

We hear from the prophet Zechariah on Palm Sunday. In effect, Jesus lived this passage when he entered Jerusalem on the first Palm Sunday, riding on a donkey. The prophet Zechariah speaks a message that reverses the expectation of the Jewish people of the time. In awaiting a messiah, many people were awaiting a militaristic, powerful, kinglike leader who would restore their nation and overcome their enemies. Zechariah, on the other hand, depicts a coming king who is meek and rides on a donkey. Jesus chose to live out this imagery from Zechariah to teach us that life in the reign of God is quite countercultural to what many people expect or want. Life in God's kingdom is the experience of oneness with God and oneness with each other in community, not having to bear the burdens of being human alone. We all have that primal need for God and the primal need for help from and connection with other people.

On the radio broadcast that Dawn Mayer and I do on Sunday mornings, I asked our engineer/producer this week to play Kate Smith's "God Bless America." My godchild, Anna Mayer, was there; I asked her, being of the Justin Bieber generation, what she thought of the song. She said she liked it. I am of the age group that knew of Kate Smith. She was on TV in the afternoon after school, and I watched her every day. I played the song because I think the Fourth of July weekend is truly a time to ask God to bless America. We have been blessed with a truly great country, a land of freedom and opportunity. Yet we know that America is also plagued by demons—addiction, violence, political corruption, too much individualism, and questionable values and behaviors associated with materialism and consumerism. Let us thank

God for this country. Let us pray for the well-being and future of this country. Let us be grateful for the many people who have given their lives for this country. Let us realize that to be a disciple of Jesus Christ, we will always live with a tension—that we need to be disciples of Jesus Christ and also be Americans. Christian discipleship should infuse and inform what it means to be a good American citizen.

Part 3

CHURCH

Roots or Up in the Air?

On this Feast of the Holy Family, perhaps we can pause to reflect a bit on what Jesus's origins were like. We are told that he grew up in the town of Nazareth. A historian-archaeologist, an expert on research on the town of Nazareth, appeared on one of the national news shows recently. He said that the Nazareth where Jesus grew up was very small, made up of about fifty buildings. There are hills around the town and a cliff. You might remember that after Jesus identified himself as someone special from God in the town of Nazareth, his neighbors and friends tried to throw him off the cliff because they felt he was being arrogant. This expert said that if Nazareth was anything, it was ordinary. It was made up of ordinary working-class people—deeply steeped, however, in Jewish culture and Jewish tradition. Jesus himself was probably raised as a Pharisee, taught to observe the Jewish law very strictly. Probably the confrontation that Jesus had with his neighbors in Nazareth indicates that Nazareth was a very clannish kind of town. Jesus tried to break with that Jewish clannishness of the time by speaking of a wide vision of the family of God and the reign of God, which was inclusive of all. Jesus, growing up in this ordinary town, knew the collusion that had taken place between Roman leaders and Jewish leaders. He knew that they were mutually benefiting each other by, at times, being abusive toward and manipulative of the ordinary Jewish folks of Nazareth and elsewhere.

Where did Jesus get his faith? It had to come from Joseph and Mary and his extended family. Notice in the gospel how the whole extended family journeys to Jerusalem to celebrate the feast of Passover. When Jesus is lost in the gospel and eventually found after three days, perhaps signifying or foretelling his three days in the tomb, he tells his mother and father, "Did you not know that I had to be in my Father's house?" He was doing his Father's will, as he understood it. If he knew he had to be in his Father's house doing his Father's will, that largely must have come from Joseph and Mary's faith and the faith of his extended family.

In fact, Scripture scholars tell us that Mary's Magnificat, in response to Elizabeth in the Gospel of Luke, is quite parallel in vision and attitude to Jesus's Beatitudes. The Magnificat prayer, the Sermon on the Mount in Matthew, and the Sermon on the Plain in Luke are mirror reflections of each other. Certainly Mary's faith influenced Jesus.

In John's first letter, chapter 3, we are told that we are to love one another as he has commanded us. The importance that Jesus placed on love, mercy, and justice, while he certainly developed these convictions on his own, was probably profoundly influenced by what he heard from his parents.

We do not know a lot about Joseph, but tradition suggests that he died early in Jesus's development after the age of twelve when he was lost at Passover time. It seems that what changed as Jesus and Mary grew older is that Jesus was always keeping an eye on his mother. She was always in close proximity to him in his ministry. She was the advocate who persuaded him to work his first sign or miracle at the wedding at Cana. She was one of his disciples. She was indeed the first evangelist physically bringing him into the world. She watched him die. She witnessed his resurrection and the birth of his movement, the Church.

Pope Leo XIII started the Feast of the Holy Family, focusing on the family of Nazareth and encouraging us to use Jesus, Mary, and Joseph as an example to look at our own families and our own relationships. Relative to looking at our own families and relationships, a principle that became very important for me in my work in religious education over the years is *family consciousness*. Family consciousness, advocated by John Paul II and also the U.S. Bishops, refers to a movement in which the Church has encouraged us to not just minister to or focus on individuals, but to minister to and care for the social context out of which individuals come. In the parishes where I worked and my work as an evangelization director, I have always spoken of the importance of evangelizing and catechizing the home and not just children. Family consciousness speaks of people who are brought together in a closely knit unit by marriage, blood ties, adoption, or choice.

This notion of choice is an interesting one. Some people have minimum or no blood ties to family, yet many people form relationships in small groups, Small Christian Communities, parishes, and congregations that become as close as regular family ties. All of these relationships are included under this notion of family consciousness.

All of us are called to become holy families. The parish that I served in before I began working at the Clare and St. Thomas in Naperville was named Holy Family; the parish's name clearly refers to Jesus, Mary, and Joseph, but also evokes the family that the parish was to become. We really tried to transform a very large parish into a network of neighborhoods, Small Christian Communities, and family-based religious education groups.

I think all parishes and all faith communities need to reimagine themselves as holy families. In our holy families, whether they are in a home, a parish, or some other sort of social network, there ought to be social learning. People ought to learn the skills of communication, confrontation, problem solving, conflict resolution, forgiveness, and reconciliation. Holy families should offer experiences where learning about faith and prayer takes place. Holy families also ought to offer experiences where love, mercy, and justice are learned as ways of life.

This feast, then, while beginning with the historical Jesus, Mary, and Joseph, encourages us to look at and appreciate anew all of our relationships. As we look at our families of origin, many of us are conscious of wounds that were inflicted on us when we were growing up. Perhaps if those wounds are still felt and evident today, we can turn to God and ask for healing and help. I think all families also have passed on gifts to each of us. Each of is a gifted person largely because of our family of origin. Let us praise God for the gifts that have come from our families. If there are any marriages, family lives, friendships, or work-related relationships in which there is hurt, estrangement, or alienation, on this Feast of the Holy Family, let us pray for the grace and the spirit to be able to work at sorrow and contrition, forgiveness and reconciliation.

A movie that received some great reviews and award nominations is *Up in the Air*, starring George Clooney. I have not seen the movie yet. Apparently it is about a man who lives a very isolated life in which he does not even realize how lonely and estranged he is. His job is to fly around to different cities to help terminate people from their jobs. For him, home is found in airplanes and hotel rooms. That is how he describes his home and his lifestyle. That Clooney character is an image and metaphor of too many people in our culture today. Too many people live lives of too much individualism, too much isolation, too much independence. Often folks are living in quiet desperation, for we have been made for relationships. On this Feast of the Holy Family, let us thank God for the people in our lives. And if ever we find ourselves drifting into isolation or loneliness, let us remember the words of our Creator in the book of Genesis when he looked at Adam by himself, "It is not good for man to be alone." It is not good for any of us to be alone. Whether we are extroverts or introverts, each of us in our own way, let us value today the value of communion and connection and work consciously at always being part of some holy family.

HAPPINESS AND HELL

I talked to a priest from the Archdiocese of Chicago recently. He spoke from a dark mood, a dark place.

He said, "Pat, our day is over. We were formed as Vatican II priests." I share this priest's view that the vision of Vatican II is fading and a pre–Vatican II spirit has begun to emerge among younger clergy and some laity. Vatican II attempted to reclaim some of the spirit and practice of the early Christian community when Christianity was a young, vibrant, livable spirituality.

Over the years, the centrality of Jesus and that early Christian community spirit were buried under clericalism and religious institutionalism. Vatican II attempted to penetrate centuries of theological debris to discover more the kerygma—the message of Jesus and the lifestyle of the early church. I have spoken and written many times concurring with this priest's observation that what prevails in the Church now is a kind of restorationism—an attempt to go back to the traditionalistic church many of us grew up in, rather than the truly traditional church that Vatican II recovered.

I was in the Archdiocese of Los Angeles this week preaching a parish mission. The pastor, who is four years older than I, concurred with the Chicago priest and my observations. He said, "Our day *is* over." It seems like the spirit of Vatican II only lasted the duration of our priesthoods, and now people are working to dismantle the Vatican II Church.

The priest's comments, as well as those of the Los Angeles pastor, made me think of an article I read recently in the *National Catholic Reporter*. It told the story of a cleric returning to the practice of saying Mass with his back to the people, and his encouragement to other priests to do the same. He referred to Vatican II–style liturgy as entertainment, and presiding at the liturgy facing the people as a stagelike theatrical experience.

Numbers 11 and Mark 9 have similar themes. In the Numbers passage, the Spirit of God has come upon more people than just Moses to help Moses with leadership of the people. Joshua and others are troubled that the Spirit has been given to many people. There is almost exclusivity in the reaction of Joshua and his colleagues. God's Spirit is to be reserved for only a very few.

Similarly, in the Gospel, John is troubled. Someone is driving out demons in the name of Jesus, though this person is not obviously a disciple, one who travels with Jesus. Both Moses and Jesus reprimand people who are trying to make their religious movement an exclusive experience. Moses says, "Would that all the people of the Lord were prophets." A prophet is not someone who predicts the future. A prophet is someone who has deep experiences of the here and now and speaks God's truth about it. Moses wishes that more people were prophets.

Jesus has to remind John and others that the reign of God is a broad concept and experience that is not limited by religious exclusivity. Jesus did not come to initiate a religious institution that includes some and excludes others. He came, rather, to help with the emergence of the reign of God. The reign of God is a vision and a way of life. It is God-centered, seeking to do what is discerned as God's will, and is about universal communion and connections. Jesus's experience of the reign of God—his understanding of the reign of God—is not that only a few belong and are saved; rather, the entire human family is ideally to be connected as brothers and sisters, as family, with God at the center of our lives. Some of the sin of religion, Christian and other denominations, is that religion is sometimes used to help some people feel better than or superior to others. Religion is sometimes used to separate people rather than to connect people.

Within Catholicism are certain factions of people who are almost Gnostic in nature. They believe that their ideology and their devotional practices are the truth. They sit in judgment about others who think differently, or perhaps behave differently, in faith matters. They judge themselves to be superior, better than others. I think it is clear that Jesus does not endorse such spiritual arrogance and separatism.

As we passed through the teen years, we all hung out in friendship groups. Many of us were sensitive to the existence of cliques. Cliques and often friendship groups can become exclusive and mean-spirited. People in a clique sometimes use the group to prove their superiority over others. The book of Numbers and the Gospel of Mark give witness that religion can become a clerical, hierarchical, institutional clique.

If Numbers and Mark warn us about the possible mistaken notions that organized religion can fall into, the reading from the letter of James warns against parallel mistaken notions. James is addressing a group of early Christians who have become enamored with the accumulations of material possessions and their own pleasure. In addition to stockpiling resources for themselves, these errant early Christians unjustly cheated poor people of resources that were rightfully theirs. James counters with statements that speak of the transitory character of life here on earth. He also reminds them of the end of their own personal lives and the end of time. He challenges his readers to grow rich in values, attitudes, and behaviors that will prepare them for that end.

I have been recommending a book by Ed Diener and Robert Biswas-Diener titled *Happiness: Unlocking the Mysteries of Psychological Wealth*. Ed Diener and his son have done extensive research, cross-culturally, into the nature of happiness. They describe happiness as including optimism and joy, feelings of calm and harmony, and other positive emotions. Happy people pay attention to the positive, interpret things positively, and live off of happy memories. The authors describe happiness as a process more than a destination. Countering the vision of the people whom James writes to, Diener and Biswas-Diener found in the research that material wealth and resources do not bring people happiness. In their findings, the pursuit of materialism actually blocks people from paying attention to other important realities that they say constitute psychological wealth. Psychological wealth involves acquiring a portfolio of physical health, mental health, spirituality, material sufficiency, life satisfaction, close relationships, meaningful work, and contributing to the lives of others. The book encourages people to work on this portfolio of psychological wealth.

I would like to expand on the notion of psychological wealth by speaking of both psychological and *spiritual* wealth. The Dieners include spirituality as one of the elements of psychological wealth. Much of the literature coming out of the positive psychology movement underscores the need that people have for spirituality.

Spirituality includes daily conscious contact with the presence and Spirit of God. Spiritual wealth includes an active prayer life, membership in a faith community and smaller faith communities, heartfelt worship, being in service to others in ministry, and an awareness of and involvement in works of mercy and justice. Those who pursue happiness often experience happiness eluding them, because they define happiness in terms of accumulation of material resources. Happiness happens when we lose ourselves in the portfolio of psychological and spiritual wealth.

As Jesus warns against the dangers of what I would call exclusive, institutionalized, organized religion, he mentions the notion of Gehenna three times. Gehenna is a Jewish apocalyptic image which Jesus was aware of that originally referred to a place southwest of Jerusalem called the Valley of Hinnom, a site of idolatrous child sacrifice. The notion of Gehenna developed in Jewish thought to become a place of fiery punishment where some people went after death. There they were punished for sins from which they had not repented. Jesus seems to indicate some kind of belief in a place of punishment after death.

In speaking of heaven and hell, I have always tried to give a realistic, existential explanation of them. Heaven and hell are not places to which God sends or condemns us. Heaven and hell are lifestyles that we begin here on earth. A heaven lifestyle is characterized by the attitudes, beliefs, and behaviors that Jesus revealed in his reign-of-God teaching and preaching. A hell lifestyle is the chosen isolation, divisiveness, and alienation that we experience in and through sin. This divisiveness and alienation can be found in the mistaken notions of religion we began talking about, and the materialistic lifestyle that some people choose that really misses the mark in life. The Scriptures, on both a religious plane and a secular plane, call us to be cautious about missing the mark in life. We all suffer from mistaken notions that are in need of reeducation, conversion, and spiritual transformation.

A Deserted Place

Why? That is the first question, the theme that runs through the book of Job: "Why?" It expresses some of the pain and existential angst that

Job experienced throughout the whole book. Briefly, let us summarize the book of Job, which has forty-two chapters and an epilogue.

The book of Job is part of the wisdom literature of the Hebrew scriptures. It is not a historical account, but rather a teaching about multiple spiritual themes. The book begins with Satan negotiating with God to tempt Job. God protests that Job is a righteous man and would never budge from righteousness and fidelity to God. God agrees to allow Satan to tempt Job. In this first trial, Job loses his resources and his children, but he maintains faith and says, "The Lord gives, and the Lord takes away. Blessed be the name of the Lord." Satan negotiates with God for a second trial of Job. This time Job loses his health—becoming covered with boils and sores. While Job still remains faithful, he is deeply distressed because of the problems with his health. At the beginning of chapter 3, Job says, "Perish the day that I was born!" Job cannot even get support from his wife, who scorns him.

Three friends—Eliphaz, Bildad, and Zophar—came to Job's home to help him with his suffering. Long conversations ensued between Job and the three men concerning the reason for Job's suffering. The three friends articulated a popular spiritual understanding: if anyone suffers, it has to do with some evil in which the sufferer had engaged. Suffering is God's punishment for people who have done wrong. Job counters that he has not done anything wrong, that he has always been a righteous man, faithful to God. The three friends encourage Job to become honest, admit his wrongdoing, seek God's mercy and forgiveness, and get on with his life. Job responds vehemently and with repetition that he has been a good and just man. Key to understanding this book is that Job had the same understanding of God as the three friends. He believed that God punished sin with suffering. But he was stumped: Why was God treating him this way, when he had not sinned?

This back-and-forth conversation goes on a long time in the book, until finally a young man steps forward. The young man's name is Elihu. He reprimands Job and the three friends for thinking that they completely understand God. They mistakenly imagined a very mechanical God, who operated in human, predictable ways. Elihu reminds the men of the power and grandeur of God, which is to be held in reverence. God then speaks of his power and wisdom, essentially telling the men that he is mystery, not to be fully understood, manipulated, or controlled.

I have always said that Job's words in chapter 42 are the most beautiful articulation of conversion or spiritual transformation in the Bible. He says to God: "I know that you can do all things, and that no purpose of yours can be hindered. I have dealt with great things that I do not understand; things too wonderful for me, which I cannot know. I had heard of you by word-of-mouth, but now my eye has seen you." Another translation that I am familiar with has Job saying, "Before I only knew you by hearsay; but now I have come to know you face to face."

As Rabbi Harold Kushner has said in his interpretation of Job, bad things happen to good people. Often there is no clear-cut answer to the question of why there is suffering in our lives. Perhaps asking why is human and natural, but often we do not receive an answer. But part of the mystery of bad things happening to good people is that they lead to spiritual transformation, spiritual breakthrough, and conversion. In wrestling with the mystery of suffering in our lives, we, like Job, can move from the God of hearsay to the God we know and see face to face. We come to understand that God has been with us in our struggles, and that God's grace has been the powerful force which has helped us endure.

How can we know that God is with us during a time of suffering or struggle? It has been my experience that we need to deliberately attend to God. I pray multiple times during the day. However, during Advent and Christmas, over the years, I have developed a habit of sitting in the dark by the Christmas tree, looking at the lights blinking and flickering, getting in touch with my life and ministry, and having a conversation with God about what is going on in my life. When the tree is down and put away until next year I still go into the living room and sit in the dark and think and pray. Doing this blesses me with a great sense of God's presence. I grow in insight. I grow in *emunah*, a Hebrew word that refers to courage for life that comes from knowing that God is with us.

We are told that Jesus, after healing Simon Peter's mother-in-law and doing many other healings and exorcisms, went off to a deserted place, where he prayed. We all need to find our own deserted place, sanctuary time and space, where we can connect with God and allow God to connect with us. This deserted space is especially important when we are in a Job mode of life.

Remember: Jesus healed Peter's *mother-in-law*. In other words, Peter, the leader of the apostles—and in our tradition, the first pope—was married. In fact, priests and bishops married and had families for years. Allow me to clarify: Celibacy has been held up as an ideal for priests since the early days of Christianity. It was a form of asceticism that some priests chose to give their total selves to Christ and the reign of God. But for centuries there was another way of being a priest: having a wife and children. Rather questionable practices were encouraged at times—for example, priests could marry, giving witness to the goodness of marriage, but not experience intimacy with their wives and to live as if they were not married. The celibacy versus married priests controversy came to a close in the eleventh century. The issue at hand was the benefice, or the inheritance of Church funds and property that priests were leaving to their wives and children. Popes like Benedict VII and Innocent II began to lay down the law that priests were not to give Church property to wives and children. This led eventually to mandatory celibacy for priests. This requirement was firmed up in the Gregorian Reform led by Gregory VII, which sought to correct abuses in the Church at the time. Priests resisted mandatory celibacy for centuries. Nonetheless, subsequent teachings maintained celibacy's status in the Church.

But now we know of married Lutheran ministers and married Anglican and Episcopalian priests who have been accepted into the Roman Catholic priesthood. I know of a Lutheran minister who became a priest, who lives in the rectory with his wife and family; there is another rectory for the celibate priests who work at the parish. This is in a suburb of Chicago.

It seems to me that the values of both celibate and married clergy demand more open and systematic discussions. As with many issues in the Church, we need more contemplative conversations, after spending time in our deserted places asking the question: Why?

GOOD SHEPHERDING

A good friend of mine and I were discussing someone recently, a religious sister by the name of Sister Carolan. Sister Carolan was a retired BVM sister when she came to volunteer in the Office for Chicago Catholic Evangelization, where I worked from 1979 to 1992. Sister Carolan was elderly; I have not kept up with her—I do not know if she is still alive. This nun was terribly stooped over, with a big hump in her back. There was a reason for her physical disfigurement. She was a teaching sister at Our Lady of the Angels parish on the west side of Chicago, the famous parish that had a school fire in 1958 that killed ninety-two children and three sisters. As the fire began to rage, Sister Carolan made a bridge of her body from the windowsill of one wing of the building to another windowsill of another part of the building, which was not on fire. She encouraged children to crawl on her body from the burning wing to a place of safety. Her back was broken in many places. Physically she never recovered. Her family presumed she had died in the fire, for they did not hear from her for three days. In fact, she was at the county morgue for three days, identifying bodies and ministering to grieving parents and families. To use an image from today's gospel, Sister Carolan was truly a good shepherd in the face of disaster.

I thought of Sister as I read and listened to news about the Vatican's investigation of religious women in America, resulting in the Vatican stripping the Leadership Conference of Women Religious of its ability to self-govern. Religious leaders maintain that American sisters are too interested in the social gospel, when they should be more interested in the church's teachings on human sexuality and contraception. So many of us who are of a certain age grew up with the comfort and challenge provided by religious sisters. My brother and I were taught by the Sinsinowa Dominicans at St. Thomas More School on the southwest side of Chicago. My cousin Dolores Lynch was a member of this order. Besides parents, religious sisters and parish priests significantly shaped many of us growing up in the 1950s and 1960s. I am greatly troubled that religious women are being treated in such a fashion in our own day.

In Ireland, priests are being silenced by religious leaders because of the questions they ask about the future discipline of the Church. Father Tony Flannery, a well-known Redemptorist author and retreat director, has been silenced. So also has Father Sean Fagan; his religious order went so far as to buy up unsold copies of his latest book so that the laity would not be polluted by it. Father Owen O'Sullivan has similarly been silenced. These are good men who have given their lives to the priesthood and to the Church, only to be exiled and unappreciated.

In a recent article titled "Spirituality, Religion Collide" in *USA Today*, author Diane Butler Bass distinguished between spirituality and religion. In her understanding, some of the mainstream Christian churches and their leadership are valuing the dictates and disciplines of religion more than valuing spirituality. Allow me to clarify: I am a Roman Catholic—and that is very important to me. Religion provides structure, organization, institutionalization, shared beliefs, shared values, shared behaviors, and common approaches to worship. But I believe that religion, this very important vehicle and structure, is at the service of a greater reality: spirituality. As organized religions and their leaders seem to be tightening up on the demands of religion, people in turn are hungry and thirsty for spirituality.

Spirituality is lived faith. Spirituality involves religious experience. Spirituality is the attempt on the part of people to connect with the mystery of God. Spirituality is an attempt to make sense of life and find meaning for life through faith—in our case, faith in Jesus Christ. Spirituality refers to what Jesus meant when he preached and revealed the reign of God. The reign of God is a spirituality which emphasizes that we should live certain values, attitudes, and behaviors. Among these are a sense of sufficiency, an understanding that wealth corrupts the spirit, a rejection of engaging in power over others, a radical belief in the equality of all human beings, a rejection of violence in all its forms, intentionally deciding for Abba/God to be the funding source of our lives, lives of prayerfulness, lives of community, lives of worship, stewardship and ministry, and justice for all.

Diana Butler Bass said in her article that the crisis facing today's churches is not liberal versus conservative, but rather religion versus spirituality. Ideally, these two realities should exist in healthy collaboration, with religion leading people to spirituality; that is how I understand these two realities. But Bass feels the two are now in tension—with religious leadership reasserting familiar patterns that include top-down control, uniformity, and bureaucracy, while many church members are seeking spirituality, religious experience, and community. Bass warns that in this tension, religious leaders run the risk of becoming CEOs of the religion business.

Jesus was not and is not a CEO. He describes himself, in John's Gospel this week, as the Good Shepherd. Jesus is our Good Shepherd. Jesus describes how he has shepherded and does shepherd us: he lays down his life for us. That is the kind of shepherding that the church of Jesus cries out for today—good shepherds who love one another with a self-sacrificial love. Quite often the metaphor of shepherd is used to describe the work of bishops and priests. The fact is, some of the best good shepherding is done by people other than ordained clerics. Spouses lay down their lives daily for each other. Parents, without measure, lay down their lives for their children. Friends who are truly friends lay down their lives for each other. Jesus speaks of good friendship in John 15. Addressing his apostles at the Last Supper, he describes the kind of friendship he has toward them: he will lay down his life for them; he has chosen them; he has revealed who he is to them; he has made himself equal to them—because of this friendship they are to bear fruit. Parish ministers, volunteering time and gifts, lay down their lives for one another. People in Small Christian Communities lay down their lives for each other—and on and on.

My mother had only two years of high school. My dad only went to school through eighth grade. They married in 1943 and have been good shepherds to each other, now, into eternity. They were good shepherds to my brother and me, in a little five-room house in Chicago. In imitation of them and so many other wonderful people in my background, I have tried to be a good shepherd as a man and a Catholic priest.

In John 10, as Jesus describes his good shepherding, he speaks of a characteristic of a good shepherding relationship—mutual knowing: "I know mine; and mine know me." Good shepherding, in imitation of Jesus, ought not to be characterized by divisiveness, tension, judgment, and ex-communication. Rather, laying down our lives for each other should lead to communion, community—the basic image of church in the first centuries of Christianity. What has happened down through history is that emerging church leadership has taken a secular power model—claiming that Jesus started the Church this way, with a top-down model of church. Leonardo Boff has written that this model of church is, at best, traditionalistic. Boff has said that a truly traditional model of church knows that the risen Jesus is at the center of the church. The glory of his risen spirit is manifest in the charisms of disciples living in communion with each other. John Paul II called Catholics to embrace the model of Church that he called a "community of disciples," a community of learners about Jesus and the reign of God. Avery Dulles embraced a community of disciples as his sixth model of church.

In the second reading from the first letter of John, we are reminded of our great dignity. We are the children of God. The passage goes on to teach us that as we pass into eternity, we will become like Jesus and see him as he is. We ought to treat one another with the respect that the children of God deserve. We are called to be communities of good shepherds, laying down our lives for each other, coming to know each other, growing in unity with each other. I believe this is how Jesus wants his church. Leaders should not continue to throw martyrs to the lions.

Lions and persecution could not stop the heroes and heroines—the martyrs—of early Christianity. In the Middle Ages, the Franciscans and other spiritual movements warned that the Church was obscuring the gospel with pomp, that it was becoming more the Church of Constantine than of the apostles. Bernard wrote to Pope Eugenius III, "All this goes back to Constantine, not to Peter."

I am glad that I experienced people like Sister Carolan—people who understood and understand what it means to be good shepherds.

Part 4

SACRAMENTS AND PRAYER

ALL SAINTS DAY

The Feast of All Saints began in the fourth century as the celebration of all martyrs, those who willingly gave their life to defend Christian faith. In the ninth century, it became a feast for the entire Church, and it assumed the date of November 1 eventually, the date that it was celebrated in Ireland in contrast to a pagan celebration that was held at that time.

All Saints . . . We remember and celebrate today the superheroes of the faith—Mary and Joseph, Peter and Paul, Monica and Augustine, Patrick, Therese the Little Flower, Teresa of Avila, and more contemporary superheroes: Dorothy Day, Oscar Romero.

In remembering and celebrating All Saints, however, we would be remiss if we just focused on the superheroes. We have all known saints—good, holy people who have over the years modeled for us faith, hope, and love. Our grandmothers and grandfathers, the patriarchs and matriarchs of our families before them, aunts and uncles, cousins, our own parents, friends whom we have known—we all have known saints and holy people who mediated to the world the presence and love of God.

And now we are on the center stage of sainthood. We are called to continue the tradition of sanctity and holiness handed on to us by both the superheroes and the lesser-known saints who have been and are part of our lives.

St. Paul, in his letters, referred to all the baptized as saints.

What exactly is the nature of this sanctity and holiness to which you and I are called? If we want to be saints in the tradition of Jesus Christ, then we must take seriously to heart what he meant by the reign of God. I think that is what the saints that you and I celebrate today finally achieved. Each of them in their unique way lived what they understood to be Jesus's vision of the reign of God.

Let's attempt a description of the reign of God, or kingdom living. To be a person of the reign of God is to *attempt to live a God-centered life*. In this lifestyle, God isn't outside of our circle of concern or at the periphery of that circle, but at the very center of our lives. We attempt to interpret all aspects of our lives through the filter of God as revealed by Jesus.

People of the kingdom, or the reign of God, are *prayerful*, regularly entering into communion with this God. Kingdom people are vigilant about the quality of life around them . . . the quality of their own lives. They are vigilant also about the horizon of everlasting life, toward which we all walk.

People of the reign of God are *nonviolent and nonaggressive*. They try to bring and make peace in all circumstances. They realize their need for what is talked about in the second reading: salvation. They are people in the process of being saved, trying to save and redeem the world.

People of the reign of God as described in today's gospel are *countercultural*. They go against the grain of the mass-mindedness of the culture, the institutions, or systems around them. Often in this countercultural lifestyle, they have discovered their dependence on another power, the power of God.

People of the kingdom *practice forgiveness, repentance, and reconciliation*.

People of the kingdom *recognize the paschal, or passage, nature of all of life*. Taking a hint from nature, they believe that all of life is about life, death, and resurrection, and that will happen one final and full time when, physically, each of us is invited over the threshold of death into eternal life.

People of the kingdom have a *belief in the apocalyptic glory that the book of Revelation describes.* They do not need to have all the answers about what heaven or eternal life is like. They hope, believe, and are convinced of the mystery. Conviction about the mystery has erased any fear or apprehension about death.

People of the reign of God *know that all this kingdom living is not done in isolation or independently.* They recognize their need for genuine oneness and community with their fellow person.

People of the reign of God are *doing their best to extend to people around them God's mercy and justice.*

The challenge to live lives of holiness and sanctity has been extended to us through our Baptism. The challenge is not to take on some sort of otherworldly direction. Rather, as saints, we are to be deeply immersed in the world, striving to transform our world more and more into what Jesus meant by God's reign.

Some words to describe holiness in the contemporary sense? *Wellness*—holy people are seeking emotional, physical, and spiritual health.

Another word? *Wholeness*—in all of their efforts, saints seek to be people of integrity.

Another word is *communion.* In all aspects of life, saints seek loving relationships of oneness with their fellow person, whether at school, in the neighborhood, at work, or with people in general.

Through the mystery of faith, as we celebrate this great tradition today, we who are called to be saints are connected with saints of all times in that wonderful reality we call the communion of saints.

Let us rejoice in the great global and celestial solidarity that we have with so many spirits and souls on this feast of All Saints.

ALL SOULS

Some Protestant Christians critique us as Catholics for praying for and to the dead. Perhaps, in an attempt to develop our own apologetical abilities, we could reflect on All Souls Day. Why do we do these things?

We pray for the dead because our love for our deceased loved ones continues. As we prayed for their well-being here on earth, we continue to express our concern for them, through God, on the other side of death. Perhaps, in praying for them we are also trying to offer ourselves some consolation that the souls and spirits of our loved ones are not just out there somewhere, but rather in the loving embrace of our God. We pray for our deceased loved ones because we love them.

None of us completely understands the mystery of eternal life. Perhaps there is the opportunity for the spirits and souls of our loved ones to grow, even after death. Should that be the case, some of us, perhaps, may pray for our deceased loved ones, that they might fully become who God wants them to become.

Relative to praying *to* our deceased loved ones, or to any souls or spirits we consider to be saints, it is not so much *to* as *through*.

We pray through their loving intercession for us. As I might have asked my mother, my father, my nephew, or a friend of mine who died of leukemia to pray for me during this physical life, I ask them also to pray for me, other people, and other situations from their position on the other side of death.

Perhaps it is simplistic thinking, but I believe that those who have died are more proximate to the divine mystery than we are. They can be powerful intercessors for us and for our needs.

All Saints and All Souls Days are times also for remembering. In that ancient Jewish tradition, we believe that as we remember, we make present again. And so, in remembering our deceased loved ones, let us feel their spirits very close and present to us. In the mystery of things, they are paradoxically one with God and one with us, a wonderful experience we call the *communion of saints*.

I have made peace with a lot of the deaths in my life. The one that still causes me significant pain is the death of my mother. I speak with her a lot. Sometimes she seems very distant, and sometimes I feel like I am bumping into her. I have experienced a lot of loneliness since she died, since so much of my energy was dedicated to taking care of her. I sometimes seek her intercession, her prayer, and the healing of that loneliness. I am not trying to replace her in my life by any means. I am asking only that the edge of sadness be less sharp. And it has become so.

Many in this Church are grieving tonight—grieving for losses that have been more painful than any that I have experienced.

I have come across two models of understanding grief. One is a linear model in which we have to go through various stages of shock, disorientation, readjustment, and resolving grief. There is truth in that model.

The one that makes more sense to me is the spiral model. This model says that death places us in a deep pit of loss, pain, and depression. The resolution of grief is to slowly spiral upward from the pit—stopping, becoming embedded in a certain part of the spiral for a while, and then moving out and moving on, hopefully upward. But then there are those days when we fall back into the pit, when we have setbacks. Through the grace of God, we can regain the distance we had achieved more quickly than in the past.

In the journey of grief, we need to keep the vision of Isaiah before us—that as we try to engage in this spiral, here comes our God with healing, help, and grace. We do not do the journey alone.

To use Paul's words from 1 Thessalonians, grieve with a great deal of hope. And we can help each on the journey through the mutual consolation that we give to one another.

Isn't it good to know that, unlike Socrates—who broached death stoically and philosophically—Jesus, who is God and human being, wept profoundly at the death of his friend Lazarus, and shook and sweat with fear as he confronted his own mortality?

Let us realize this night that Jesus knows this pain we know of being human, and whenever life hurts, he is there to help us.

LEARNING FROM TWO BLIND MEN

Grieving the loss of a loved one until the good news of resurrection lessens the pain . . . having a profound insight into the meaning of one's life, especially the meaning of suffering and struggle in one's life . . . going to the Sacrament of Reconciliation regularly to seek God's mercy for a pattern of sin . . . making a decision, with the help of God, to change a habit or pattern of sin with immediacy . . . the story of Bartimaeus in Mark 10, coupled with another story in Mark's Gospel . . . together these elements explain, at least in part, the process of conversion.

As my examples indicate, conversion, or spiritual transformation, for some of us involves a process of coming to see in a new way. At other times, the coming to see in a new way can be an abrupt experience. For Bartimaeus, his coming to see life in and through Jesus happens through a *momentary* encounter with Jesus. In Mark 8, another blind man is given his sight by Jesus, but that sight only comes *gradually.*

So it is in each of our journeys of faith. At times, spiritual transformation takes awhile. At other times, that transformation, or coming to see in a new way, happens quickly. Both experiences are valid and true, and all of us have both kinds of experiences.

"Coming to see in a new way" is frequently used in all four of the Gospels to explain what faith is. Faith is a lot of things. It is a relationship with God. It is an intellectual appropriation of certain creedal elements. But faith is also epistemological. It is a way of knowing and seeing the world around us. This new coming to see, this faith, does involve insight, new values, a changed philosophy of life, and a whole new lifestyle involving thoughts, feelings, and behavior. Jesus called this new sight "life in the reign of God." Whenever we have conversion events or processes, whenever spiritual transformation is occurring in us, we are coming to see in a new way.

Bartimaeus exemplifies *persistence*, a value that is very important for disciples of Jesus Christ. I suggest that we understand persistence in two ways. Persistence speaks to me of living a life of discipline when it comes to conversion and spirituality. In other words, on the journey of faith, we are not just reactive or waiting for things to happen to us willy-nilly. Rather, we intentionally pay attention to the movement of God in our lives. And as we sense that God movement or hear God's call and will, we intentionally change, act, and allow ourselves to be transformed in response to God. This spiritual discipline is a kind of vigilance, attending to God in our lives, and attending to the quality of our lives in the face of God.

Persistence admits of another connotation. Bartimaeus wanted something; he wanted his sight, so he persistently cried out to Jesus, "Jesus, Son of David, have pity on me!" People tried to silence him, but he cried still louder, "Have pity on me! Have pity on me!" When we perceive something as our daily bread, something that we genuinely need or want, we ought to go with faith and integrity and persistence to our God. It is okay to pray for what we want as long as we understand what we want as holy, good, and congruent with God's will.

We are told that Bartimaeus's persistent prayer makes Jesus stop. And so it is with God and us. When we are persistent in asking for our daily bread, *God stops for us*. Though God might not give us exactly what we ask for, we are assured, in the teachings of Jesus in the Gospel of Luke, that God always gives the Holy Spirit to those who pray. Whenever we pray, we are touched by or filled with grace and Spirit. This grace and Spirit empower us to face all the challenges of our lives. Let us be persistent in terms of discipline for the spiritual journey, and persistent in honesty in our prayer. God stops and attends to us when we pray, the gospel teaches us.

When Bartimaeus receives sight, we are told he follows Jesus on "the way." "The way" is codified language. It meant something to the early Christians. "The way" was a life of discipleship; this life of discipleship, this "way"—ultimately for Jesus and for all disciples— led and leads to Jerusalem. Jerusalem is a symbolic spot referring to where Jesus Christ was put to death, buried, and then rose again, transformed and glorified.

The ultimate goal of the new sight we receive, either quickly or in a process sort of way, is to understand better and to embrace the paschal mystery—that what life is all about is the mystery of living, dying, and rising, over and over again, with Jesus, until finally our bodies stop and we enter into a new dimension of being that we call eternal life. New sight, new sight on "the way" is always a gradual embracing, with conviction and hope, of the mystery of life, death, and resurrection. That mystery is going on in each of our lives in different ways. We bring that mystery to this table every time we offer the Eucharist. We become one with each other, and one with Jesus, in the mystery of living, dying, and rising.

Let us be glad today that, as Jeremiah prophesied, God always walks with us, through our joys and difficulties, ultimately leading us to new or eternal life. Let us thank Jesus for that which the letter to the Hebrews speaks of: by dying on the cross and rising for us, Jesus has revealed to us the meaning of life, which is life, death, and resurrection.

Supply Concerns

Worldwide, a very prevalent disorder is addiction. Addictions develop in people at all socioeconomic strata. Addiction is characterized by a growing need for something, a need that becomes a compulsion—a compulsion that begins to rob people of life and health, a compulsion that, if not stopped, leads to death. Some people are addicted to alcohol. Some people become addicted to drugs. Some people become addicted to work. Some people are addicted to sex. Some are addicted to money, and on and on. Wherever there is an unhealthy dependency, obsession, or compulsion leading to the deterioration of life, there is addiction.

One symptom of addiction is supply concerns. The addicted person needs to make sure that a good supply of whatever feeds the addiction is available, whether it's alcohol or drugs or money or work or sex partners. Supply concerns are an addict's self-focused preoccupation with having enough—or more than enough.

Maybe all of us in a consumer and materialistic culture suffer to some degree with supply concerns. We are all concerned that we have enough of what we perceive to be necessities for us. The recent economic difficulties have made us even more supply concerned. Many people lost a lot of money in the stock market and other investments. On the other hand, to the degree that some people have had to cut back because of the recession, some people have learned that their supply concerns were unwarranted—that, in fact, they can get by with less. Some people have learned that the "more" they were living with was unneeded; perhaps it even blocked happiness or intruded on relationships. To what degree do all of us as American consumers have supply concerns?

The widow whom Elijah meets in 1 Kings in the area of Zarephath must certainly have had supply concerns. Yahweh had brought a drought in response to the king of Israel's sinfulness. The king at the time was Ahab. The drought extended to the area of Zarephath, which was a territory largely populated by worshipers of the pagan god Baal. With the drought occurring also in the land of Baal, Elijah was trying to demonstrate to the people that Yahweh is the almighty God, not Baal. Yahweh can control rainfall and drought even in the land of Baal. Elijah asks the woman for a cup of water, which she goes to get; then he asks for a piece of bread. The woman responds that she has only a little flour left and very little oil, and that she is going to make something for her son and herself. Then, because of the drought, both of them will probably die. Elijah asks the woman to do something that almost seems selfish. He says, before you cook for your son or for yourself, make something for me. And then he assures her, "The Lord God Yahweh has promised that the jar of flour will not run empty or the jug of oil run dry until the day when the Lord sends rain upon the earth."

This passage closes with the information that the woman and her son were able to eat for a year with what God provided them. The woman was called to place faith and trust in a God she did not even believe in: faith and trust that God would always extend providential love toward her and her son, faith and trust that there would always be something for them to eat. She was called beyond supply concerns. She was called beyond concern for herself and her son to a generous, self-sacrificial love for a stranger, Elijah.

Even more profound is the generosity of the widow who appears in Mark's Gospel. Jesus was speaking against the scribes, the interpreters of Old Testament law. They were, in effect, an early form of lawyers. These lawyers loved to show off, wear fine robes, and demonstrate how much Jewish law they knew. Often, as the gospel refers to, they used their legal ability to cheat people. Working for widows, they often would make themselves trustees of the widows' estates, eventually claiming some or all of the widows' resources. Perhaps a contemporary analogy of these men would be crooked televangelists who defraud people with their preaching. Up against the scribes, and many rich people who are putting money into the treasury of the Jewish community, there is this poor widow who has two small coins, worth a few cents. The rich place large amounts of money in the treasury. The large amounts of money are not that much of a sacrifice to them, for they have much, but Jesus tells us that the widow gives from her poverty all that she had. The Greek version of this passage reads, "She gave her whole life."

These two widows remind me of my maternal grandmother, Margaret Canty. I have only vague recollections of her, since she died when I was five years old. My memories are that of an older woman who simply sat in a chair in the living room, coping with heart disease and arthritis. She was in her mid-seventies when she passed away. I was told that as a younger woman, she was a vivacious Irish redhead. She had eight children of her own with her husband, Patrick Canty. She was committed to bringing Irish immigrants over to the United States to help them get on their feet and establish a home here. So many people, after they had left Ireland, would stop at Maggie Canty's house to stay there for a while and get a good meal. I am told that she never counted the cost. She always believed there would be enough for her family and anyone else who was in need. She also helped bring over to the United States a number of young men who went to American seminaries and became priests.

The people in the gospel who had large amounts of money were obviously people of power. Before I was ordained a priest, a sister who I believed liked me asked to see me, and she gave me this sage advice: "Pat, in the priesthood, always try to be a powerful person, but never be a person of power." Those words have stayed with me, and I try to live them. Maggie Canty was a powerful person, but she was not a person of power. The widows spoken of today in their generosity and self-sacrifice are powerful people, but not people of power. People of power can step over others to get what they want. Powerful people engage, rather, in the care and service of others.

The widow in the gospel seems to have had no supply concerns. She gave everything she had for the well-being of others, who benefited from what was put in the treasury. The story of the widow precedes the passion narrative, the story of Jesus's death in Mark's Gospel. The generosity and self-sacrificial love of the widow is almost a prologue to the total self-gift that Jesus engaged in through his crucifixion and death. We are told in the letter to the Hebrews that this one act of sacrifice—Christ's death and his resurrection—has reconciled the human family to God. No further sacrifices are needed. The one perfect sacrifice has been effected through the cross of Jesus Christ and his glorious resurrection. Through his life, death, and resurrection, Jesus has totally united the human family to Abba, our loving Creator and Parent.

When we offer the Eucharist together, we are not offering one sacrifice after another every time we celebrate Mass. Rather, every Mass re-presents or makes present again the one perfect sacrifice of Jesus and allows us to share in the power of that event. In the face of the troubled economy—with many of us having taken financial losses, with many people concerned about whether there will be enough resources for their retirement—the gospel calls us away from supply concerns. The gospel calls us to self-sacrificial love and generosity. The gospel calls us to trust in the providential love of God for us. The gospel calls us to trust that somehow, even in difficult times, God will always provide. God is for us, and God will always take care of us. Let us learn from two poor, trusting widows.

My Body and Blood: Do This in Remembrance of Me

What was on Jesus's mind the night before he died, when he gave to disciples of all time the gift of the Eucharist? I think it is important to pay attention first of all to his use of bread and wine. We hear of a parallel meal of bread and wine offered by Melchizedek with Abram in Genesis 14. In Jewish tradition and culture, people believed that when the Messiah came, he would share a meal of bread and wine with his followers as Melchizedek did with Abram. Jesus was equivalently saying to his apostles, those who were with him Holy Thursday night, "I am the Promised One."

Why did he use the words "body" and "blood" over the bread and wine? In the Greek version of the Scriptures, body is represented by the word *soma*, meaning "one's very self," and blood is expressed in the word *haima*, meaning "life force." In giving us the Eucharist, Jesus was saying, "I am giving you my very self."

Why did Jesus use the Passover meal as the context for giving us the Eucharist? The Passover meal was the central act of worship for the Jewish people. As they remembered God's saving deeds done through Moses as they left Egypt and passed through the Red Sea, they believed that those mysteries in the past became present for them again. The past became present and led them out to a new future. When Jesus transformed the Passover meal, he was saying, "When you remember me in my acts of living, dying, and rising, those past mysteries become present."

Why, in general, did Jesus choose a meal for this gift of the Eucharist? Because through meals, ancient peoples internalized mystery. They took the mystery, in a sense, inside of them. When we celebrate the Eucharist, we become one in the mystery of life, death, and resurrection with Jesus and with one another.

As Paul says, Jesus handed on to us what was handed on to him. On the night before he died, Jesus took bread. After he had given thanks, he took it and said, "This is my body for you. Do this in memory of me. This is my body and blood. Do this in remembrance of me." Does Jesus want us to repeat the Eucharist? Does he want it to become a staple for our spiritual diet? Yes. When he says "Do this in remembrance of me," I think he is speaking more broadly also. Jesus not only gave us his body and blood in the Eucharist and in the Good Friday through

Easter events. Jesus gave his body and blood, his very self, in many ways during his public ministry—in his teaching, in his preaching, in his healing, in his foot washing. In his service to others, Jesus always gave his very self and his life force to others. Jesus wants us to give our very selves. Jesus wants us to give our life force. Jesus wants us to give our body and blood to one another.

Mothers certainly give their body and blood as they carry their children, give them birth, and raise them with their spouses. Fathers give their body and blood to their children in work, service, and love. Spouses ideally give their body and blood, their very selves, to each other in the ongoing deepening intimacy of marriage. Pastoral leaders, people in ministry, volunteer ministers in a parish—all give their body and blood in service of others. So many people in their professions give of their body and blood for others: teachers, those in the medical profession, soldiers who give their lives for their values and their nation. Ordinary people often go to work not with the agenda of just making a salary but being of service to one other. Many people with heightened consciousness give their body and blood to and for one another.

On this Feast of the Body and Blood of Christ, are we conscious of giving our body and blood for the well-being of our fellow person? The Eucharist is not a holy thing to be observed and adored. The Eucharist, as we celebrate it, is prayerful activity and worship with a community of people. As Augustine once said, "Be who you are, Body of Christ; become what you eat, Body of Christ." The Eucharist is spiritual food. It transforms us into the living Body of Christ. But the Eucharist is also, in a real sense, a *way of life*. The way of life is all of us trying to give of our whole selves to one another in love and service.

Some forces at work in our world keep us from holistic, adequate Eucharistic celebration and Eucharistic living. For some people in this consumer culture, their goals in life are very self-centered. They want to achieve success and material resources for themselves. They do not much care about giving their body and blood for others. Robert Putnam, in his works *Bowling Alone* and *Better Together*, has talked about the breakdown of community in Western society. Many people live individualized, isolated lives. Their lifestyles are contrary to the notion of becoming the Body of Christ in the world.

Time magazine ran an article on another subject that perhaps deters people from Eucharistic celebration and living: the scandals that have rocked the Church for the past ten years. The article said that even a solidly Catholic nation like Ireland is at a point of saying to Church leaders, "There is no longer a need for the kind of church that the Catholic Church has become." Parishes need to really work at overcoming these obstacles to Eucharistic celebration and living and invite people to the mystery of the Eucharist.

In the gospel we hear a story that is traditionally interpreted as Jesus multiplying the loaves and fish. The setting is one where Jesus has healed and taught over five thousand people. The apostles are concerned that the people are getting tired, hungry, and thirsty. They encourage Jesus to send the people off so that they can find lodging and buy food. Jesus insists on a kind of immediacy in response to the people's needs. He challenges the apostles to do something to feed and care for the crowd themselves. The apostles maintain that they have only five loaves and two fish. Again we are told that there are at least five thousand men in this gathering. Jesus encourages the apostles to have them sit down. He takes the loaves and the fish, raises his eyes to heaven, says a blessing, and gives them to the disciples to distribute to the crowd. All had their fill. In fact, there were twelve baskets of fragments left over.

What was at the core or essence of this miracle of Jesus? Did he multiply the five loaves and the two fish literally, or did the people indeed have resources with them that perhaps they were hoarding for themselves? Was the miracle that Jesus effected here a miracle of getting people to break out of self-sufficiency and self-concern to genuinely become community, sharing blessed, prayed-over food with one another? Whatever the nature of the miracle, this story is certainly a prefigurement of the Eucharist. It was a celebration of sacred and human presence to each other. It was a celebration of people becoming connected with each other and with God, and indeed it was a life lesson—one that would become clarified at the Last Supper. In memory of Jesus, we are always to share our body and blood, our true selves, with each other. To celebrate this great feast, let us get a feeling for the expansiveness of the Eucharist. Let no liturgical reforms objectify the Eucharist and turn it into a holy thing that causes people to feel unworthy or distant. May this Feast of the Body and Blood of Christ remind us of our need for this spiritual food and challenge us to give our whole self for the life of the world around us.

ASH WEDNESDAY

As I asked myself the questions of what I want to do for Lent and what I want to say on Ash Wednesday, some words spontaneously jumped into my mind. They are the words of the Lord's Prayer. During Lent, I encourage us to live the Lord's Prayer.

God, hallowed be your name . . .

Let these days that we begin together be times of praise and thanks. Let us become conscious of the wonders of creation, and the many blessings and gifts that God has shared with us. Let us be people of thanks, for praise and thanks are signs and indicators of a converting heart—signs and indicators of a person striving to become more God-centered.

Your Kingdom come . . .

The reign of God is what Jesus was most about.

Let us take these days and try to understand more deeply and live more intensely the attitudes, values, and behaviors that are God's reign.

Your will be done . . .

That is a scary request. It is much more comfortable that we live out of our own wills. But God's will is always the way to truth, the way to peace, the way to love. We can know God's will through greater attention to God. This Lent, let us pray for the knowledge and the courage to do God's will.

Give us our daily bread . . .

Let us turn to God for what we need, but in terms of material things, let us not be greedy or stockpile resources for ourselves. Let us become more concerned about daily bread for people who are victims of injustice.

Forgive us our trespasses . . .

Through our own devotion and prayer, through the penitential rite of the Mass, through the Sacrament of Reconciliation, let us go to God in sorrow and contrition, seeking God's forgiveness. God's forgiveness is always available for us.

As we forgive those who trespass against us . . .

Let these be days when we truly study and try to put in practice the abundant research that is now available on forgiveness. In forgiving others, let us liberate those who have hurt us from guilt and shame. Let us liberate ourselves, with the help of God, from anger, anxiety, and depression.

Lead us not into temptation . . .

To be tempted is to become conscious of choices in life that lead us away from God's will. To be tempted is to be seduced into false security, false happiness—seduced into sin, which is missing the mark in life. Let us pray for wisdom, that we might understand and know when, indeed, we are being tempted.

Deliver us from evil . . .

Sin is real. Let us become more and more conscious of the patterns of sin within and around us. Let us strive to live in an environment of grace and love.

We can find some direction for Lent in the model prayer, the Lord's Prayer. We find further instructions for our Lenten journey in the Scriptures.

Joel teaches us that we are to rend our hearts. Lent is a time to go into our hearts, to go into the deepest part of ourselves, and to engage in activities that are spiritually therapeutic, that restore and renew spirit within us. Let us not be afraid or reluctant to go into the deepest part of ourselves this Lent.

"Be reconciled!" Paul shouts to us from 2 Corinthians. We should be reconciled to God, if any distance has emerged between God and ourselves. This is a time to try to close that gap.

God is always available to us for reconciliation, but reconciliation demands that at least two parties do the work of growing closer. We must attend to our relationship with God and, as I said earlier, try to make it more the central relationship of our lives.

Lent is a time also for us to look at our own personal relationships and to pray for the grace, wherever possible, to reconcile with other people from whom we are estranged, unless doing so would cause greater harm or danger.

Jesus gives us, in Matthew, the three principal tools for the Lenten journey. He calls us to *almsgiving*, to deeds of charity and mercy toward our fellow person, to deeds of justice toward our fellow person.

He calls us to *fasting*. Fasting can be understood in a broad sense. To fast is to engage in some sort of discipline—doing or perhaps not doing some thing or things that might result in growth, that might allow God to transform us.

Prayer: Each one of us must find our own unique style for praying. But Lent is a time to try to find more time, more room to enter into communion with the power and the Spirit of God.

What unique spiritual program this Lent will take each of us to the deepest part of ourselves, our hearts; that will help us confront sin and turn away from it; that will help us be reconciled to God and one another; and that will help us live the Lord's Prayer?

The ashes we use today remind us of our own mortality. All of us live in terms of the horizon of death—our own and that of the people we love. If we begin with the end in mind, as Stephen Covey encourages us to do, let us keep in mind that the end is our own physical death, and our hoping to go on to eternal life.

Let Lent become a call to us to greater integrity, wholeness, and wellness. May Lenten ashes challenge us to become better disciples, or learners, of Jesus Christ.

Let us take a moment to try to define or name what ashes are calling us to this Lent.

HUNGERS AND THIRSTS

Cathleen Falsani, a freelance writer for the Chicago *Sun Times*, wrote a touching article titled, "Moving Is Much More Than Packing Up the Furniture." Falsani and her family, she said, are among 20 million who will move to a new place, a new home, this summer. She speaks of the process of moving as the quest to create and find a new home—a haven, a sanctuary, a place of love that is warm, welcoming, and safe. For some months now, I've been in the pursuit of a new home. Though I have chosen working at the Clare and working at St. Thomas the Apostle, things do not feel like home yet. Home is a psychological, spiritual experience. Home is a network of relationships. It takes time for home to emerge.

I don't like "new." I like things the way they were, the way they are. Falsani said in her article that moving is one of the most stressful things that people engage in, along with getting married and divorce. I can attest to that. In these months of getting ready to move, moving, and now post-move, I have felt a lot of anxiety and I have experienced a lot of grief. When I get anxious or upset, I go into a unique pattern: I lose my appetite. I can be even physically hungry, but I have an aversion to eating. Though my appetite is not good, this period of anxiety and grief has made me aware of some profound hungers and thirsts.

In the midst of moving, I am hungry and thirsty for inner peace in the face of some of the anxiety and stress that I feel. I am hungry and thirsty for hope in the midst of the grieving I am going through. I am hungry and thirsty for the resolution of grief, which is the ability to remember loss with less pain. I am hungry and thirsty for the presence and assurance of the Holy Spirit of God. I am hungry and thirsty for new life to come from the life, death, and resurrection process. I am hungry and thirsty to feel at home, to have a new faith home. I am hungry and thirsty for community. I am hungry and thirsty for old relationships, seasoned friendships—people with whom I do not have as much contact as I once did. And I am hungry and thirsty for the birth of new relationships. I am hungry and thirsty for support. I am hungry and thirsty for friendship, mentoring, and guidance. I am hungry and thirsty for a sense of meaning and purpose. I am hungry and thirsty for healing.

I am hungry and thirsty for fewer psychosomatic symptoms. I am hungry and thirsty for more energy when I get physically depleted. I am hungry and thirsty for the ability to concentrate more. I am hungry and thirsty for a new spirit and attitude of surrender, of being able to let go and let God.

In this period of anxiety and grieving, in this period of poor appetite for food, I am getting in touch with deep hungers and thirsts that reside deep in my heart, deep in my spirit.

Let us reflect on John 6, Jesus's famous bread-of-life discourse. John 6 says to all of us that, somehow, the deepest hungers and thirsts of the human heart are satisfied and quenched through the person, ministry, and teaching of Jesus. He is food for our souls. Often, as the apostles articulate in John 6:1–15, and as Elisha's servant does in 2 Kings, we are conscious of our scarcity—that we do not have enough food or resources for our hungers and thirsts. Jesus and Elisha teach us that, in and through God, an abundance of resources is available to satisfy that for which we are most painfully hungry and thirsty.

Thomas Groome, the great religious educator from Boston College, has said in his teaching and writing that what Jesus taught about the reign of God—that way of life, that new vision of God, that new set of convictions and values—is really the satisfaction of the heart's deepest hungers and thirsts.

I have shared with you some of my hungers and thirsts. At this point in your lives, what might you be hungry and thirsty for, psychologically and spiritually? One of the messages of the gospel is to go to Jesus and ask for his help with our deep hungers and thirsts.

Besides the emotional and spiritual hungers that we sometimes feel, there are more physically hungry people in the world than ever. According to the UN Food and Agricultural Organization, one-sixth of the planet's population is going hungry. Those who suffer the most are in the developing world; 642 million people are malnourished in Asia and the Pacific. Among the developed countries, some 15 million people go wanting in the richest countries of the world. The hunger crisis is due to the global economic slowdown coupled with persistently high food prices. This situation has pushed some 100 million more people into chronic hunger and poverty this year. As we go to Jesus for help with some of our interior hungers, the bread-of-life discourse also challenges us to greater solidarity with those who are actually physically hungry.

One way to support the hungry and poor is to become part of the Catholics Confront Global Poverty movement, a Catholic Relief Services and U.S. Conference of Catholic Bishops program. Catholics Confront Global Poverty is an awareness, action, and prayer program. This national effort is seeking Catholics to sign up on the Internet to indicate solidarity with the poor. Those who sign make a commitment to engage in one or some of the following activities: prayer, education, advocacy, and action. As we become more aware of the poverty and hunger in our world and in our own nation, let us do our best to express solidarity with those hungry and poor.

Back to moving: Cathleen Falsani found a prayer that she used for her move. It's called "*A Prayer for New Beginnings,*" and it speaks of the anxiety and hope that come with moving to a new home. I include the prayer:

A Prayer for New Beginnings

God of new beginnings, we are walking into mystery.
We face the future, not knowing what the days and months
    will bring us or how we will respond.
Be love in us as we journey.
May we welcome all who come our way.
Deepen our faith to see all life through your eyes.
Fill us with hope and an abiding trust that you dwell in us
    amidst all our joys and sorrows.

Thank you for the treasure of our faith life.
Thank you for the gift of being able to rise each day with
the assurance of your walking through the day with us.
God of our past and future, we praise you.
Amen.

THE BATH OF REBIRTH

In Titus 2, Paul writes that Jesus "saved us through the bath of rebirth." The bath of rebirth is what Baptism was for the first Christians. For the first three centuries of Christianity, as the Catechumenate or the Rite of Christian Initiation of Adults developed, those who were interested in becoming followers of Jesus took a very disciplined journey toward conversion of mind, heart, and behavior. The original Catechumenate involved evangelization, catechesis, exorcism, anointing, and worship. It resulted in this bath of rebirth that took place at the Easter Vigil. Those being baptized were plunged into water three times. They were baptized in the name of the Father, and of the Son, and of the Holy Spirit. The plunges were timed with the mention of each person of the Trinity. Scholars tell us that, three times, people were held down in the water, simulating or giving the feeling of drowning. What the Church intended was for the baptized to feel they were dying to one way of life and rising to another. As they rose from these waters of rebirth, they were given a white garment and a lit candle, and were anointed with chrism as a sign of the new life begun in and through Christ. By the fourth century, the Catechumenate was already in decline. Constantine had made Christianity the religion of the empire. No longer was work done on conversion. People were baptized en masse, without scrutiny or discernment about whether a life change or growth in discipleship had taken place. The Church increasingly took on an institutional motif. Baptisms multiplied, while conversion became minimized.

As Augustine and others emphasized the doctrine of original sin and the need to baptize infants in the face of widespread disease and death among children, Baptism morphed into a sacrament for infants. The life change, the death to one way of life and resurrection to another, fell by the wayside. Baptism became the sacrament that saved children, erasing original sin and promising heaven for children who might die. Without Baptism, they would be relegated to another experience called limbo.

As sacraments evolved and emerged in Catholic tradition and culture, they unfortunately became holy things that people received. We lost the original meaning of *sacramentum* that Tertullian, one of the Church fathers, encouraged. Sacramentum was borrowed from the Roman military. It meant vow or pledge. Soldiers took a sacramentum to Caesar. In the early Church, Baptism, Chrismation (which became Confirmation), and Eucharist were each a sacramentum, or a vow or a pledge to live in a covenant with God through Jesus in the context of Christian community. Augustine's theology of sacrament as a sign of something happening to individuals beyond observation and appearance began to prevail.

Many of us grew up with this form of sacramental theology. I have heard that in Irish culture, sometimes the parents of an infant would not even go to the church for the Baptism. The godparents took the child. The notion of home as domestic church and parents as the pastors of their children certainly disappeared.

Not until the Second Vatican Council mandated that the Rite of Christian Initiation of Adults be restored did we began to retrieve the catechumenal spirituality of Baptism. A temporary rite was produced in 1974. I remember trying to do the RCIA at St. Hubert's using a manual that was in Latin. In 1988 the norms for how to do catechumenal ministry were established for North America by the Bishops of North America; we still operate out of those norms.

I mention this history and this theology on the Feast of the Baptism of the Lord. The Baptism of the Lord by John the Baptist provides us with an opportunity to reflect on the meaning of our own baptisms. Many evangelical Protestant churches still emphasize the importance of saving Baptism for adults. As Roman Catholics, we are a two-track church. We still baptize infants, but the baptism of adults has become normative for us again. The steps of the Catechumenate of evangelization, catechesis, proximate preparation, vowing, and mystagogia, or follow-up after sacramental celebration, have become normative for preparing for all of the sacraments.

What happened to you and me when we were baptized? First, we were given a relationship with the Trinity. We were baptized in the name of the Father, and of the Son, and of the Holy Spirit. We were not baptized so much into the immanent or theoretical, abstract Trinity. We were baptized into the economic Trinity or the experiential Trinity. The Trinity is an experience that we live. Baptism has given us a relationship with God, our Parent and Creator, and a relationship with Jesus, whom Paul reminds us has saved us. Baptism brings us a special imparting of the Holy Spirit. We never walk alone in life, because we have been baptized into the Spirit of God.

Paul adds in Titus that in Baptism we receive the hope of eternal life. We were baptized into the life, death, and resurrection of Jesus, immersed in the mystery. We live that experience of life, death, and new life over and over again throughout a lifetime until we are called home to God; and then we pass from death to eternal life. Baptism was a bath of rebirth into existential meaning for life.

We are told that when Jesus was baptized, the people around him heard the voice of God saying, "You are my beloved Son." I think similar words were spoken over each of us and all of us when we were baptized. I think God said to us through the ritual of the sacrament, "You are my beloved." Baptism has given us such a positive self-image, such great dignity, such great importance. We are God's beloved. That ought not to give us any false pride, but rather great feelings of self-worth. There are so many experiences, institutions, and patterns of sin in daily living that rob people of the dignity that they were given at Baptism.

I believe that God's words, "You are my beloved," really are spoken over all people whether they are baptized or not. The Sacrament of Baptism reminds us of the lovability, the importance of every individual. Having been baptized, we have a responsibility to treat all human beings as God's beloved and work for renewal and justice that all human beings be seen and experienced as God's beloved.

Our Baptisms were not just Baptisms into God. We believe that the Spirit of God resides in relationships and in community, so Baptism also was an immersion into the reign of God as it is embodied in the Church, in communities of faith. We have been baptized into a universal Church that tries to foster communion and connection worldwide. We have also been baptized into local churches that we are a part of as we grow and age. We are baptized into Small Christian Communities, small cells of church. We are baptized into the domestic church, which is the home.

The Baptism of Jesus began Jesus's mission to the world, to transform the world more and more into God's reign. Baptism for each of us has also sent us on a mission. In fact, each sacrament that we celebrate missions us out to the world to be agents of change and transformation for the world of which we are a part. We are to do our part; we are to use our gifts to help with the emergence of the reign of God.

Isaiah 40–55 is called the book of Consolation. The chapters were written to give comfort to the Jewish people in exile in Babylon, announcing that their liberation and renewal were forthcoming. Isaiah 40 reads, "Comfort, give comfort to my people, says your God." Every year when I directed the Office for Chicago Catholic Evangelization, we had a conference called Comfort My People Day based on Isaiah 40. The purpose of the day was to bring comfort to African American Catholics who were dealing with the struggles, the violence, and the poverty of inner-city life. Today, as we celebrate the Baptism of the Lord and recall and appreciate our own baptism, God extends to you and to me great comfort in that we have been given the bath of rebirth. Let that bath of rebirth influence us daily, and let us always try to transform the faith communities that we are part of into truly catechumenal communities founded on the bath of rebirth.

MOTIVATION

We all know of people who have gotten into ways of life for the wrong reasons. A person can begin a role or career with good motivation, and then allow it to deteriorate into something problematic. Some priests become ordained, and some become too comfortable with the trappings of clericalism or hierarchy. The privilege of the role and power can begin to corrupt the priest. The comforts of rectory life make some priests too comfortable—and underwhelmed. Some people enter political life with great promise, offering people hope or a changed world. Sometimes such people let go of dreams and ideals, and become satisfied and gratified, again with power, or financial gain. People who enter the field of crime prevention and the protection of people can become accustomed to wielding excessive aggression or violence toward others.

James and John are rather above board in their motivation as they talk about their future roles with Jesus. They want to be at his right and left hands when his kingdom comes to fruition, when he enters into glory—both of them probably still misunderstanding the mission of the reign of God. James and John want privileged positions with Jesus. They want power. They want to be able to lord it over others. Jesus reverses the expectation of James, John, and the other apostles. Jesus says that anyone who wants to be his follower must have the motivation of a servant. Jesus equates service with greatness, reminding his followers that he did not come to be served, but to serve and to give his life as a ransom for many.

This theme of self-sacrificing love and service is found also in Isaiah. There are four servant songs in Deutero-Isaiah: 42:1–7; 49:1–7; 50:4–9; and 52:13–53:12. It is unclear who the suffering servant is in Isaiah—Isaiah himself or the whole nation of Israel—but the theology of the passage is that the servant gives his life for the well-being of others, and through his suffering "justifies many." The servant, through his suffering, brings new life to others.

A similar theme is stressed in the letter to the Hebrews. The Jewish notion of sacrifice is implicit in Hebrews. The ritual of Jewish sacrifice is something that connected the people with God. In giving of himself as sacrifice, Jesus is depicted as leading the entire human family to oneness with God. Jesus is referred to as a high priest who can identify with our weakness because he himself has been tested. For years, in parish work, I stressed the image of servant leadership as being the proper motivation of a disciple of Jesus Christ who is trying to live the reign of God.

We have a wonderful example of this type of servant leadership in a man who was recently canonized a saint: St. Damien, the Leper. Born Jozef De Veuster in Belgium, Damien would pray each day before a picture of St. Francis Xavier, the patron saint of missions and missionaries. All that Damien ever wanted to do was to be a missionary who helped people; however, he was judged to not be intellectually fit to be a priest. He became a lay brother. When a person who was being sent as a missionary to Hawaii fell ill and was unable to go, the religious order approached Damien; he went to the island of Molokai as a lay brother. Damien eventually was ordained a priest. At the time, Hawaii was a kingdom, and the king of Hawaii quarantined all people with diseases like leprosy, or Hansen's disease, on the island of Molokai. Damien gave his life in dedication to caring for the outcasts of society, namely the lepers. Not only did Damien take care of the pastoral and sacramental needs of the residents of Molokai, he built houses for the lepers, he ran schools and educational centers, he opened an orphanage, he made coffins, and he dug graves.

After spending significant time with the lepers of Molokai, Damien contracted the disease himself and died in the late nineteenth century. The story goes that one day after he had been diagnosed with leprosy, he introduced himself to his leprous community as "we lepers." He totally identified with the plight of the people he served, in a spirit of selfless service. This man, who was deemed unacceptable to be a priest, became a servant to the poorest of the poor. He was an extremely dynamic man in doing his servant work for the residents of Molokai. As he was dying, he wisely found a team of people who would take over after his death and continue his work. Damien the Leper, a servant leader, died at age forty-nine.

Some of us work full-time in the church. Some of us have stepped forward to respond to the baptismal call we all have for ministry—many in an unpaid, volunteer role. Many of you go to work each day, whether church work or secular work. Many of you care for loved ones and families. God's Word reminds us that in all matters, our motivation must be to serve. We lead by service.

I quote Stephen Covey frequently. He is the author of *The 7 Habits of Highly Effective People* and *The Eighth Habit*. *The Eighth Habit* is a book about discovering what Covey calls "voice." Voice is a convergence of getting in touch with one's gifts and one's passion. Voice is getting in touch with conscience, or the voice of God speaking within us. People discover voice, then bring gifts, passion, and conscience to bear on real-life needs surrounding them. Covey laments that few people live their lives this way. Many Americans, many consumers around the world, are motivated by a desire for wealth, the accumulation of resources, to be the best at what they do, or to separate themselves from their fellow person—either by rank or the amount of resources that one may have.

Covey says that other people go through life simply trying to make a buck. They are not in tune at all with the realities of gifts, passion, conscience, or needs. In late adolescence or early adulthood, such people get on a career track and just keep walking, trying to be relatively comfortable in life, paying one's bills. Research has shown that all any of us needs is material sufficiency. We do not need abundance to be happy. Covey contends that people would find happiness if they were more deliberate and intentional about trying to discover this reality of voice—the convergence of gifts, passion, conscience, and need. Living out of voice helps people experience much more fulfilling lives.

When I was the pastor at Holy Family, we had a process in the parish called Gifted. For years we tried to help thousands of people discover their voice. We tried to help people marry their gifts, passion, and conscience to the needs of the community. Many people over the years reported what a countercultural experience Gifted was. They said, "I always knew what was *wrong* with me. I never took the time to ask the questions: 'What's good about me? How am I blessed? How am I gifted?' I was blind for years to the needs that were around me." Through the Gifted process, many people were helped to engage in that convergence that is the discovery of voice. God's Word challenges us—in our ministry work, our day-to-day work, our interactions with our families, and our interactions with people in general—to seek only to be servants. In serving, we are to work for the common good and the glory of God. Such purified motivation in all that we do would certainly help with the emergence of what Jesus meant by the reign of God.

Why do we do the things we do? The answer that Jesus, Isaiah, and the letter to the Hebrews pushes us toward is that we do what we do so that we might be servants.

A Creed

We believe in one God, a God who is beyond gender.

We believe that God is the Creator of the universe, the Creator of multi-verses, who holds all things in balance.

We believe that God is the Loving Parent of us all, who has intended that each one of us come to life.

We believe that God, our Loving Parent, loves each of us, and all of us, unconditionally. We believe that God cares for us with a providential love, and that God, our loving Creator and Parent, works all things for our benefit.

We believe that this God transcends us, is mystery.

We believe that we will never completely understand, nor can we control, this God, but we believe also that this God is immanent, with us in all aspects and experiences of our lives.

We believe in Jesus Christ.

We believe in the reign of God, which was, and is, his central mission.

We believe in what He taught, that only God can be God, and that we need to build our lives on the foundation of a relationship with God.

We believe that Jesus is the human face of God. The way Jesus was and is the way the God of mystery is.

We believe that our God, like Jesus, is loving, merciful, forgiving, and just..

We believe that Jesus calls us to imitate the love, mercy, forgiveness, and justice of God.

We believe that Jesus is the model human being. We believe that He is the fulfillment of the evolution of the human family. We believe that the human family is now striving to be like Jesus, the model person.

We believe that Jesus calls us to connection, to communion, with each other and with God.

We believe that Jesus has revealed the essence of the mystery of existence, and that is the paschal mystery. We believe that He has revealed that life is passage-like in nature. We believe that He taught that we constantly are living, dying, and rising to new life during our days on earth; and we believe in his promise, revealed to us at Easter and in his ascension, that through the experience of physical death, we pass over to eternal life. We believe that heaven is essentially a mystery that we cannot know a lot about, but we believe that it is eternity with God, with all who have preceded us in death, and with those who will remain here after we die. We believe in this communion of saints.

We believe in the Holy Spirit.

We believe in the presence of God in our lives.

We believe in the sacramental principle, that God's presence is shot through all of existence.

We believe in the power of God at work in our lives.

We believe in the presence of the Risen Christ at work in our lives.

We believe that the Spirit is how we experience God.

We believe that when we pray for the Spirit to fill us, we tap into wisdom, peace, understanding, insight, compassion, and justice that are beyond our human powers.

We believe that it is the Holy Spirit that connects us with our fellow person.

We believe that we share in the power and presence of God.

We believe that each one of us has been given a manifestation of the Spirit for some benefit.

We believe in the Body of Christ, the Church.

That is, we believe in ourselves.

We believe WE are called to help with the emergence of God's reign, in imitation of Jesus.

We believe that through the Eucharist and the other sacraments we are connected with Catholic Christians throughout the world.

We believe that the reformers in our tradition spoke and speak truth to a Church whose leaders did not and do not want to listen.

We believe that Christ is calling us to ecumenism, to a new experience of oneness with those Christians who are not Roman Catholic.

We believe that there is truth to be found in the religions of the world that are non-Christian, and that all of these spiritualities are attempts to articulate what Jesus meant by the reign of God.

We believe that Jesus Christ will come again, and lead the human family to the completion of God's plan for the human family.

We believe that God—Abba, Savior, and Spirit—are life-changing realities.

When we give our hearts, minds, and total selves to these three different experiences of God, our lives are dramatically changed. We can find meaning and purpose for every aspect of being human if and as we live the Trinity.

Delusion versus Mutuality

If I were to tell you that God spoke to me today, or that I spoke with God, you might suspect that I was having delusions or hallucinations, indicative of psychosis. Yet the ability to hear God speaking and to speak to God is at the core of our faith. As Catholic Christians we believe that we can have a relationship of mutuality between ourselves and God. I especially want to focus here on how God speaks to us.

The readings this week are about God's Word. Deutero-Isaiah, the second part of the book of Isaiah, is addressed to the Jewish people still in captivity in Babylon. God, speaking through the prophet, describes his word that goes forth from his mouth. God says his word shall not return void. His word shall do his will, achieving the end for which he sent his word.

We believe in revelation. Revelation is that aspect of our Christian tradition which holds that God is not distant, remote, and noncommunicative. God is always manifesting himself to us and to people around the world. But God's Word is not spoken in a direct, concrete way that could be interpreted as delusional or hallucination-like. God's Word is often spoken indirectly. God's Word is mediated through human experiences. I believe that God sometimes speaks to us through our thoughts. God speaks to us through our feelings. God speaks to us through physical experiences that we have.

We will not begin to hear God's Word or interpret it if we do not engage first in an activity that positive psychology has come to call mindfulness. *Mindfulness* is making space and time to get in touch with our inner worlds, to get in touch with thoughts and feelings. Mindfulness necessitates, at times, solitude and deep listening to the self. Eugene Gendlin started a movement many years ago he called Focusing. Gendlin's work encouraged people to make time and space each day to get in touch with thoughts and feelings. Thoughts, feelings, and physical sensations all can be preludes to an encounter with the divine.

God can speak through other people. God can speak through human experiences. I think that when God communicates with us, we have a felt sense of that in our minds and in our hearts. We have a felt sense that we have just encountered more than meets the eye. For many years I have produced materials for Small Christian Communities. One of the first steps that people took in the small communities that I directed at Holy Family was the step of sharing "God sightings." God sightings referred to momentary encounters with God, glimpses of God that people had since their last small group meeting. Small-community members were encouraged to talk about the experiences of their lives in recent days, what was going on in the news, what was going on in the parish, their neighborhoods, or their families. The exercise of focusing on God sightings very much put people in a posture of attending to God's presence in everyday human experience.

God speaks to us through experiences we have within us—interior experiences. God speaks to us in relationships and events. God speaks to us in community, in and through our connections with fellow believers. We believe as Catholic Christians that God speaks to us through God's scriptural word. As Catholics, we are not literalists or fundamentalists when it comes to the Scriptures. We do not interpret all of the books of the Bible as literal, historical truth. Catholics are contextualists. A contextualist tries to get inside a piece of Scripture to analyze when it was written, why it was written, by whom, and what the historical situation was when the passage was written, as well as other contextual issues.

Contextualists engage in two movements in reading, studying, or listening to Scripture. The first movement is *exegesis*. Exegesis is a kind of scientific method. It is a movement backward to uncover contextual issues. After gathering some wisdom about a particular passage of Scripture, contextualists make a movement forward; that is called *hermeneutics*. What does this passage of Scripture say to us today in our present situation?

Quality Scripture study and interpretation necessitate these movements of exegesis and hermeneutics. Hermeneutics is a kind of art form. It is the ability to interpret Scripture for our own day. When we experience the Liturgy of the Word together, if the proclamation of Scripture, attending to Scripture, and preaching on Scripture all work together, the community worshiping can experience a jump of the imagination. That jump of the imagination is an intuition of incarnation and revelation, a sense that God is present, God is alive in the human story, God is speaking to me, God is speaking to us: "I hear a message from God in this experience of Scripture." To not approach Scripture in this way is at times to engage the Scriptures and miss the forest for the trees.

How can people engage in this contextual approach to the Scriptures, to God's word? There are two instruments that I would like to recommend. First, have a good Catholic edition of the Bible with good footnotes and good introductions to the various books of the Bible. I strongly recommend the *Catholic Study Bible*, which is a version of the *New American Bible*. It is very helpful in aiding people to engage in exegesis. Another helpful instrument is the *Jerome Biblical Commentary*. I would recommend the most current edition, titled the *New Jerome Biblical Commentary*. This is a rather expensive book, but I think we need to ask ourselves, "What do we value?" If we say hearing and experiencing God's Word is important to us, then I think we should buy for our loved ones and our homes tools that help us encounter God's Word and understand it in meaningful ways.

Many different periodicals can help with hermeneutics or interpretation. Two that I find helpful are a weekly article on the weekend's readings in *America* magazine, a Jesuit publication, and the *National Catholic Reporter*, which has a reflection on the Sunday readings each week.

In some parishes where I have worked or done consultation, thousands of people have engaged in the experience of Small Christian Communities. Many of these groups were lectionary-based, that is, they discussed and prayed about the Sunday readings that were coming up the following weekend. Many of those good people went to Mass on the weekends having already studied, prayed, and talked about the Sunday readings. The Liturgy of the Word at Mass became a much more meaningful experience for them, almost becoming the cherry on the sundae, the fulfillment of prayer and work that they had done individually and in community during the week.

The Book of the Prophet Isaiah is broken up into three distinct sections. First-Isaiah constitutes chapters 1–39. These chapters seem to have been written by the original Prophet Isaiah. Deutero-Isaiah makes up chapters 40–55. They were written by an anonymous author in Isaiah's tradition to bring comfort and hope to the Jewish people in exile in Babylon. This section is frequently called the Book of Consolation. Trito-Isaiah makes up chapters 56–66. These seem to have been written some years later by a school of people in Isaiah's tradition. Let us keep in mind whenever we hear chapters 40–55, often a message of hope is being spoken to us, especially if we are feeling exiled or troubled in some way. Paul, in Romans, addresses the problems of struggle, suffering, and death. Paul articulates the Christian hope and conviction that all of life's struggles are moving toward new life here on earth and eternal life on the other side of death. Paul writes, "All creation is groaning in labor pains . . . as we await the redemption of our bodies."

Jesus uses the imagery of seed and ground to speak of the Word of God. Jesus is teaching that God is in an ongoing process of self-revelation, sowing seeds of self-communication in each of our lives. Jesus states that sometimes the ground is receptive to seed, takes it in, and produces fruit—the ground being us. But sometimes the ground is not receptive to the seed of God's Word, and God's revelation is not fruitful in the lives of such people. I know it is very easy for me when the message of God's Word is comforting to take in that word of comfort, but when God's Word is challenging—calling me away from sin or unhealthy attitudes or behavior, calling me to greater, bigger investment regarding charity or justice—sometimes I am slower to take in God's challenging Word. Keep in mind that we believe that Jesus Christ is the *Verbum Dei*. Jesus is the Word of God spoken to the human family. We need to listen to and attend to Jesus's teachings, Jesus's miracles, Jesus's revelation about the reign of God. God speaks powerfully through his Son, Jesus. Let us take on the posture this week, "Speak, Lord, your servant is listening."

Corpus Christi

When I was growing up in the 1950s and early 1960s, that's what the feast was called: *Corpus Christi*—Latin for "the body of Christ." This feast focuses on the gift that is the Eucharist.

Back when some of us were children, there were processions around the neighborhood, inside the parish church—with the pastor or associate pastor at the end of the procession with a monstrance, carrying the Blessed Sacrament. This day and its traditional festivities were oriented toward showing reverence to the real presence of Christ in the Eucharist. I was and I am an advocate for Catholic devotion. I was influential in creating a Eucharistic Adoration Chapel at the parish where I served as pastor for fourteen years. Many people came to that chapel for quiet prayer, meditation, and contemplation. All of these activities have great value, joined to the celebration of the Eucharist in community.

But back in those old days, and now, we run the risk of engaging in mistaken notions and behavior regarding the Eucharist. As I said earlier, I am an advocate for devotion that complements the Eucharist: Eucharistic adoration, Benediction. But we must beware that we do not treat the Eucharist as if it is a holy thing to be looked at from afar. One of the problems that the Catholic Church has is that too many people have turned all the sacraments into holy things that they observe, look at, take, or receive. In rendering sacraments holy things, we rob them of their evangelical and conversion power. The original meaning of *sacramentum*, before it meant "sign," was "vow" or "pledge." The early Christians engaged in a process, a journey of conversion, that we now call the Rite of Christian Initiation of Adults, which resulted in the threefold sacramental celebration of what we now call Baptism, Confirmation, and Eucharist. Rather than acquiring holy things, our ancestors in faith engaged in conversion that resulted in sacramental moments. The sacraments were, and should be now, celebrations of conversion.

Rather than a thing, I prefer to experience the Eucharist as action or activity. When we gather as a community for the Eucharist, we experience together a memorial meal. The Jewish understanding of a memorial meal was that, in remembering a past sacred event, that sacred event became present again. When we celebrate the Eucharist we remember the life, death, and resurrection of Jesus. In remembering these sacred events, the past becomes present: his life, death, and resurrection are not simply historical events, but rather present realities.

When Jesus tells us that he is giving us his body and blood, he is saying that he is giving his very self to us. In each of our lives, our body and blood constitute our very selves. Through the action of the Eucharist, we encounter Jesus himself in the mystery of his living, dying, and rising. When we take the sacred food into ourselves, the consecrated bread and wine transformed into the real presence of Jesus, we become one with Jesus in the paschal mystery. Not only that, we become one with each other and one with disciples around the world who are celebrating the same holy meal. Not only do we receive Holy Communion, we *become* Holy Communion: with Jesus, the assembly, and disciples around the world. We become connected with those who have preceded us in death; we celebrate the communion of all saints. We should show great reverence to the consecrated bread and wine. We should not, however, reify the Eucharist. It is not a holy thing; it is a sacred, communal action and activity.

Let us turn again to the bread-of-life discourse from John 6. In the statement today from 6:51, Jesus says, "I am the Bread of Life; whoever eats this bread will live forever"; but earlier in 6:35 Jesus states, "I am the Bread of Life; whoever comes to me will never be hungry. Whoever believes in me will never thirst." Notice the movement in John's theology. We are to come to Jesus personally and communally in conversion and celebrate that life change by eating the holy meal.

Themes that we fail to develop sufficiently in talking about the Eucharist are *hunger* and *thirst*. These themes are spoken of beautifully in the book of Deuteronomy: "The Lord your God has directed all your journeying in the desert. . . . He therefore let you be afflicted with hunger, and then fed you with manna. . . . In order to show you that not by bread alone does one live, but by every word that comes forth from the mouth of the Lord. . . . Do not forget the Lord your God who brought you. . . . Out of that place of slavery; who guided you through the vast and terrible desert. . . . Who brought forth water for you. . . . And fed you in the desert with manna."

Some years ago, in his classic, *Christian Religious Education*, Thomas Groome spoke of the reign of God as the satisfaction of the heart's deepest hungers and thirsts. What are human beings' deepest hungers and thirsts? We are hungry and thirsty for meaning; we want to believe that there is deep-down purpose in the lives that we live. We are hungry and thirsty for love: God's love, love with each other, giving and receiving love. We are hungry and thirsty for significance. We want our lives to make a difference in the world. Life has to be more than a job and paycheck. We hunger and thirst for justice: commutative justice, honesty in all that we do; distributive justice, working so that the resources of the world are shared equally by all of God's people; social justice, working to change systems that abuse or dehumanize people. Jesus and his vision and lifestyle of the reign of God satisfy these and other deep, human hungers and thirsts.

If the reign of God satisfies these deep hungers and thirsts, the Eucharist is that sacred meal which celebrates and helps with the emergence of God's reign. In his book *Dining in the Kingdom of God*, Eugene LaVerdiere wrote that the Eucharist is a lived, prayed experience of the gospel, the reign of God. The Eucharist is like a booster shot of all that Jesus is and is about.

Nonetheless, we hear especially from younger people that they find the Eucharist boring or irrelevant. I think, at times, those of us responsible for the celebration of the Eucharist, on the level of appearances, rob the Eucharist of its passion and power. The Eucharist is presided over by older male celebrants who are often quite distant from the experiences of their parishioners. The music accompanying the Eucharist in some parishes is dreadful. The male dominance at the Eucharist robs those at worship of both a female and married perspective. The goal of Eucharistic preparation and celebration should be to help people have a religious experience as they celebrate the Eucharist. Unfortunately, in many faith communities this does not happen.

As I was driving to work one day, I was pushing buttons on the radio and came across Catholic Relevant Radio. Monsignor Michael Boland, the director of Catholic Charities in the Archdiocese of Chicago, was hosting a program on the problem of real, physical hunger in the Chicago metropolitan area. He spoke of the thousands of families and children who do not have adequate food in areas like Roseland, Englewood, and other neighborhoods on the south and west sides of the city. He and his guest, who also works at Catholic Charities, talked about the thousands of meals that their organization provides for thousands of poor, hungry people in the Archdiocese.

One of the most meaningful days I have had recently was to spend a day, along with other people who work in Franciscan communities, at an organization called Feed My Starving Children. As many other volunteers have done at this organization, we spent the day packing food for hungry people around the world. I left that place with the feeling that I truly did something meaningful and worthwhile that day. I encourage any of you who are called by God to engage in such service to check out this organization located in Aurora, Illinois, or perhaps in an area near you.

As we focus on the Eucharist as that which helps us with spiritual hungers and thirsts, let us remember that there are people quite proximate to us who are hungry. As Jesus feeds us, so also we should do something to feed people who are physically hungry and thirsty. Find out where the nearest Catholic Charities office is. Get the address and phone number, and share resources or time to feed the hungry.

Jesus wants us to care for the poor and hungry. It was he who said in Mark 8, "My heart is moved with pity for the crowd, because they . . . have nothing to eat."

Part 5

RELATIONSHIPS

FORGIVENESS AND DOUBT

I find it interesting that Jesus's first word from the cross as he died was about forgiveness. "Father, forgive them, for they know not what they do." We hear him talk about the same issue on the first Easter night, the evening of the resurrection. Unlike Luke, who has the Holy Spirit coming at Pentecost, John depicts Jesus imparting the Spirit on that first Easter night as he breathes on the disciples. Curiously, with the imparting of the Spirit comes a mission, and the mission is connected with forgiveness. The disciples are to speak of God's forgiveness toward the human family. They and we are to live and teach the importance of forgiveness among human beings, in relationships. Forgiveness was very important to Jesus and his vision of the reign of God. (I should mention that Jesus also says at this commissioning for forgiveness that if the disciples retain people's sins, they also will be retained. This is very similar to the notion of binding and loosing regarding sin in Matthew 18 and Matthew 16. Jesus is giving a larger mission to us, his disciples: to be a source of moral authority to the world around us. We are to speak out prophetically about things that we perceive to be sinful and wrong.)

As I have done research into forgiveness, both academically and with control groups during my doctoral dissertation, I discovered that forgiveness contributes to health. People who forgive lessen their anxiety, depression, and aggression. People who refuse to forgive have a tendency to grow in these realities.

Robert Enright is a psychologist who has made his life's work the study and promotion of forgiveness. He speaks of several phases in the forgiveness process, the first of which he calls *uncovering*. In the uncovering stage, people have to admit and confront they are in denial about the hurt. When we have been hurt, we have a tendency to say, "No big deal," perhaps to calm ourselves or delude ourselves that everything is okay. Enright says that when we get beyond the denial phase, we begin to admit how terribly hurt we are; then other emotions kick in: anger, hatred, and resentment. For a while, some of these things might be good to feel because they are signs that a person has some self-respect. But often in the uncovering stage, people begin to obsess about the hurt. They keep on playing the hurt over and over again in their minds. Eventually a person awakens to the fact that this position is not healthy.

The person then progresses to another phase, which is the stage of making a decision. *Deciding to forgive* is not forgiveness itself; however, it is a key step. The person, through deciding, moves in the direction of the third stage of forgiveness.

The *work phase* of forgiveness demands that we develop within ourselves empathy and understanding, not just generally, but very specifically. We need to develop empathy and understanding toward the specific person who has hurt us. We need to ask questions about the person who hurt us. What was his or her background? What was going on in that person's life at the time of the actual hurtful event? How might the person who hurt us actually be hurting himself or herself? After being hurt, there is a resistance to such empathy and understanding, but empathy and understanding are crucial if the process of forgiveness is to continue and progress. If the forgiving person can get into the skin, into the shoes of the person who has done the hurting, that facilitates the next step in this work of forgiveness, which is *absorbing the pain*, not needing to retaliate or hurt back. There follows then the *granting of forgiveness* as a free, altruistic gift. In fact, the person whom we are forgiving very well might not objectively deserve the forgiveness, but we give it nonetheless.

Forgiveness is expressed in many different ways. It might be directly communicated to the person who has hurt us, through an encounter. It might be sent in written form. Perhaps it is largely an intrapsychic experience in which we let go of our need to retaliate or hurt back. I think it is best when forgiveness is somehow communicated to the person we are forgiving. Often, with the granting of forgiveness, there begin some of the healthy benefits that come with the act of forgiveness.

In the *postforgiveness* or *deepening* phase, Enright says that several things happen. People perhaps engage more deeply in the work of forgiveness, sensing perhaps that some of the forgiveness they have engaged in so far has been superficial or pseudo-forgiveness. Forgiving people begin to experience themselves as people with the potential to hurt others. They begin to wonder who else should be forgiven or to whom should I or we be saying we are sorry for any hurt we may have caused others. Enright says that when we become serious about forgiveness, forgiveness begins to become part of a person's philosophy of life or vision and strategy for life.

On the night of his resurrection, Jesus commissioned us to be people of forgiveness. At times, I think I have forgiven people when, in fact, I probably have not, because I have not been as deliberate and intentional as I should have been. I can vaguely forgive, sort of forgive, but I do not think that sometimes I give the intentionality to the process of forgiveness that Enright encourages. Without such intentionality, we get obsessed with the past, and we are not freed up for the future that God is calling us to, and the interior freedom he wants us to have.

If we are asked to think, pray, and act on the issues of forgiveness, the gospel places before us another obvious issue: the reality of doubt in our lives of faith and spirituality. Thomas probably had good reason to doubt. Many Jewish people at the time had no belief in life after death or the possibility of resurrection. Also, like the other apostles and disciples, Thomas must have been greatly disturbed and disappointed regarding what happened to Jesus. So much of his hope and joy must have been lost through the crucifixion of his teacher and mentor. Doubt is part of the process of faith. We all have times when we doubt. We have doubts about God. We have doubts about other relationships that we have with human beings. We can doubt ourselves. Doubt is normal; doubt is human.

We ought not to stay in doubt, however. Staying in doubt is like holding one's breath. To be a fully functioning human being, we need to inhale and exhale. Staying with doubt cripples and paralyzes us. Like nonforgiveness, it keeps us from the future. Doubt seeks to be resolved by developing conviction. That certainly is what happened to the first disciples of Jesus Christ. The confusion of Good Friday—and possibly even Easter, and the days after Easter—eventually became conviction around the time of Pentecost. The apostles became so convinced and convicted about the life, death, and resurrection of Jesus that they were wiling to give their lives to teach, preach, and share what they perceived to be the good news about the meaning of life that they found in Jesus.

Many years ago, James Fowler did extensive research and writing on the stages of faith. He describes the faith of young children, which is often tied up in stories and symbols. He talked about the faith of older children who, in a sense, swallow their religious tradition whole. Then, in Fowler's system, there is the beginning of adolescence and young adulthood. As the brain expands and intellectual power is greater, young people begin to look at their faith tradition more critically, which is not to be discouraged. Certainly doubt is present in this adolescent, young adult era. As we move into adulthood, we continue to have periods of doubt, but we more or less settle down and settle into our faith tradition. Fowler says that some few people go beyond this conventional settling into deep, profound spirituality.

One of Fowler's findings is that many people, because they do not take working at their faith or studying about their faith seriously, stop growing in faith around their childhood or adolescent years. People can be in their forties, fifties, or sixties and have an arrested development of faith of late childhood or early adolescence. Much of the research that I have done over the years into evangelization has led me to see as a Catholic problem that we have been focused primarily on children and not enough on helping adults grow in their faith. The parishes that I have worked in have really tried to make Small Christian Communities and other ongoing adult formation opportunities a very important part of the parish's discipline. Let all of us, at whatever age we are, be committed to a growing faith, one that is not stuck in some arrested, underdeveloped stage.

A closing thought on doubt has to do with people's relationships with organized religion and the Church. Recent studies by the Pew Forum have found that more and more Americans have trouble with organized religion, though they profess to be spiritual, praying every day. Certainly, credibility problems have grown between ordinary Catholics and Catholic leaders in the face of what now appears to be a worldwide sex abuse scandal involving priests, bishops, and even higher authorities who have tried to cover up the scandal rather than dealing with it. One cardinal, defending the pope and the Church, spoke of reports of child abuse of children in Europe as petty gossip. If hundreds of children have been abused, and these situations have not been handled properly—and if, indeed, cases have been covered up to protect the Church—that is much more than petty gossip. Catholic people desire greater integrity, transparency, moral truth, and concern for the well-being of children from those who call themselves shepherds. Until and unless that is forthcoming, there are going to be a lot of doubting Thomases regarding the institutional Church.

MINDFULNESS

I learned a lot through the transition from being a pastor. I learned a lot about human nature. I learned that you can think you know people and you really do not. I learned that sometimes hidden under a lot of theological jargon and pretense can be a lot of aggression, need for power, and need for control. Paradoxically, among those who claim to minister, there can be very poor motivation. For years I have emphasized that servant leadership is the model that people ought to engage in if they feel called to parish ministry. I think those words, "servant leadership," are rather hollow as spoken by at least some people I have encountered.

I mention some of these examples because they seem to fit some of the themes of Scripture. The "just one," spoken of in the book of Wisdom, confronted some apostate Jews for their lack of faith. They, apparently, had grown far from God and the Mosaic law, and saw life as a matter of here and now, and pleasure. The "just one's" call to conversion only solicited aggression and anger from these people. They plotted how to hurt him, even how to kill him, trying to see whether there is a God who really would protect him or save him.

I was reminded recently of the work of Dr. Martin Luther King Jr. in the 1960s. I grew up on the south side of the city of Chicago, where King would sometimes march and hold nonviolent protests against racism. The nonviolence of King and his followers seemed to elicit from some of my white neighbors hatred, anger, and aggression. Things were thrown at King and people who were part of his marches—again, lessons about human nature, lessons about how, within the hearts of many, there is much negative energy.

The letter from James seems to confront a similar problem. The letter reminds us that sin dwells first in the level of attitudes. James confronts the attitudes of some in the early Christian community who seem to be in need of power and control over others. He warns that this need for power and control is causing division in the Christian community. He calls them to seek the wisdom that is from above.

Mark tells us that Jesus predicts he is going to suffer and die at the hands of his enemies. Saying that the disciples did not understand Jesus's second prediction about his passion, Mark paints a negative picture of the disciples. They do not understand who Jesus is or what his mission is about. Later he discovers that they had been arguing about who among them was the greatest in the movement.

Jesus teaches a very countercultural vision of what good leadership looks like. To be a leader in his community of disciples, one must become the servant of the rest. If we are involved in pastoral ministry, if we volunteer in any way for some cause, if we work a job to make a living, Jesus is calling us to develop and deepen the motivation of service in all that we do. We are to lead by serving others.

The reason that Jesus picks a child—and he talks about the importance of accepting a child—is that children in that culture had no legal status. They were, in a sense, nonentities. They could do nothing if someone did something to serve them to reciprocate or give back. Jesus is saying that through the use of a child, we should be willing to serve; we should be willing to be for others without any hope of reciprocity. Jesus says that if anyone accepts someone like a child, that person is accepting Jesus, and whoever accepts Jesus accepts the one who sent Jesus. Jesus is reminding us of the imminence of the Spirit of God in every person and in all creation. The world is shot through with the spirit and presence of God. We ought to live in a spirit of awe, wonder, and reverence toward this imminent God.

I have been doing a lot of research into a movement called positive psychology. Positive psychology deemphasizes a preoccupation with disease and what is wrong with people psychologically, and rather focuses on the ingredients of wellness, health, and happiness, and asks people to concentrate on those positive building blocks. Positive psychology calls people to a healthy plan for self-care. One of the key concepts of positive psychology is mindfulness. Mindfulness refers to a process, and eventually a lifestyle, in which we are increasingly in touch with our attitudes, our feelings, and our thoughts. Rather than allowing these inner dynamics to control us, we peacefully observe them, learn from them, and if any of them have become dysfunctional and problematic, try to change them. I encourage us to become more and more mindful of things like anger, aggression, the need for control, ambition, thinking and living in quantitative categories, focusing on how much and how many, jealousy, resentment, a refusal to forgive, a refusal to say we are sorry, and a refusal to reconcile.

Let us pay attention to any of the negative material that is so much a part of human nature. A big part of mindfulness in the positive psychology movement is heightened awareness through meditation; such inner work should be done at least twice a day. Let us find some prayerful words from Scripture or our tradition as we try to grow in mindfulness, and let us use prayer and meditation to try to transform our negative energy into positive attitudes, oneness with the Spirit, and oneness with God's presence. Let us become more willing to be servant leaders in all that we do.

THINK IT OUT

I receive consolation from the book of Wisdom, which reminds us God gives a share of his wisdom to us when we attend to the presence of God's Spirit with us. I feel great hope when I am reminded of the good news of resurrection, that life is eternal, in and through the risen Jesus. I grow in confidence when I am reminded that God unconditionally loves me and forgives me. Indeed, Christianity is a spirituality and faith of *great consolation*.

But the gospel also offers unique *challenges* to any of us who wish to take it seriously. I am reminded of a missionary who spoke with a number of us some years ago. He said at one point in his career he found himself preaching and teaching the Church more than the person and the teachings of Jesus, and so he made it his life's work to attend to and share with others what he called the *naked gospel*, his attempt to get to the very heart of what Jesus was most about.

In addition to words and messages of consolation, the naked gospel of Jesus Christ, with the church varnishing taken off, can be quite a challenge. Not only are we assured of resurrection and eternal life, Jesus also teaches us that the cross, in various forms, is an experience that the disciples of Jesus Christ must accept and embrace. We are also taught that we are to love our enemies, love people who have hurt us, forgive people who have hurt us, over and over again. In this world of materialism, we learn from Jesus that we are not to find security or identity in material resources. In addition, we are challenged to be people of peace, people who never unnecessarily use aggression to get our way.

Paul's letter to Philemon presents the challenging nature of the gospel. Onesimus was a slave who ran away from Philemon. Paul wrote Philemon and told him to take Onesimus back, not as a slave, but as a brother, an equal. The naked gospel calls us to recognize the radical equality of all human beings in God's family. From the perspective of the naked gospel, not only are all people equal to each other, God's family is connected one to another not just by blood ties, but rather in and through the Holy Spirit. I think that is, at least in part, what Jesus means when he teaches us that we must let go of mother, father, and family to be his followers.

One of the challenges of Jesus's preaching and teaching is that we are to be people of justice. *Commutative justice:* We are to be just in all of our dealings with each other. *Distributive justice:* We are to be concerned about the fair and equal sharing of God's resources among all members of the human family. *Social justice:* We should be concerned about changing any social structures that hold people captive in situations of injustice. The radical, naked gospel does not only offer consolation to the world but also great challenge. To be a disciple of Jesus Christ is to think, feel, value, and behave in ways that are totally countercultural to the dominant culture around us.

Jesus calls us to be a calculating people. He says that if we were to build something, would we not carefully plan out such a project? If we were going to war with others, would we not plan to win? In just the same way, if we claim to be disciples, discipleship is not mass-minded conformity. Rather, discipleship is a choice, a choice that we deliberately make to embrace both the consoling and the challenging aspects of gospel living.

Jesus challenges us to think out and to weigh the implications of discipleship. We sometimes speak of smorgasbord Catholicism, wherein people choose to emphasize aspects of Catholic discipline and culture that they like, while discarding others. Well, there is an even more insidious phenomenon, and that is *smorgasbord discipleship* or *Christianity*, wherein we take the comfort of the gospel but try to avoid those aspects of the gospel that make us uncomfortable, or that make us stretch and grow.

We explain the Sacrament of Confirmation as the completion of a young person's initiation into the Church. We explain it also as a celebration of God's promise that the Holy Spirit of God will always be with us. We explain Confirmation, especially the preparation for it, as a time to scrutinize and discern one's gifts for the work of the reign of God. We especially emphasize that Confirmation is the individual's choice; that Baptism and Eucharist, the first two steps of initiation, were decided on by parents. Confirmation, the final step in initiation, is to be chosen by each individual.

I once heard someone say that Confirmation ought to be a repeatable sacrament. The person saying that was trying to emphasize that faith in the gospel, faith in Jesus, is at least in part a choice, a decision that each of us must make. As we grow, as we age, we should understand the gospel and all of its implications better and more. As we grow and age, we are constantly challenged to embrace more significantly, more profoundly, the entire truth of the gospel, not just the easy or consoling parts.

I encourage us to constantly look on ourselves, whatever our ages, as people in the process of confirming faith. At each stage of our lives, let us open ourselves to the entire gospel message and try to both intellectually believe in and behaviorally act on the whole message of Jesus Christ.

I frequently refer to Dietrich Bonhoeffer and his classic work, *The Cost of Discipleship*. Bonhoeffer reflected on how Hitler overcame Europe, pushing over and controlling so many people who claimed to be Catholic or Protestant Christians. Bonhoeffer, reflecting on this phenomenon, said that the only way he could understand it was that the followers of Jesus Christ had allowed their faith to become tepid. He said too many Christians were living lives of *cheap grace*. He went on to popularize the title of his book as a theory, the *cost of discipleship*. To really be a disciple of Jesus Christ is to not just have a comforting, consoling faith, but rather to be willing to pay the price that true discipleship demands: a life of self-sacrifice and self-investment in what Jesus understood and taught to be the reign of God. If any of us are living lives of discipleship that do not cost us anything, we are not truly living discipleship, but rather empty religion or cheap grace.

Do we really want to be disciples of Jesus Christ? Think it out. Sort it through. Decide. Act. And throughout our lifetime, let us continue to confirm our faith.

ALL YOU NEED IS LOVE

UCLA's Higher Education Research Institute sponsored a survey recently on 220,000 college freshmen at 297 institutions. This institute has been researching college students since 1966. In trying to analyze what freshmen consider important about the present and the future, the survey found that the highest-ranking concern of college freshmen, ranking at 78.1 percent, was "being well off financially" in the future. This concern among young people was more important than the other choices, including raising a family or helping others in difficulty. A similar study of freshmen was done in 1969. At that time only 42.2 percent expressed a concern about being well off financially. The highest statistic in 1969 at 84.9 percent was to develop a meaningful philosophy of life. The study went on to say that perhaps the recession and a shortage of funds among young adults and their families have contributed to these statistics.

I have been trained in Adlerian psychology. Alfred Adler broke with Sigmund Freud because of Freud's determinism, especially about sex drives and aggression. Adler emphasized that human beings are in pursuit of something: love, connection, and belonging. Adler and his disciple Rudolph Dreikurs said that many people, unfortunately, do not reach this goal of love, belonging, and connection in their lives because they develop mistaken notions about how to achieve these realities. For Adlerians, love, belonging, connection, and social interest are the meaning of life. Adlerians talk about mistaken notions and misguided priorities that keep people from love—giving it and receiving it. Among the Adlerian love-blocking priorities are the excessive need to live a life of comfort, a strong need for power over others, an inordinate need for pleasure, and the need to please others; the last priority results in people usually accepting the crumbs of love rather than having genuine love in one's life. From the Adlerian perspective, the college freshmen who want to be assured that they are going to have lives of financial success may indeed reach their financial goals, but nonetheless find their lives rather empty and lacking in meaning and purpose.

I begin with these thoughts about college freshmen and what is important in life as a way of getting into Paul's famous 1 Corinthians passage on love. Paul reminds us of three important spiritual values in life: faith, hope, and love. He singles out love as the greatest. Paul gives some beautiful descriptions of love: how love is patient, kind, and enduring.

Let us add to Paul's reflections. Love is not just a feeling. Love is a decision, a commitment we make for another or others. Love is self-sacrificing. In love, we forgo some of our own immediate needs to meet the needs of others and address the issues of other people. Love is abiding. It is enduring. True love is forever.

When we love another person, we practice a lot of the attributes that Paul highlights in his 1 Corinthians passage. We also try to encourage the people whom we love, helping them to know what is good and beautiful about them. When we love someone, we affirm their gifts, their beauty. When we love someone, we comfort them. Sometimes when we love someone, we have to disagree with and challenge that person. In loving relationships, we can be angry with one another and hurt one another; but where there is love, there is always an attempt to build a bridge of reconciliation. Remember the 1970s movie *Love Story* and that famous line, "Love means never having to say you're sorry." The fact is that love involves contrition and forgiveness, over and over again, in our relationships. Love in its deepest form is a covenant bond with another person or with other people, an unbreakable bond of affection and commitment. To love another person is to be *for* another person. As Paul says, love is the most important activity in which we can engage. Ideally, love is also characterized by mutuality.

The same kind of self-sacrificial giving is present between and among people. We do not just give love; we also must receive love.

Love is being a creative influence in other people's lives, and love is having other people who are creative influences in our lives. As I said earlier, we all need and deserve love. If we are short on receiving it, if we are short on giving it, then I believe God's word is calling us to ongoing conversion. Our number-one priority needs to be the giving and receiving of love. Those college freshmen have a rude awakening coming their way.

In the book of the prophet Jeremiah, God uses a word—Paul refers to it also—that I think captures what love is. God says to Jeremiah, "Before you were born, I knew you." Paul, speaking of God's love for him, says, "I am known." Love is knowing someone, coming to understand someone, coming to accept and respect someone as that person is. Love involves the acceptance and tolerance of another person's weaknesses and vulnerabilities. True love is unconditional acceptance and commitment.

There are all different kinds of love. There is the love of spouses for each other, of parents for their children, and of children for their parents and siblings. There is friendship love, which Jesus describes in John 15, in which we reveal who we are to another, make a decision for another, recognize the equality of the other, lay down our lives for another, and make life better for another. There is the love of a faith community for each other, be it a small group or a large congregation. There is the love of ministers who care for people. As followers of Jesus, we must also love the stranger. There is the profound love of intimacy, and there is also love that manifests itself in mercy, compassion, and deeds of justice.

There is the love of God for us, which is eternal and unconditional. As I said earlier, Jeremiah and Paul speak of this love. Truly believing in and trusting in God's unconditional love for each of us can radically change our lives.

Too often, too many of us have been cheated out of the love that we need and deserve. That is largely due to the mistaken notions and priorities that many people experience in family-of-origin and other enduring relationships. If we somehow do not have mutual love in our lives, we need to take action to change that. It is a human need. We experience how people cheat each other out of love in the gospel when the extended family and neighbors of Jesus refuse to accept him as he has grown and become, and try to lock him in past stereotypes, arising from their own small-minded clannishness.

In a recent edition of the *Sun Times* in the wellness section, Roger Ebert wrote an article titled "Nourishing Memories." Ebert has written some interesting things recently about his own battle with alcoholism and his ongoing struggle with surgeries for cancer. This latest article is about how Ebert, because of recent surgeries on his tongue and in his mouth area in general, has not been able to eat, drink, or speak for years. He talks about his struggle in missing food for some time, but he has reached a point now where he has lost his craving for food. What soothes him now are memories—memories of lunches and dinners he had with people over a lifetime. He has come to see that eating, for him, was not just taking nourishment into himself. Eating was about enjoying people and relationships. The next time we sit down for a meal with another or others, or when we look around church and see people gathered for the Eucharistic meal, let us remember that what matters at such meals is the love and connection and communion we share with one another and with God. It is striking that Jesus left as his final gift a memorial meal, the Eucharist, in which we are forever one in love with him and one another.

KNOWING

I received an email this week from someone who has been paying attention to the Gospels of the Easter season. The gentleman was confused as to why the apostles and disciples often did not recognize the risen Jesus when they first encountered him. I attempted an interpretation. I wrote back that I believe the words from the Acts of the Apostles describe the experience of the first witnesses of the resurrection. In the

Acts passage this week, Luke speaks of the first Christians as "coming to believe." That notion is repeated in other passages of the New Testament. The first witnesses of the resurrection came to believe; it was a process. They would see Jesus; then he would disappear. He was the same Jesus. His identity was intact, but he was changed. He was transformed. He possessed what theologians have come to call a "spirit body." He was no longer subject to the laws of time and space. Thus, the first witnesses would sometimes recognize him, and sometimes they would not.

Let us stay with the notion of coming to believe. Faith can be explained in a variety of different ways. Faith is intellectual assent to a body of convictions like those we express in the Nicene Creed. Faith is knowing about God, Jesus, the Spirit, and the Church. In the Gospel of John, Jesus introduces us to a different understanding of faith. He uses the verb "know." He said his followers listen to his voice, and "I know them." This quote from John 10 comes after the famous good-shepherd teaching in John 10 in which Jesus talks about himself and us: "I am the Good Shepherd; I know my sheep and mine know me." At its most profound level, faith is coming to know Jesus, to know God through Jesus, and allowing ourselves to be known by God through Jesus.

Think of people whom you believe that you truly know. We can have the same kind of relationship with Jesus. We can know him. We can know his values. We can know his vision. We can know his patterns of thought. We can know his style of behavior. We can know and experience his presence. We can know Jesus; we can learn Jesus; and we can live Jesus. This is what Christian discipleship is about. Disciples are learners trying to grow in Jesus's way of life.

Coming to know him and allowing ourselves to be known by him involve some discipline. We come to this mutual knowing with Jesus through a variety of activities. We come to know Jesus through prayer, and in praying we ought not to hide behind rote prayer all the time. Rather, we ought to be transparent with Jesus, sharing with him who we are at given moments in our lives. We come to know Jesus through worship, through the sacramental life, through our prayerful reading and study of Scripture. We come to know Jesus by imitating him in ministry, and in mercy and in justice. We come to know Jesus in community, in our families, in small groups, and in large groups with which we worship on weekends. We can come to know Jesus. As it is in other relationships, coming to know Jesus and allowing ourselves to be known by Jesus are progressive acts. We can halt the process any time we want, but we also can deepen the process. The process becomes deepened through intentionality, being deliberate about our relationship with him.

One of the finest movements in which I have taken part during my priesthood is the Marriage Encounter movement. Marriage Encounter is a retreatlike experience that couples take on a given weekend. There might be twelve or fifteen couples taking the weekend and ten or twelve couples ministering the weekend. The common experience that I have noted since the late 1970s, when I first experienced Marriage Encounter, is how far apart couples often can become. Couples have the potential for the most intimate of relationships within the marriage covenant, but many people, both in taking and giving Marriage Encounter weekends, talk about how they have drifted from each other or perhaps have never really known each other. Husbands say, "She doesn't know who I really am." Wives say, "He doesn't know who I really am." The weekend is oriented toward getting couples in the process of coming to know each other. Are there any relationships in our lives in which distance has set in, and we ought to try to come to know that person anew?

This drifting or distance can happen in our faith relationships also. If we want to deepen the coming-to-know experience with God through Jesus in the Spirit, we must develop a discipline like the discipline of dialogue that couples learn in Marriage Encounter, a discipline that keeps us in that process of coming to know Jesus.

We need to keep something in mind about the similarities in our relationships. Though we may grow in intimacy with another person and grow in knowing another person, another person always remains partly a mystery to us. There is always more to come to know about another person. So it is with Jesus. We can know Jesus, but Jesus always remains a mystery. Like the early apostles and disciples, we recognize the risen Jesus at times, and at other times we very well may miss his presence and not recognize him in given encounters.

The apocalyptic imagery of the book of Revelation gives us a highly symbolic, mystical glimpse of the risen Jesus. He is portrayed as the Lamb seated at center of a throne. Implicit in this statement is an ecclesiology or vision of church. In the early church, Jesus was very much the center of faith. As word of his resurrection spread and was present in the communities of believers, people used their gifts and charisms for the common good in the context of community. This dynamic ecclesiology centered in Jesus was gradually replaced by a vertical, top-down ecclesiology that grew to emphasize the importance of hierarchy, patriarchy, and the power of the ordained. Laity were rendered as infantilized consumers of religion services at the bottom of a top-down diagram. In our scandal-ridden Church, there is an opportunity for purification and perhaps for attracting alienated people back to the Church if we once again become a more Jesus-centered church rather than an institution- or hierarchy-focused church. I believe in and want to give my time and effort to a Jesus-centered church. The other model of church is seriously flawed and is causing people to move away from the church in significant numbers.

In the context of the themes of coming to know God and God coming to know us, Revelation reminds us that the Lamb seated at the center of the throne, seated at the center of our lives, can wipe every tear away. Jesus, in the gospel, reminds us that we are in his hands, and there is no snatching us from the hands of Jesus. He goes on to say that we are in the hands of the Father, and there is no snatching us from the hands of the Father. Let us feel peace and rest in the protective intimacy that we have in our relationship with God, through Jesus, in the Spirit.

Part 6

MERCY AND JUSTICE

Truth and Consequences

When I was in grade school in the 1950s, there was a popular TV show titled *Truth or Consequences*. On the show, participants were asked ridiculous questions that really had no serious answer. If they did not give the answer that the host was looking for, they were judged as having answered incorrectly and given consequences. The consequences were usually some difficult, embarrassing, yet funny experiences that they had to endure. I enjoyed *Truth or Consequences*.

Ezekiel and Mark's Gospel focus on the phenomenon of prophecy. Ezekiel and Jesus were both prophets. Over the years, prophets have been misunderstood as people who can predict the future. While prophets have intuitions about the future, they really were and are intensely focused on the present. Prophets are sensitized to what is going on in the world, and they are sensitized to the voice and revelation of God. Prophets listen to, listen for, and hear divine truth. In some of the stories, prophets are reluctant to respond to God's call to speak divine truth. They realize that God's truth is a phenomenon that people and culture both resist. Prophets usually overcome their resistance to God's call and perform their unpopular ministry.

Prophets speak God's truth. In speaking God's truth, it was not and is not a matter of truth *or* consequences, but rather truth *and* consequences. Prophets pay a price for the truth they speak. In the case of Ezekiel, he saw the leadership of Jerusalem increasingly oriented toward secular power. They wanted to play ball with the big powers—Assyria, Egypt, and Babylon. They lost their contact with Yahweh and commitment to the covenant with Yahweh. Ezekiel prophesied to the people that they should return to a theocentric way of life. Eventually, the people of Jerusalem were overtaken by Babylon and taken into exile. Ezekiel accompanied the people to Babylon and continued to do his prophecy in exile with his people. His prophecy always involved two realities: he challenged the people toward conversion, and he offered hope and support. He challenged the people to accept the Lordship of Yahweh, greater morality, and greater responsibility for their lives. In his prophecy, he was met with great rejection, resistance, and rebellion. He nonetheless continued his work. In Mark's Gospel, Jesus returns to his family and friends and begins to teach God's truth. Mark tells us that they were offended by his prophetic teaching. They rejected him. Jesus was troubled by their lack of faith.

Why do people reject prophets? Because they speak God's truth, which is countercultural to mass-mindedness and private logic. God's truth makes people uncomfortable. God's truth challenges people and calls them to change. Often we want to maintain the status quo of our lives. We do not want to listen to prophets; we want to get them out of the way. Let us pray for God's grace that we might be more open to the prophecy of the Hebrew Scriptures, to Jesus, and to the prophets who are in our midst.

Not only are we to listen to prophets, we need to realize that we are all called to be prophets. When we were baptized, we were anointed to become priests, prophets, and kings. Whenever I do a baptism of an infant, child, or adult, I explain those words. In baptism, we were anointed to be people of holiness, people who listen to and live God's truth, and people who lead both in church and in society.

Prophecy is like leadership. The call to leadership is not just to a few; it is a call to all. So also is the call to prophecy—would that all the people of God were prophets. Prophecy is a journey; it is a process that takes a lifetime.

Prophecy is listening for and living God's truth in the present. I have mentioned the work of Rushworth Kidder, who wrote the book *Moral Courage*. Kidder's notion of moral courage is similar to prophecy. He says that people with moral courage operate out of moral principles. Such people know that speaking and living moral principles are dangerous actions; there can be painful, ongoing consequences. People with moral courage nonetheless persist in speaking and living what they perceive to be truth.

We cannot be prophetic or morally courageous if we do not take the time to be people of discernment. I had a moral theology instructor many years ago who said that we all know or have the capacity to know the truth. He said it was a matter of listening deeply within ourselves. Deep within ourselves prophetic moral truth emerges. This does not mean that all of us listening to ourselves become laws unto ourselves. What is emerging as divine moral truth always has to be in dialogue with others, specifically a faith tradition and community. Emerging truth from within, in dialogue with others, results in common sense, prophetic truth and moral courage.

Not only do I have a doctorate in psychology, I was the recipient of psychotherapy for years for problems I had with anxiety. While I did not want either the problems or the therapy, that years-long process taught me to be a person who looks at every aspect of life and myself, always pursuing the truth and God's truth. Seeking the truth and speaking the truth have become passions for me. People have told me that I sometimes make them feel uncomfortable when I speak. I guess what I am trying to do is what Ezekiel did: speak God's truth—offering challenge, support, and hope. I know that such ministry does involve consequences. But as Martin Luther said, "Here I stand; I cannot do other."

If we fail to be prophetic people, I fear that we simply live lives of codependency and enablement with institutions, organizations, and people who are afraid of or running from the truth. Such codependency and enablement fail to help with the emergence of divine truth and the reign of God. Let us embrace God's call to be prophetic people, knowing that the truth—listened to, spoken, and lived—will always have consequences. It is not a matter of truth or consequences; it is always truth and consequences.

A Spirituality of Cultural Resistance

The recent economic downturn has particularly sensitized me to people who have abruptly lost their jobs. Work is a sacred activity in which we cocreate the world with God. Work is the source of our livelihood, giving us and the people whom we love the resources and means we need to live. For many people, work contains meaning for life. Many documents in Catholic social teaching speak of the dignity of work and the dignity of the worker. Some people have lost jobs because of an organization's lack of resources to pay them a wage, but I fear that at times in this whole experience of work loss, laborers and workers are not respected as people, but are cast off as if they are things.

Reflecting on the plight of such people reminded me of the work of John Kavanaugh, a Jesuit priest who wrote a classic some years ago, *Following Christ in a Consumer Society*. Kavanaugh describes human living under two umbrella terms: "commodity form living" and "personal form living." In commodity form living, which Kavanaugh says is the essence of consumerism, we live in a society that no longer values the interior life, a society in which, frequently, significant relationships become broken. In commodity form living, a craving exists for things such as the source of our identity and security. There is a depersonalization of living that creeps toward injustice. There is a flight from the experience of weakness and woundedness. Commodity form living is about marketing and consuming.

Kavanaugh says that commodity form living and consumerism can affect the way we think and feel, the way we look on other people, our spouses, our children. We tend to look on each other as commodities. Not only does the truism "You are what you eat" contain truth. We also "are what we consume." In commodity form living, we are what we possess, but we are also possessed by our possessions. We become produced by our products. We are remade and revealed as commodities. We are robbed of our humanity.

Kavanaugh has a litany of terms he uses to further describe commodity form living:

Thinghood	It is all about technique
Productivity	Coolness
Consumption	Hardness
Quantity	Accumulation
Noncommitment	Invulnerability
Passivity	Having
Violence	Hedonism
Devaluation of life	Skepticism
Competition	Doubt
Retention	Isolation
Sexuality as mechanics	Addiction
Your body is a machine	Flight from self
Live with fear	Degradation of persons
Do not be committed	Death

Kavanaugh concludes his section on commodity form living by characterizing it as a contemporary expression of idolatry.

In contrast to commodity form living, there is personal form living. Personal form living is based on a Christian anthropology that the human person has great dignity. Personal form living is rooted in the faith and covenant with God of the Hebrew scriptures. We find our dignity because we are loved children of God. Personal form living is another expression for what Jesus Christ preached and taught in his reign-of-God preaching and teaching. Personal form living involves a discipline of self-critique, interiority and action, moral responsibility, unity in the midst of diversity, and freedom. Personal form living values community, prayer, shared worship, living a vowed life, and resistance to the culture around us. Personal form living values interiority, relationships, simplicity in life, and laboring for justice. Finally, personal form living does not run from, but embraces the woundedness involved in human experience.

As he did for commodity form living, Kavanaugh also has a litany of words that he uses to explain personal form living:

Intrinsic value of the person	Body as temple of the Spirit
Finding worth in who you are	Fear not
Giving yourself as gift	Covenant
Faith and trust	Meaning
Quality	Uniqueness
Freedom	Tenderness
Covenant living	Compassion
Engagement	Love
Acceptance of weakness	Generosity
Forgiveness	Being
Healing	Faith
Exaltation of the least person in our midst	Hope
Sharing and giving	Solitude
Sexuality as a sign and sacrament of personhood	Simplicity
	Justice
	Life

Kavanaugh's book is subtitled *A Spirituality of Cultural Resistance.* To live as a disciple of Jesus Christ is to strive to resist the dominant culture of commodity form living and to engage in ongoing conversion toward personal form living.

Other writers have written on the theme that Kavanaugh has developed in his writings and speaking. Similar thoughts can be found in Gabriel Marcel's *Being and Having* and Christopher Lasch's *Culture of Narcissism.* John Paul II wrote extensively on the dangers of consumerism.

I offer these reflections during Advent. Like anyone else, I am concerned that I have not been Christmas shopping yet and done my share of consuming—even if I do that in the name of love. The paradox of

Advent and Christmas as a holiday season is that so many people are spending time and money chasing after things in the pursuit of joy and happiness when we know that things cannot truly make us happy. I have written and spoken before about material sufficiency. All we need is enough. We do not need more and more.

The third weekend in Advent is traditionally called Gaudete Sunday because of the emphasis on joy that is present in the first and second readings. *Gaudete* is Latin for "rejoice." The usually somber prophet Zephaniah begins today in chapter 3 with, "Shout for joy. . . . Sing joyfully. Be glad and exalt with all your heart." Then the prophet goes on to explain why people should feel such joy. He says twice, "The Lord is in your midst. . . . The Lord, your God, is in your midst."

In his letter to the Philippians, Paul engages in an imperative: "Rejoice in the Lord always. I shall say it again: rejoice!" Then he adds a statement that has changed my life: "Have no anxiety at all, but in everything, by prayer and petition, with thanksgiving, make your requests known to God. Then the peace of God that surpasses all understanding will guard your hearts and minds in Christ Jesus." Gaudete Sunday reminds that we can find joy by experiencing God in our midst. Gaudete Sunday reminds those of us who live in this consumer culture that peace can replace anxiety if we become people with a discipline of prayer.

In Luke 3, John the Baptist seems to be warning against early experiences of commodity form living in his own day. The crowds asked John the Baptist after his teaching, "What should we do?" His reply was, "Whoever has two cloaks should share with the person who has none. And whoever has food should do likewise." We are told that tax collectors came and said, "Teacher, what should we do?" And his response was, "Stop collecting more than what was prescribed." The soldiers asked him, "What should we do?" and he told them, "Do not practice extortion, do not falsely accuse anyone, and be satisfied with your wages." John the Baptist speaks a vision of charity, mercy, and justice for those who are listening to his teachings.

The Scripture readings converge today to remind us that we are called to a different way of life, and that different way of life—different from the dominant culture around us—is the reign of God, personal form living, and valuing *being* rather than *having*.

If we believe there is truth in John's words, he makes a comment that speaks to us about the proper mood of Advent. He says, "One mightier than I is coming." This is what we pray about and celebrate— the coming of the one who is mightier than John the Baptist: Jesus. It is he who brings us the full revelation of the reign of God. It is he who can be spiritually reborn in our hearts and lives this Advent and Christmas season. Let us finish Advent and move into Christmas more willing to live the spirituality of cultural resistance.

BIGGER BARNS

Shirley Sherrod was an official with the U.S. Department of Agriculture. Last March, she gave a talk at an NAACP gathering. Someone took a snippet of her talk and began to pass it around electronically. In this snippet, Ms. Sherrod, who is African American, said that a white farmer came to her over twenty years ago for help in holding onto his farm, which was being taken away from him. She said her first reaction was, "Why should I help this white man when so many black folks, like myself, have lost their farms?" When Shirley Sherrod told the story of her reactions to the white farmer—that initially she did not want to help him—she was met with applause from the African American audience at the NAACP meeting that she was addressing. That was the snippet of the talk that eventually ran on FOX News, which beat its chest and said that the other networks would not even cover this story.

After this part of Ms. Sherrod's talk was posted to the Internet and replayed on TV, she received a phone call while driving her car. It was from the Department of Agriculture. She was told to pull over to the side of the road and formally resign from her position. She was told that this is what the "White House" wanted. In turn, the NAACP called for her resignation. Being a loyal servant, Shirley Sherrod resigned her position. What came out later was that that small part of Shirley Sherrod's talk did not convey her full message. She said that encounter with the white farmer who was going to lose his farm was a spiritual transformation for her. She came to her senses and said, "This isn't about race. This is about people in need, whether they are African American, White, Hispanic, whatever racial/ethnic group they might be part of. This white farmer is in need. I am going to help him." And she did; she helped the man save his farm.

The carefully cropped passage from Shirley Sherrod's talk, which presented her as a racist, did not reveal another truth about her life. Her father was killed by a white man in 1965. In the full body of her talk Shirley Sherrod said this:

> *What it is really about is those who have versus those who don't. They could be black; they could be white; they could be Hispanic. I have come to realize that I needed to work to help poor people. God helped me to see that it is not just about black people; it is about poor people. I have come a long way. I knew that I couldn't live with hate. I have come to realize that we have to work together. It is sad that we don't have a room full of whites and blacks here tonight because we have to overcome the divisions that we have. We have to get to the point where, as Toni Morrison said, "Race exists, but it doesn't matter."*

My first reaction to this story was amazement at how people can manipulate the truth and manipulate information to hurt others and promote their own ideology. A man carefully took snippets of a talk about spiritual transformation and conversion and used it to cause harm to a good and just woman. This story has reminded me of the danger to all of us when we rush to judgment.

I myself have been the victim of information about me being manipulated and half-truths being told about me. I could identify with Shirley Sherrod.

It also struck me that there was racism on the parts of the whites who propagated the shortened form of her talk, as well as the African Americans who were listening to her and who applauded her initial resistance to help the white farmer.

After the whole truth came out about Shirley Sherrod, the secretary of agriculture called her and offered her another job. He asked for her forgiveness, and she told him that she does forgive him. But the last I heard, she does not know whether she wants to return to that former place of employment. What a tremendously just and spiritual woman. Not only has she gone through a spiritual transformation that has helped her transcend racism to focus on care for the poor, but she has even moved to the position of being able to forgive people who ruined her career. This story of Shirley's spiritual transformation, I am sure, has invited the secretary of agriculture; the president, who has called Shirley Sherrod; and many who have experienced this story to our own conversion and spiritual transformation.

Her story stands in sharp juxtaposition to the main character of the parable in Luke 12. Jesus teaches about the importance to guard against greed. He says that one's life does not consist of possessions, and then he tells a parable of a rich man whose land produced a bountiful harvest. Listen to what this rich man says in the parable:

What shall I do? I do not have space. This is what I shall do. I shall tear down my barns and build larger ones. I shall store all of my grain. I shall stay to myself, "Now as for you, you have so many good things stored up for many years, rest, eat, drink, and be merry!" (emphasis added)

Unlike Shirley Sherrod, who had a spiritual transformation that led her to the care of poor people, the man in the parable is a portrait of narcissism. Did you notice how many times he used the pronoun "I," speaking about what he was going to do for himself, not for others? The man is guilty of narcissism, materialism, and consumerism. He finds his security in what he has. God appears in the parable and calls this man a fool. He tells him, "This night, your life is going to be demanded of you; and the things you have prepared, to whom will they belong?"

Jesus, in the parable, warns all of us about storing up treasures for ourselves, but not being rich in what matters to God. Well, what matters to God? What matters to God is what Shirley Sherrod discovered. What matters to God is mercy toward our fellow person. What matters to God is compassion. What matters to God is generosity. What matters to God is justice, especially distributive justice—sharing our resources with people in need, assuring that the goods of this world, the resources of this world, are shared with all the world's inhabitants. What matters to God is forgiveness. What matters to God is communion with our fellow person and with God. The gospel reminds me of the story of Oskar Schindler, a wealthy man who, during the course of the Nazi persecution of the Jews, used his wealth to protect Jewish people from Nazi squads and to help Jewish people escape to freedom. It is said he saved twelve hundred Jews from death. Schindler had an awakening that his vast wealth was not to be used for himself, but for the well-being of others. Schindler himself died penniless.

I have mentioned before the work of Edward Diener and his son, Robert Biswas-Diener, both psychologists in the positive psychology movement. The Dieners and others in positive psychology have discovered that we have a materialism/consumerism set point. In other words, for most of us, after we have acquired a certain amount of wealth or material resources, gaining more does not make us happier. Happiness is not really found in stockpiling wealth and resources. Happiness is found in spirituality, in our connection with other people, sharing with other people, good relationships, love, and investing in the well-being of others.

The author of the book of Ecclesiastes identifies himself as Qoheleth. The name is mysterious. Its root seems to mean *assembly*, so the name appears to refer to someone who teaches wisdom to an assembly, someone who assembles wisdom for others, or both. Qoheleth says that most of the things to which people give their time and energy miss the point of life, or miss what matters to God, to use the words of Jesus. "Vanity of vanities; all things are vanity. . . . What profit comes to man from all the toil and anxiety of heart with which he has labored under the sun? . . . Even at night, his mind is not at rest."

In Colossians 3, Paul speaks of greed—exemplified in the man in Jesus's parable—as idolatry. Paul says to any of us for whom greed, materialism, or consumerism are problems, "Put to death . . . the greed that is idolatry. . . . Be raised with Christ."

Let us learn from the Scriptures that most often the right direction is to not to build bigger barns for our stuff, but rather, in concern for our fellow person, to be more willing to share our resources with those who are in need.

Socialist?

I was called something last Sunday that I had not been called before. I have been called a lot of things in my lifetime, but this title was striking. I had been speaking about the Shirley Sherrod situation, in which she lost her job because of a quote taken out of context from a larger talk she gave on overcoming racism. I mentioned that I first heard about this whole situation on FOX News. One of the FOX reporters was prevailing, saying that, indeed, Shirley Sherrod should be fired. Something that I was not aware of, which people brought to my attention since my presentation last week, is that Bill O'Reilly was one of the people who negatively reported on Shirley Sherrod, and when he learned the whole story, he apologized. When I was speaking of this situation, I also commented that I had heard that the Obama administration was afraid of what FOX personality Glenn Beck might do with this whole situation—and that is why Obama's leaders wanted Shirley to step down. I did not make any sort of qualitative or judgmental statement about Glenn Beck. After Mass, a woman walked by me and said, "Glenn Beck is a patriot. You are a socialist." That is what I was called last week—a socialist.

I have done some research into the source of that comment. On March

2, on his radio and TV programs, Glenn Beck warned people to beware of religious leaders who talk about economic or social justice. He said that those were "code words" for socialism, Nazism, and communism. He said that if religious leaders persist in talking about social or economic justice, people ought to leave their parishes or congregations.

After I was called a socialist, a couple of other people came up to me expressing concern about my reference to distributive justice in the closing prayer of the Mass. I have become surprised at the devotion so many people have to Glenn Beck. His extreme views have led him to gain millions of viewers and listeners and millions and millions of dollars.

I need to set the record straight about being Roman Catholic and being concerned about justice. In last week's Scriptures, Jesus cautioned us against greed in all of its forms and reminded us that life is not about possessions. Jesus tells us, in Luke, that God has given us the kingdom of God, and that we are to sell our belongings and give alms to the needy. He tells us that whatever we treasure has really captured our hearts, and he calls us to be vigilant about the quality of life. One of the things we are called to be vigilant about as Catholic Christians is justice. This call to justice goes back to Jesus himself, and is also found in the theology and spirituality of the Hebrew Scriptures. This call to justice is part of the Hebraic Christian tradition.

In more recent times, the Catholic Church has developed a body of work that has become known as **Catholic social teaching.** The timeline below lists the most significant documents and outlines the issues they address.

1891 *Rerum Novarum*, Leo XIII	Concern for the poor, rights of workers, and the duties of both workers and employees.
1931 *Quadragesimo Anno*, Pius XI	Respect toward workers, creation of a just social order, and warnings against inherent dangers in both capitalism and socialism.
1961 *Mater et Magistra*, John XXIII	Just wages for workers.

1963	
Pacem in Terris, John XXIII	Concern for common good, disarmament.
1965	
Gaudium et Spes, Vatican II	Encouraging Catholics to pay attention to the signs of the times, and to work for justice and peace.
1967	
Populorum Progressio, Paul VI	Structural injustice, calling the world to a new, healthy humanism.
1971	
Octogesima Adveniens *(Call to Action)*, Paul VI	Worldwide justice.
1971	
Statement of the Synod of Bishops	Justice as a gospel mandate.
1975	
Evangelii Nuntiandi, Paul VI	Evangelization as incomplete if not joined to works of social justice.
1981	
Laborem Exercens, John Paul II	Spirituality of work.
1988	
Sollicitudo Rei Socialis, John Paul II	God's radical option for the poor, structures of sin in the world.
1988	
Statement of the Pontifical Justice and Peach Commission	Warning against racism and encouraging conscience formation.
1990	
Redemptoris Missio, John Paul II	Poverty.
1992	
Catechism of the Catholic Church	Justice.
1995	
Evangelium Vitae, John Paul II	Abortion, euthanasia, and the death penalty.

Another significant work is *Economic Justice for All*, prepared by the U.S. Conference of Catholic Bishops in 1986. That document spoke of the three classical divisions of justice in Catholic culture. We are to be about *commutative justice*, in which we practice honesty in all of our dealings with each other. We are to practice *distributive justice*. We are to be concerned about and act on proper distribution of the world's goods so that all of God's people have at least minimal resources to live happy and full lives. This has nothing to do with big government trying to reach into people's pockets and redistribute their wealth. The document also called us to *social justice*, that is, to challenge and change systems that hold people in bondage and keep them from living the fullness of humanity.

As much as people might like or enjoy Glenn Beck, his admonition to leave your church if your church speaks of justice is something that flies in the face of Catholic identity.

Someone who has helped me understand the call to justice better than I have in the past is Jim Wallis, founder of the Sojourners Community, in Washington D.C. The Sojourners Community is a faith community in which to belong, people must make a commitment to justice. Writing in his classic *Call to Conversion*, Wallis has said that too many Christians live a kind of political conformity and a spiritual lukewarmness that are not inclusive of justice consciousness and justice work. To be a Christian, he wrote, one must live with and spend time in proximity to the victims of injustice, working with them and helping them. The issues of justice, Wallis said, must become part of our prayer lives and become part of our worship lives.

Unfortunately, despite all of the qualitative writing that has been done on social justice in Catholic history, often people have not been helped to discover practical steps by which they can become involved in the various dimensions of justice.

Someone who helped Holy Family, where I worked for a number of years, is a man by the name of Michael Cowen, who with Bernard Lee wrote the classic *Dangerous Memories* on Small Christian Communities. I asked Michael to come to the parish to talk to Small Christian Communities about how to get practical about social justice missions in their groups, challenging groups to not just be into self-nurture but also justice. Cowen said that justice is something that cannot just be worked on alone. People need a community to work with on issues of justice. He said that in the context of community, people ought to share with each other all of their concerns about mercy and justice, to get all of them out on the table. After that has been done, there ought to be discernment as to the one issue on which the group is willing to come together. Discussion must take place about how much time people are willing to give to the justice project, what would be the starting point, and what would be signs of success or effectiveness. He encouraged groups to bring in people who have worked in whatever area of justice they are concerned about, to resource them and to serve as consultants. Cowen's methodology made at least some groups able to get their arms around issues of mercy and justice.

Wisdom 18 and Luke 12 call us, as people of faith, to be prepared and vigilant. That vigilance seems to involve an eschatological dimension, being prepared for the end of time. I think the vigilance issue also has a very day-to-day meaning. We are to pay attention to what is important and to what matters in life. As people of faith, we are descendants of Abraham, who is talked about in the letter to the Hebrews. As people of faith and descendants of Abraham, one of the aspects of human life that we need to be attentive to is justice.

In conclusion, I need to be honest about something, and I take some ribbing from other people about this. I am, in fact, a FOX News junkie. Rupert Murdoch and Roger Ailes, who put together FOX News some years ago, have significantly trounced CNN and MSNBC in the ratings. FOX broadcasts have great production value and good reporting. I find some reporters on the station to be rather shrill, and I cannot stay with them too long, but I enjoy the station. Some reporters are more "fair and balanced" than others. My particular favorite is Megyn Kelly.

Finally, I am not a socialist. I am an Irish Catholic, an independent voter, a person trying to be a disciple of Jesus Christ—someone who tries to live the reign of God.

HEAVEN—NOW AND LATER

The April 16, 2012, issue of *Time* magazine had an interesting cover story titled "Rethinking Heaven," by Jon Meacham. The article begins with the author discussing conventional understandings of heaven. He says that the images that many of us jump to when we think of heaven can be found in the best-selling book *Heaven Is for Real*, by Todd Burpo with Lynn Vincent. The book tells the story of four-year-old Colton Burpo, who reported that he visited heaven during surgery for appendicitis. The child was indeed seriously ill and close to death. He told his parents about seeing Jesus, sitting on his lap, meeting John the Baptist, meeting his grandfather, and meeting a deceased sister about whom he knew nothing. He saw Mary, who acted like a mom toward Jesus. Meacham talks about how art, tradition, and religion have influenced our understanding or concepts about what heaven will be like.

But the author presents other views, other than the traditional, to help us understand heaven. He quotes John Blanchard, executive pastor of Rock Church International in Virginia Beach, who said,

> *I don't believe we are going to be floating around with little wings looking like Cupid playing harps, for all eternity. Heaven isn't just a place you go—heaven is how you live your life. What's trending is a younger generation, teens, college-aged, who are motivated by causes—people who are motivated by heaven are also people motivated to make a positive difference in this world.*

Meacham also mentions N. T. Wright, the former Anglican bishop of Durham, England. Wright has a very existential, here-and-now approach to heaven. Heaven is God's space; the followers of Jesus should be trying to bring God's space to the earth, transforming our world into how God would have it. Wright speaks of trying to create heaven here on earth. The alleviation of pain and injustice in the world, in this view, is the ongoing work that Jesus began, and the means of bringing into being what the early Christians meant when they spoke of heaven. Believers should be hard at work making the world godly and just.

Which is correct—*The Heaven Is for Real*, traditional understanding of an afterlife awaiting us on the other side of death, or this more existential approach that suggests heaven is our work now, as we live on earth? I think that there is truth in both understandings.

In the Gospel of John, we hear the famous story of doubting Thomas. Thomas would not believe in the risen Jesus until he saw him and probed his wounds. Jesus appears again a week later after his first appearance. In both instances, he calms his followers' fears with the word, "Peace." I believe that Thomas represents all of us: we all have moments and periods of doubt. To a degree, it is true that we all have some agnosticism in us, in that we know we do not know all things about God, Jesus, eternal life, heaven, and so on. But Thomas is paradigmatic for how faith works. He moves from doubt to a direct experience of Jesus; he has a religious experience. This religious experience leads him to "come to believe." As with the other first witnesses of the resurrection, his religious experience leads him to convictional faith. He becomes convinced that Jesus is risen—his identity intact, but nonetheless transformed, different than he was before.

So it is with you and me: We can doubt; we cannot know; but we also have experienced Jesus as risen. We have come to believe; we are convinced about resurrection: Jesus's and, eventually, ours.

This encounter with the risen Jesus speaks of the transcendent nature of resurrection. Jesus was the same, but he was transformed. His identity was intact, but he was no longer subject to the laws of time and space. He passed through doors and walls. He appeared and disappeared. He was recognized, and sometimes he was not recognized. This spirit-body of the risen Jesus reminds us of the mysterious, transcendent, ethereal nature of resurrection and eternal life.

But there is a quite down-to-earth, existential approach to resurrection also contained in this passage from John. Jesus breathes the

Holy Spirit into those gathered in that room, and he sends them on a mission. The mission has a curious, challenging direction. It is to be a mission of sharing with people God's forgiveness, while challenging them to forgive each other, in imitation of God.

The real-life, here-and-now implications of heaven and resurrection are also spoken of in Acts 4. The group of people who abandoned Jesus, denied him, and betrayed him are described by Luke as completely transformed:

> *The community of believers was of one heart and mind, and no one claimed that any of his possessions were his own; but they had everything in common. With great power the apostles bore witness to the resurrection of the Lord Jesus, and great favor was accorded them all. There was no needy person among them, for those who owned property or houses would sell them, bring the proceeds of the sale, and put them at the feet of the apostles, and they were distributed to each according to need. (4:32–35)*

This glimpse of the early church speaks of people who were trying to create heaven on earth. This portrait of the early Christian movement speaks of the miracles that flowed from Easter and the resurrection of Jesus. In the second reading, from the first letter of John, we are told that we who believe in the risen Jesus are victors over the world. In John's theology, the world represents all that is anti-Christ and anti–reign of God. Here again, the here-and-now, existential implications of the resurrection as mission are discussed.

Many years ago, I was very impressed by the theologizing of a priest, Roger Troisfontaines, who wrote the book *I Do Not Die*. In this book, Troisfontaines speaks of eternity as a process. Some people choose to be in the process of heaven by living the values and behaviors of the reign of God as taught by Jesus. Heaven people pass over the threshold of death, and heaven continues for them. In a similar way, some people choose to live hell-oriented lives. They are alienated from others and from God, self-centered, narcissistic, oriented toward power or pleasure, or both. People who begin such a lifestyle here on earth also pass over the threshold of death. Troisfontaines believed that people with a hell lifestyle probably continue that lifestyle in the hereafter. In this view, God does not send anyone to heaven or hell; rather people choose how they want to live eternally. I believe this view is tempered by the story of the good thief who died with Christ, who repented in the last moments of his life and was assured paradise by Jesus. I know people who translate the tradition of purgatory as follows: maybe the spirits of some people continue to strive toward conversion and repentance, even after death. Perhaps people can change the direction of their lives after they have died.

There is much that we do not know about heaven. I believe in both of the dimensions of heaven discussed in Meachem's article. I believe that after death we move, as Jesus did, into a different dimension of being. We become spirit, one with God, one with those who preceded us in death, and one with those who remain here on Earth. Our identities will be intact, but we will be transformed. But I also believe that indeed in John's Gospel and in Matthew 28, Jesus has sent those of us who believe in resurrection on a mission: to bring God's space into the world, to bring heaven to earth. Perhaps that is just another way of saying that the believers in Jesus are called to help with the emergence of the reign of God in the world.

I was with my aunt Ag the night she died, after a brutal fight with cancer. Ag had lost her only son, her only child, years before to kidney disease. Later she lost her husband to the same disease. Ag was a woman of loss and suffering. Nonetheless, during her years on earth, she brought much joy, happiness, and love to many people. Moments before she died, although she was unconscious, tears began to flow down her cheeks. I said something about it to the people standing around her bed. One of the medical people in the room said that her tears were simply her autonomic nervous system at work, involuntary movements. But I don't think so. I think her tears were tears of love for the people standing around her deathbed, and tears of joy as she saw her son, Ronnie, and her husband, Johnny—and all who preceded her in death—with whom she was about to be rejoined. That is not to mention the vision of God she may have been experiencing. She was journeying to a new dimension of being. I had similar experiences with my parents and so many other people whom I was with when they died.

Heaven? It truly is now and later.

LEPERS

When I was a kid, I was not very good at sports. I was a severe asthmatic, and running or getting excited sent me into episodes of wheezing and having difficulty breathing. I liked sports, but when we would gather in an empty lot for baseball games, no one would pick me to be on their side—with the exception of my brother, who would reluctantly take me, and warn me to not be a klutz. When I was not picked, I would simply go home and do something by myself—the beginning of my introversion! At other times, "the cool guys" would gather in one of the guys' houses to goof around. My brother was the natural leader of this group. As we would enter the house, the door would be slammed in my face. They did not want me hanging around with them. I would go home, and do something by myself. I learned how to be comfortable alone. By the time I reached junior high I had developed the ability to form my own friendships, some of which endure to this day.

Obviously, this rejection as a child influenced and shaped my self-concept. It made me feel unwanted, unacceptable, odd, and disliked. I became a very shy kid, reluctant to take the initiative in relationships and in other realities. I engaged in a lot of self-doubt. Children being unkind to other children obviously did not just happen in the 1950s. We hear current stories in the news of children who are mocked, rejected, and bullied. Some become so devastated that they become quite depressed, and some have actually taken their own lives to escape the pain and rejection.

In my own case I could identify with the article in the February 6, 2012, edition of *Time* magazine. This cover story is titled "The

Power of Shyness," by Bryan Walsh. The author distinguishes between shyness and introversion. Shy people have anxiety over social situations; introverts renew themselves by being alone. There is obviously overlap between shyness and introversion. But Walsh feels that shy or introverted people develop an interiority that provides power for the challenges of life, which some extroverts may not develop.

I begin with a reflection on my childhood, because of the centrality of the disease of leprosy in Leviticus and the Gospel of Mark. At the time of the writing of both Leviticus and Mark, people with the disease of leprosy were declared unclean, unacceptable, and excommunicated from the community. To be close to a leper, to touch a leper rendered a person unclean. Lepers were the rejects of the human community. They could not worship or have any meaningful connection with other people. The unclean nature of leprosy was twofold. First, there was the danger of physical contagion, catching the disease from the leprous person. Second, lepers were considered spiritually unclean. Spiritual uncleanness was also transmitted to those in contact with lepers.

Knowing what Jewish people thought and felt about lepers makes what Jesus did in the gospel astounding. The leper knelt before Jesus and said, "If you wish, you can make me clean." We are told that Jesus was moved with pity; he touched the man and said, "I do will it. Be made clean." We are told the leprosy left the man immediately, and he was made clean. Note the pity and compassion Jesus felt toward the man. His pity and compassion transcended any religious or legal restrictions that had been placed on the leper. In effect, Jesus allowed himself to be considered unclean, unfit for synagogue worship, because he actually touched the leper.

I felt like I was a leper in certain circumstances when I was a kid. Have you ever felt like a leper? Do any of us now? Who are today's lepers? What people or groups are judged, looked down on, rejected, or cut off from meaningful connection with other people? People with AIDS? Those with emotional problems? The addicted? The homeless? The poor? The hungry? The unemployed? Those who take prophetic stands regarding the Church or society?

St. Paul in 1 Corinthians 10 calls us to be imitators of Christ. In part, I think that means that we need to reach out and touch, in different ways, those who are considered and treated as today's lepers.

In his interesting book titled *The Alienated and Bored Church Member*, Dr. John Savage analyzes, across denominations, why some people become inactive and alienated from their church of origin. He said that some people have a cluster of pain in their lives; the pain can involve troubled relationships, emotional problems, financial or work-related problems, marriage or family problems, and on and on. Such people hope that their religious congregation would help with their cluster of pain. Savage found in his research that rather than helping with the cluster of pain, the parish or congregation often was part of a negative event that actually made the pain worse. In a process like this, the person in pain, hurt by the church, begins to stop going to church. In many congregations, the person's absence is not even noticed. They are forgotten. Savage says that they are *screened out*. No one seeks them out or tries to find out what the problem is. The hurting person becomes more deeply alienated, ceases church attendance, and often withdraws children from religious education. Savage described such parishes as *screening congregations*. In other words, in many cases, the local church is at the heart of the "inactive problem." Savage's recommendation is that parishes need to engage in proactive visitation of their inactive population. We should try to reach out and touch people who have been made to feel like lepers by their own faith communities.

Father Bill Rowe, seventy-two years of age and a priest for forty-seven years, has pastored St. Mary's Church in Belleville, Illinois, for a number of years. He has not taken a salary from the parish; rather he lives off of a military retirement salary. Father Rowe has had the practice of changing some of the prayers in the Roman Missal, to make them more understandable for the congregation. The bishop called him to a meeting some months ago and told him that he had to say the words from the new missal exactly as they are printed. The priest wrote the bishop a letter and said he could not do that; that was not prayer for him. He offered his resignation, if that is what the bishop wanted. The bishop did not respond for months. On February 2, 2012, the bishop wrote Father Rowe and accepted his resignation. In his letter, he said: "Make every provision in the rectory to make it comfortable for your successor. Please make sure that all appropriate books for the celebration of the Eucharist are in accord with the new translation of the *Missale Romanum* are in place. Please also make sure that all appropriate sanctuary furnishings are in place." The principal of the school defended the priest, saying that everything he did was for the well-being of the parishioners and the students. Nonetheless, an aging priest was rendered a leper because of his pastoral approach to liturgy.

We have been a church known for our excommunications.

When the leper said to Jesus, "If you wish, you can make me clean," Jesus replied, "I do will it." Let us keep in mind this approach that Jesus has toward all of us. He wants to reach out and touch us—if and when we feel like lepers. We would be better imitators of Christ, as individuals and as a church, if we reached out and touched people who seem to be today's lepers. There would be much healing in our world and in our church. Take it from an old leper.